Jury Trials and the Popularization of Legal Language

Linguistic Insights

Studies in Language and Communication

Edited by Maurizio Gotti,
University of Bergamo

Volume 162

PETER LANG
Bern · Berlin · Bruxelles · Frankfurt am Main · New York · Oxford · Wien

Patrizia Anesa

Jury Trials and the Popularization of Legal Language

A Discourse Analytical Approach

PETER LANG
Bern · Berlin · Bruxelles · Frankfurt am Main · New York · Oxford · Wien

Bibliographic information published by die Deutsche Nationalbibliothek
Die Deutsche Nationalbibliothek lists this publication in the Deutsche Nationalbibliografie; detailed bibliographic data is available on the Internet at ‹http://dnb.d-nb.de›.

British Library Cataloguing-in-Publication Data:
A catalogue record for this book is available from The British Library, Great Britain

Library of Congress Cataloging-in-Publication Data

Anesa, Patrizia
Jury trials and the popularization of legal language : a discourse analytical approach / patrizia anesa.
p. cm. – (Linguistic insights studies in language and communication, ISSN 1424-8689 ; v. 162)
Includes bibliographical references and index.
ISBN 978-3-0343-1231-8 (alk. paper)
1. Law–Language. 2. Jury. I. Title.
K213.A54 2012
340'.14–dc23

2012030077

ISSN 1424-8689
ISBN 978-3-0343-1231-8

Joy in looking and comprehending is nature's most beautiful gift. (Albert Einstein)

Acknowledgements

This book, based on my PhD thesis, would not have seen the light without the support offered by the Department of Foreign Languages at the University of Verona, where my PhD programme was conducted.

I also owe a deep debt to the Aarhus School of Business, and in particular to the Department of Business Communication and the Research Group in Knowledge Communication, not just for all the useful comments and help received, but because it is the kind of place where ideas develop and grow. Special thanks go to Jan Engberg, Peter Kastberg, Carmen Daniela Maier and Constance Kampf for their constant help.

I have also been blessed with the good fortune to work with Maurizio Gotti, whom I would like to thank for his dedication to this project and all the hours spent sharing his precious ideas with me, as well as for his continual encouragement and for being a great inspiration.

I am also grateful to the anonymous referees that have read the manuscript of my volume for the precious comments and suggestions that they have given me.

Finally, I am hugely indebted to my family and friends for their patient support and love, and because so many days together were organized around the writing of this book.

Contents

1. Introduction

No law or ordinance is mightier than understanding. (Plato)

The ever-increasing prominence of studies of language and the law in research agendas is often borne out of the acknowledgement of the fundamental role the law plays in everyone's life. In particular, trials, whether considered from a linguistic, communicative or social perspective, are highly complex, as well as critically important, events.

This work focuses on spoken discourse within the context of jury trials, and aims to obtain a fuller understanding of how the language of jury trials operates, and how specialized legal knowledge is communicated across professional barriers. More specifically, the objective is an analysis of the communicative dynamics taking place in a criminal jury trial, and one of the main areas of interest in the current work are the various strategies and techniques which are used to communicate specific legal concepts, principles and procedures across knowledge asymmetries. In particular, this study will focus on the communication of specialized legal knowledge between experts from within the legal profession and laypersons. The privileged field of analysis of this work will be a jury trial within the U.S. context. In particular, the present study focuses on the communication processes which take place between legal experts and non-experts in some specific phases of the trial, namely the jury instruction phase, the opening statements and the closing arguments.

The choice to focus on the jury trial system does not reflect an aim to reach a critical decision about which mode of trial is preferable, but rather to gain better awareness of the importance of knowledge asymmetries in this context, and to develop a deeper understanding of how they are exploited. By definition, a jury trial brings together a broad cross-section of society and, from this perspective, I will try to explain what mediational and communicative strategies are employed between legal experts and jurors, and what reasons lie behind these choices.

The attempt is to contribute to a better understanding of how knowledge is communicated in this context, with the awareness that no analysis will answer such a complex question in a universally satisfactory manner. Therefore, the aim is not to resolve this ongoing dilemma on the validity of generalizations drawn from one case; rather, this work aims to understand how and why certain processes take place in a particular communicative event. More specifically, I intend to undertake the exploration of this event through a linguistic and discursive analysis.

After the introductory chapter, this work offers some reflections on the inextricable interrelation between law and language and provides an introductory review of research on legal language with a specific focus on courtroom settings. In particular, courtroom interaction has been investigated in relation to the crucial role played by different kinds of power relations in the construction of meanings within the trial (Danet 1980, Maley 1994, Jackson 1995, Cotterill 2003). Considerable attention has been devoted to the examination phase, focusing on the interaction between attorneys and (expert and eye) witnesses (e.g. Atkinson/Drew 1979, Matoesian 1993). Even though no introduction can adumbrate the complex concept that courts may be seen as *fora* for the appropriation of discourse, chapter Two also attempts to address issues related to the institutionalization, authorization and appropriation of legal discourse.

The next chapter moves on from a review of the literature to describe the research framework that will be employed in the present work. It presents the research interest and rationale as well the theoretical and methodological background with the aim of illustrating the theoretical tenets and the methodological approach, the tools of analysis and the perspectives adopted for discussing real-world issues in interactions and, more specifically, for investigating courtroom discourse.

In particular, starting from the assumption that the study of discourse has become a major interest in research in a vast array of disciplines and can be approached from a variety of perspectives, it is deemed necessary to specify the theory of discourse adopted here, while nonetheless acknowledging the complexity and the fluidity of this concept. The chapter offers a brief discussion of Discourse Analysis and shows in particular which aspects of Critical Discourse Analysis (CDA) this investigation draws on. In this respect, it may be argued that

> [t]he move away from the analysis of individual decontextualised texts to look at the socio-cultural factors that lie behind the production of particular types of texts is a defining feature of Critical Discourse Analysis (Barlett 2010: 137).

From this perspective, it is clear that the analysis of the texts cannot be meaningfully carried out in isolation from reflections on the contexts of production, as well as the legal and procedural constraints that, in a trial, may determine the use of certain language items. However, it should also be pointed out that CDA does not simply 'move away' from the observation of 'decontextualized texts', in that from a CDA perspective the very nature of texts is indissoluble from their contexts, and the decontextualization of a text would be a mere artifice. The approach that I will embrace is not only suited to the description of language in a specific social context, but it is also based on the analysis of emerging discursive issues and of knowledge and power asymmetries, which in turn shape and are shaped by their social context(s).

As Stygall notes, "[l]inguists, by and large, look at what's there, not what's not. In doing so, we may be missing some of the main effects of the interaction of institutional power" (Stygall 1994: 28). The observation of the actual talk and the development of discourse will be the point of departure of this analysis; however, some reflections on what is excluded from the discourse will be attempted, especially in the light of the linguistic constrictions imposed by the institutional setting of a criminal jury trial. The aim is to combine the description and the analysis of language structures with a wider approach in which the context is of primary importance.

From a methodological perspective, I discuss the possibility of combining an overall qualitative approach with a quantitative one. In particular, considerations deriving from discourse analytical perspectives are complemented by the use of two main tools, namely

AntConc and Wmatrix, in an attempt to combine their respective strengths; for instance, the very intuitive accessibility of AntConc and some of its specific tools, such as the Concordance Plot, are integrated with the use of Wmatrix, which encompasses other valuable analytical tools, such as the semantic tagger.

I will engage myself in a form of localized discourse analysis, as the aim is not to focus on general or generalizable patterns but primarily on a specific discourse event. Some research trends highlight the general idea that "far less reliance is placed on quantifiable and/or general patterns" (Swann 2002: 59), but this study requires a more specifically-focused approach because of the inherently localized nature that discourse assumes in this work and because of the specificity of the discourse situation under investigation. Quantitative specifications, however, have also been made in this analysis. Indeed, although affirming that "discourse analysis, as with many other varieties of qualitative research is more difficult than positivist number crunching" (Parker/Burman 1993: 156, cf. Banister *et al.* 1994) highlights the complexity of qualitative research, it does not consider the valuable contribution quantitative approaches may offer.

In other words, the complementary use of several research approaches is a key aspect of this study; on this basis, the use of a quantitative perspective is considered to supplement rather than contradict what is, in the final analysis, a qualitative methodology. This choice is not merely borne out of an awareness that "investigators are increasingly stepping beyond their original disciplinary boundaries" (Iedema/Wodak 1999: 6), but is deemed necessary in order to enable this investigation to bridge the paradigms of theory and practice, descriptive and prescriptive studies, micro and macro analysis.

Chapter Four provides an overview of communicative dynamics in courtroom settings, and in particular in jury trials. Some of the principal features of the legal system and of the jury system are highlighted. In particular, crucial issues related to the jury system, such as fairness, impartiality, representativeness and competency, are introduced. The inherent communicative complexity of a jury trial is also described, by focusing on the role played by knowledge and power asymmetries.

The focus of the analytical chapter is on one specific communicative event. Indeed, chapter Five is concerned with the analysis of a specific trial, namely *California vs Westerfield*, 2002. From a practical point of view, the choice to focus on this trial lies in a personal familiarity with the specific legal system, the accessibility of language, and the possibility of accessing data in a time- and cost-effective manner. Moreover, the U.S. is particularly representative of the trial by jury system, as it is in the U.S. that the highest proportion of jury trials takes place, as will be shown.

In light of the consideration that language utterances can be made sense of and interpreted in relation to the situation and the cultural context, chapter Five offers a discussion of different phases of the Westerfield trial, by first introducing some thoughts on the situational context, and offering a discussion of some of the procedural and legal constraints. In an attempt to avoid slipping into the discussion of the epistemology of legal issues, which are already commonly addressed in academic legal study, the main focus of this work is on the discursive construction of a specific communicative event. However, Galdia (2009) reminds us that there would be no Legal Linguistics without Law; it is therefore inevitable that some reflections upon the specific legal contexts, procedures and principles will be briefly introduced, not least to better enable the investigation to take into account the legal reasons underlying certain communicative and linguistic choices.

The courtroom represents an arena not only for dispute resolution but also for constructing and maintaining a certain professional identity (Bogoch 1999: 1) and in fact, as we shall observe, competing identities are continually fighting to emerge and to be recognized. The concept of identity is not here left as an unproblematic matter and the analysis observes some of the processes through which the construction and maintenance of professional identities take place. The main phases of the trial to be analyzed are jury instructions, opening statements and closing arguments. The analysis of the instruction phase focuses in particular on the communicative relationship between the judge and the jurors. The focal point of the analysis of opening and closing statements is, instead, on the dynamics that characterize the communication processes between attorneys and jurors. This chapter also focuses on accommodation strategies adopted by legal experts in their interaction with laymen and on the emergence of different forms of hybridity in courtroom discourse.

This investigation constantly warns against the temptation to assume an automatic generalizabilty of the observations which emerge from the analysis. Moreover, the study takes into consideration the fact that "the semiotic resources at our disposal are so rich and subtle that our command of them at the conscious level is necessarily limited" (Richards 2006: 3); at the same time discourse, especially when relatively planned (see Tannen 1987a, 1987b, 2007), includes specific choices that stem from a strategic repertoire.

The concluding chapter recapitulates and reframes the main insights gained into the linguistic and communicative dynamics that characterize the specific event under scrutiny; it also affirms the need for further investigation in the field, especially in the light of the consideration that trials are generally considered the most manifest realization of the process of doing justice, or injustice (Merry 1990).

2. Legal language

But do not give it to a lawyer's clerk to write, for they use a legal hand that Satan himself will not understand. (Cervantes)

2.1 Law and language

Law and language are not simply inter-disciplinarily related, but they form an indissoluble nexus by their nature. It may be argued that language is the essence, and to some extent the pre-condition, of any reflection upon the theory and practice of law. This is not meant to imply that the relation between language and law is strictly hierarchical but to highlight the fundamental role language plays in the very existence of law.

The expression 'Law and Language' is sometimes used to refer to studies focusing on the interrelation (and to some extent the interdependence) between the two spheres. Following Galdia (2009: 63-64), the expression 'Language and Law' is preferred here, given the assumption that language may be seen as a constitutive element, or an essential requirement, of the law. In other words, it may be argued that there would be no law without language, as the role of language as a pre-condition for the existence of law could not be substituted by any other means. As Fletcher (2003: 85) crudely remarks, "[t]he idea of law without language is about as plausible as the idea of baseball without balls and bats". A discussion of the intrinsic nature of law would go beyond the scope of this work, but it is conceptually worth pointing out that attempts to analyze law as a phenomenon independent from language are very limited[1]. In fact, it is plausible to assume that any formalization of law is inalienable from the use of language.

More specifically, Goodrich (1984: 173) remarks that "both legal theory and legal practice are, and have always been, heavily dependent upon the tools of rhetorical and linguistic analysis". From a historical point of view, the modes of self-representation of legal language may be said to be predominantly exegetical and philological and therefore intuitively linked to, and indeed inalienable from, linguistic methods and theories.

Developments in the study of legal language have also generated crucial reflections upon its fundamental social role, starting from the considerations related to the pervasiveness of law in each society. The investigation of the influence of law on our lives cannot be dismissed as a mere intellectual experiment. As Galdia (2009: 55) remarks, "[i]n everyone's biography the presence of law is sensible at least in some extent". Obviously, the impact it might have on each individual is considerably different, but, in the light of the high level of regulation and institutionalization (see section 2.1.3) of modern society, law is inevitably present (although it may be argued that it is not omnipresent) in everybody's life.

2.1.1 Legal vs ordinary language

In his definition of legal language, Cornu (1995: 16) suggests that legal language is a particular usage of ordinary language. It has also been argued that legal language is an elaboration, an extension of ordinary language, and that it is inexorably through ordinary language that a specialized language is acquired. The relation between the concepts of *legal* and *ordinary language* is not self-explanatory and must be problematized for the interpretation of the notion of legal language adopted here to be illustrated effectively (see section 2.1.2).

---

1 See Leibnitz's attempt to formalize law as a *more geometrico* in *Dissertatio de arte combinatoria* (1666) and *Nova methodus discendae docendaeque jurisprudentiae* (1667), discussed in Galdia (2009: 63-64).

A distinction between what is often generically labelled as 'ordinary' language and 'legal' language is intuitively undeniable. In particular, if we consider the widespread perception that the legal world is based upon an overwhelmingly unfamiliar, archaic, unintelligible, opaque, and even deceptive language, it is easy to conceptually discern it from 'everyday' language. However, this distinction is highly problematic and fails to address the obvious issue that the 'legal' world and the 'ordinary' world are unavoidably interdependent; once one engages in a more detailed analysis, the line between the two (intuitively identifiable) languages appears to be finely drawn.

In this respect, there is wide consensus upon the idea that one distinctive feature of legal language lies in its power to transfer and confer legal relevance and validity to everyday language and modify it accordingly (Greimas 1976: 92). What is particularly interesting from a discursive point of view is to see through which mechanisms this process takes (or does not take) place (see Goodrich 1984: 183), and to illustrate how different phenomena may characterize the interplay between what is simplistically seen as 'ordinary' and 'legal' language in different (legal) contexts. What emerges is generally not a mere transformation or translation from the former into the latter: ordinary and legal language cannot be understood as two opposite poles that may occasionally influence each other but as deeply interrelated spheres which constantly intermingle and amalgamate.

Another common oversimplification springs from the heuristic temptation of establishing the nature of legal or ordinary language according to the primary category of users, and therefore establishing that legal language corresponds precisely to the language used by legal professionals. This assumption is intuitively incontrovertible and seems to strike at the core of the nature of legal language itself. Nevertheless, the supposition of a direct causal correlation between language users and language types may disregard the complexity of legal language use, the variety of contexts of production and the diversity of (potential) users.

Of course I am not arguing that legal language cannot be seen as the language used by lawyers, but that a clear-cut distinction between legal and ordinary language may be a partial and even misleading interpretation of a much more multifaceted phenomenon (especially, as will be shown, in particularly complex contexts such as trials). The language of the courtroom is a clear example of the indivisibility of legal and ordinary language and of the interdependence of these two spheres.

2.1.2 Defining legal language

Legal language is present to a more or less significant degree in our lives (see *inter alia* Stygall 1994); the awareness of its pervasiveness and the understanding of its crucial social role are some of the factors that have determined the constantly growing interest in this area of study.

2.1.2.1 Beyond the language of lawyers

Legal language has often been treated as a monolithic entity, as "a unity to be understood as the social image of the argot or language of élite or professionalised power" and has been defined as "the language of authority, which takes the discursive form of monologue, distance (temporal and hierarchical), and specialization" (Goodrich 1984: 187). In particular, considerable research has been devoted to the study of the language of the law, understood specifically as the language of legal documents (see section 2.3). For instance, Mellinkoff (1963: 3) describes the language of the law as "the customary language used by lawyers in those common law jurisdictions where English is the official language", insisting in particular on its use by a specific professional category.

The conception of legal language in this research is more inclusive (see section 2.2.3): it extends beyond the idea of legal language as the preserve of a specific professional class and emphasizes the complexity of this multi-faceted concept, attempting to give a more comprehensive account of the ways in which it accommodates change and constantly shapes and reshapes itself. In view of this theoretical platform, it will be seen that the complex nature of legal language finds its apotheosized crystallization in the context of a jury trial (see chapter 5).

Sharing the view that concepts such as class, gender, status and professional expertise are not self-explanatory (see *inter alia* Cameron 1990), Stygall (1994: 5-6) also points out that "studies in legal language have assumed that the social explanation for the existence of such a language is the simple correlation between the existence of legal profession and of distinguishable legal language".

I argue for a more complex interpretation of the concept of legal language for two main reasons. Firstly, professional categories and their boundaries cannot be automatically defined; secondly, assuming a mechanical correlation between belonging to a specific professional group and the use of a certain typology of language is an oversimplification, especially in the context of a jury trial, given the variety of participants involved, the relational dynamics between them and the complex processes (such as accommodation and reciprocal influence) which take place.

At a deeper level, a strict definition of legal language as the language of lawyers implies the pre-existence of specific professional identities and cultures that make use of a specific language. Conversely, I would also like to highlight the crucial role played by discourse in shaping professional identities and cultures, which within this work are not considered to be completely pre-defined and static entities, but fluid, shifting and evolving concepts (Gunnarsson/Linell/Nordberg 1997).

2.1.2.2 The notion of legal language

The problematization of the interpretation of the expression *legal language* is fundamental to any subsequent analysis. A wide range of interpretations may be offered; it has been suggested, for instance, that legal language should be treated as a *technolect* (Mattila 2006), a language *variety* (Charrow *et al.* 1982, Crystal 1995, Tiersma 1999a) a *dialect*, a *register*, a *domain*, or a *sublanguage*[2]. In particular, in the attempt to offer a definition of legal language, it has been pointed out that it may be seen as a *technolect*, (Mattila 2006: 3), as it is often identified with the language of legal specialists; it is also clear, however, that legal messages inevitably concern ordinary people, too. Le-

2 For a deeper discussion see Kurzon (1997: 123-134) and Danet (1980: 470-474).

gal language tends to be so pervasive and to govern in some ways all domains of social life that the idea of a *technolect* appears limiting. Adopting a broader perspective, Cornu (2005: 17) describes legal language as a professional language, mainly used by people operating in the legal world, whether directly or indirectly. In Cornu's view legal language does not belong to one single professional category, namely lawyers, but it is rather used by a wide range of different professions.

In the following passage, Crystal adopts the expression *variety of language*. He points out the complex nature of legal language and stresses the social importance it assumes as well as the responsibility that this type of language inevitable carries with it:

> Legal language is always being pulled in different directions. Its statements have to be so phrased that we can see their general applicability, yet be specific enough to apply to individual circumstances. They have to be stable enough to stand the test of time, so that cases will be treated consistently and fairly, yet flexible enough to adapt to new social situations. Above all, they have to be expressed in such a way that people can be certain about the intention of the law respecting their rights and duties. No other variety of language has to carry such a responsibility. (Crystal 1995: 374, emphasis added)

The notion of legal English as a *variety* of language, has often been used in order to highlight its differences from the stereotypical interpretation of ordinary language, without assuming that it may for this reason be seen as a different language.

Legal language has also been defined as a *dialect*, but this designation does not appear appropriate if the idea of dialect is understood to refer primarily to notions of geographical location. From another perspective, Tiersma (1999a: 133) also mentions legal dialects and distinguishes, for instance, between the legal English spoken in British contexts and American contexts[3]. Some interesting examples related to (in particular lexical) differences between the two spheres are mentioned by Tiersma (1999a: 134):

---

3 More specifically, it should be pointed out that there is no 'British legal system', and therefore the legal languages used, for instance, in England and Wales display considerable differences in relation to the legal language used in Scotland.

> Sometimes one word has different meanings in various jurisdictions. In American legal English, a *judgment* is the disposition or outcome of a case. In England *judgment* also refers to the statements of reasons for the disposition, something that American lawyers call an opinion. An appellate court *affirms* or *reverses* a lower court's judgment in the United States, while it *allows* the appeal or *dismisses* it in England. A *brief* is an argument to the court in the United States, while it is a written case summary for the guidance of a barrister in England. *Corporate law* in America is *company law* in England. Legal idioms may also differ from place to place. An American lawyer is *admitted to the bar*, while a British barrister is *called to the bar* and may eventually *take silk* (become a Queen's Counsel). (Tiersma 1999a: 134)

The terms *jargon* or *argot* are also occasionally used to identify specific professional languages, but they often tend to be associated with an aura of complexity and incomprehensibility. Similarly, expressions such as *legal lingo* and *legalese* tend to be attributed a relatively negative connotation and are not frequently used. With particular (but not exclusive) reference to the language used in the courtroom, Danet (1980) talks about *language in the legal process*, and Levi and Walker (1990) often use the expression *language in the judicial process*. On a practical note, scholars have also remarked that there has been a tendency to avoid the term *legal* in order to circumvent potential confusion with *lawful* (Mellinkoff 1963).

2.1.3 Institutionalization, authorization and appropriation

It is generally agreed that legal language finds its lifeblood in its institutionalization; in particular, it has been noted that the process of institutionalization of language is based on a sort of 'secret pact' between the text and the institution that it represents (Lenoble/Ost 1980: 87). Moreover, because of its highly institutionalized nature, the language of the law intrinsically brings with it the fundamental issue of authorization. As Goodrich (1984: 188) remarks, "legal discourse is socially and institutionally authorized – affirmed, legitimated and sanctioned – by a wide variety of highly visible organizational and sociolinguistic insignia of hierarchy, status, power and wealth".

The Foucauldian 'régime of truth' on which a society is based may be seen as the precondition for this process of authorization, intended as the affirmation, legitimization and sanctioning of legal discourse. More specifically, Foucault affirms:

> Each society has its régime of truth, its 'general politics' of truth: that is, the types of discourse which it accepts and makes function as true; the mechanisms and instances which enable one to distinguish true and false statements, the means by which each is sanctioned, the techniques and procedures accorded value in the acquisition of truth; the status of those who are charged with saying what counts as true. (Foucault 1980a: 131)

Beyond the interdependence of legality and institutions (Lenoble/Ost 1980: 83), the issue of authorization is here intended as the process through which "the appropriation and institutionalization of meaning and discourse" (Goodrich 1984: 185) takes place in a specific context. From this perspective, the following oft-quoted Bakhtinian remark strikes at the very heart of this crucial issue of the appropriation of meaning:

> Every discourse has its own selfish and biased proprietor; there are no words with meanings shared by all, no words 'belonging to no-one'. [...] Who speaks and under what conditions they speak, this is what determines the word's actual meaning. All direct meanings and direct expressions are false, and this is especially true of emotional feelings and expressions. (Bakhtin 1981: 401)

It seems obvious that meanings, and in particular meanings emerging in legal practices, cannot be seen as a static and predefined product to be contemplated and must be understood and problematized within a specific discursive framework. Indeed, the interdependence between meanings and discursive contextual factors is a fundamental postulation, even in the analysis of the apparently fixed, unalterable and stagnant language of the law.

As has been mentioned, the social institution of 'the law' has often been defined as "the locus of a powerful act of linguistic appropriation" (Mertz 1994: 441) that emerges from the transformation of ordinary language into specific legal categories imposed by the state. The complexity underlying the concept of linguistic appropriation finds its exemplar illustration in the domain of law. More specifically, the question of linguistic authorization concerns the generation of the social legitimacy of legal language, the definition of its paradigms and their acceptance within a society, as well as the affirmation of its discursive practices; in other words, it may be seen as "the question of the social production and control of meaning in the form of an order of discourse which determines what can and should be said" (Goodrich 1984: 185).

2.2 Towards a taxonomy of legal language?

The concept of legal language is vast and protean, and its intricacy and its versatile character have often been highlighted. As has been shown, legal language, with its pervasiveness (and at the same time its uniqueness), has drawn considerable scholarly interest. Different approaches have been adopted in order to offer a categorization or taxonomy of legal language. Considering the multifaceted nature of legal language, and the number of areas it penetrates, such categorizations are inevitably highly heterogeneous.

2.2.1 Suggested categorizations

Legal language has often been primarily considered a question of style (Dölle 1949). Following Joos's (1961) taxonomy of styles (namely, *frozen*, *formal*, *consultative*, *casual*, and *intimate*), Danet (1980) offers a categorization of different areas of legal language according to their level of formality. Focusing on Joos's first four categories, Danet associates *frozen* style with written documents, but she also indicates that some types of events mainly characterized by the use of the spoken mode, such as civil marriage ceremonies, could be considered *frozen*. According to Danet, *formal* language is encountered in statutes, lawyers' briefs and appellate opinions, as well as in lawyers' examinations of witnesses in trials, lawyers' arguments in trials, and expert witnesses' testimonies. Instead, lawyer–client interaction constitutes an example of *consultative* style. Finally, *casual* style characterizes informal conversations, such as lawyer–to–lawyer conversations. Danet does not consider Joos's notion of *intimate* style to be attributable to any aspect of the language of the law.

To some extent this categorization may be seen to be fallacious, as different areas of legal language may in turn be characterized by very different styles. For example, the language of the courtroom, which constitutes our field of analysis, includes, as will be shown, an intricate series of sub-domains, communicative situations and styles, and a categorical distinction would therefore be misleading. In other words, the styles of different legal domains (especially in trial processes) do not arise *sui generis*, but from the intermingling of different factors (contexts, settings, participants involved and the relationships between them, procedural constraints, etc.).

It has been stated that legal language can be theoretically divided into sub-genres "according to the various sub-groups of lawyers", distinguishing, for instance, between "the language of legal authors, legislators (laws and regulations), judges, and administrators, as well as advocates" (Mattila 2006: 2). However, this approach will not be adopted in this study. Indeed, this categorization does not seem to sit well with the concept of interdiscursivity (see *inter alia* Fairclough 1992a, Candlin/Maley 1997, Candlin 2006) adopted here. Moreover, even though a distinction made according to the (primary) users does not automatically neglect the collective nature of some instances of legal discourse (and the collective process of production which lies behind it), it does not emphasize the essentially intertextual and interdiscursive character of such discourses. Finally, the very activity of identifying different 'sub-groups of lawyers' may raise issues related to the interconnections between such subgroups and the presence of reciprocal influences between them; this categorization may also call for a reflection on the inevitable exclusion of all other professional categories who do not prototypically belong to the specific professional category of lawyers (and its sub-groups), but who may still be significantly involved in the use of legal language.

The classification suggested by Galdia (2009: 91) also draws to some extent on the concept of language users:

- Language of statutes (language of legislation);
- Language of legal decisions including fact description;
- Language of the legal doctrine;
- Language used by lawyers in professional discussions and pleadings;
- Language used by laypersons in legal contexts (testimony, comments on legal decisions);
- Language used by administrative clerks.

What emerges, especially in regard to the last three categories, is the use of language users as a categorizing criterion. This criterion will not be employed in the taxonomy suggested in this work, in light of the fact that the definition of different groups of users is not self-descriptive, and, moreover, the interactions between them determine crucial influences and contaminations.

Another theoretical division may be made "into sub-genres on the basis of branches of law" (Mattila 2006: 5). This criterion also appears both problematic, because it is based on the principle of a mechanical correlation between branches and sub-genres, and limiting, in that it relies on pre-existing categories, and does not emphasize the (potential) interrelation between different branches. Consequently, despite the difficulties inherent in any attempt to describe the highly complex concept of legal language, the use of more open and dynamic categories (see section 2.2.3) is suggested in this work.

2.2.2 The complexity of legal language categories

As has been shown, the world of legal English comprises a variety of types of texts which fulfill different functions and a clear-cut distinction is often not possible. Gibbons (2003) remarks that legal language could essentially be divided into two main areas, namely the codified sphere of language (which is mainly written) and the language of the legal process:

> The language of the law can be broadly divided into two major areas – the codified and mostly written language of legislation and other legal documents such as contracts, which is largely monologic; and the more spoken, interactive and dynamic language of legal process, particularly the language of courtroom, police investigation, prisons and consultations among lawyers and between lawyers and their clients. (Gibbons 2003: 15)

The border between these two areas is, however, often unclear, because of the intertextual nature of the texts we are dealing with. The examples are innumerable; for instance, it is evident that codified texts are not only referred to continuously in the legal process, but they also play a fundamental role in the development of the process and its outcomes.

In his interpretation, Kurzon (1989) identifies the *language of the law* and *legal language* as two distinctive spheres, where the former is used "in documents that lay down the law", and the latter refers to the language "used when people talk about the law" (Kurzon 1989: 283-84). More specifically, in a later work Kurzon (1997: 120) offers the following categorization:

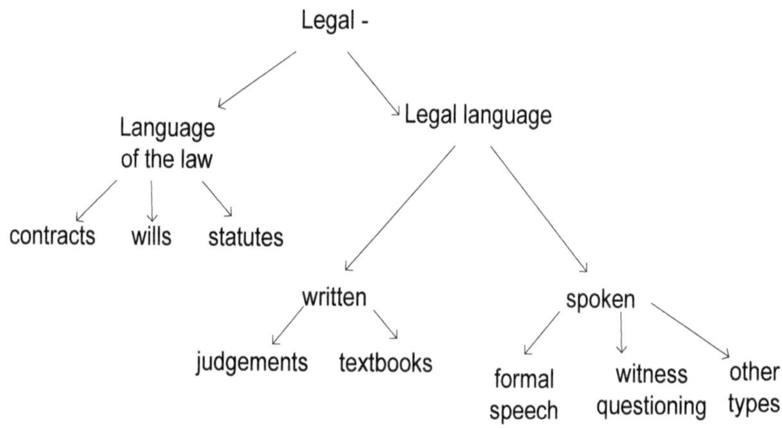

Figure 1. The language of the law and legal language (Kurzon 1997: 120).

According to Kurzon, *the language of the law* represents a narrower use of language in specific legal domains, whereas the expression *legal language* refers to the remaining domains (where the language of the law is not prevalent). Within the area of *legal language* Kurzon also identifies *law talk*, specifying that "this subtype is in a spoken form only, i.e. spontaneous speech used, for example, when a lawyer questions a witness, or when the judge speaks to the jury, or when two lawyers get together and speak about legal matters" (Kurzon 1997: 120). However, limiting this concept of *law talk* to spoken texts seems to neglect the complexity arising from the constantly growing interconnection and interdependence between modes. For instance, on a more practical note, lawyers may "get together and speak about legal matters" in a mode that is not necessarily purely spoken. Similarly, client–attorney consultation would presumably fall into the category of *other types* of spoken legal language, but it is evident that such a definition may be restraining, in that it would not consider potentially hybrid forms of consultation, such as online interaction.

It is not my aim to neglect the existence of a potential categorization into written and spoken texts, but this distinction would not be fruitful for the approach adopted in this analysis. First of all, at a general level, it may be argued that the written–spoken dichotomy appears unsuitable because new technologies allow for a constant interplay and interchange between these two modes to the extent that they may even appear indiscernible (see Gunnarsson 1995: 112). Moreover, texts may often be seen as the result of a complex interrelation between spoken and written modes and this process is particularly evident while analyzing the language of the courtroom (see section 4.6). In her bibliographic work on legal language Levi (1994) identifies three major categories:

- Spoken language in legal settings;
- Language as a subject of the law;
- The written language of the law.

She also describes forensic linguistics as a separate applied class. The first category identifies a variety of events, from lawyers' speeches to judges' directions in court, but it is also plausible to assume that these events are not necessarily carried out through the spoken mode. For instance, in a jury trial the jury instruction phase may be seen as typically oral, but it is generally based on written instructions, and juries may be given the written version of the document (see section 5.3).

The second category is inevitably linked to the other ones, in that issues related to *language as the subject of the law* may be dealt with in legal settings and are presumably governed by what Levi defines as *the written language of the law*. The second category is also so strictly interconnected with the concept of *forensic linguistics* (identified by Levi as a separate applied class) that it may at times appear impossible to discern them.

Trosborg's (1995) interpretation of the concept of legal language is particularly revealing in that it complexifies the issue by identifying different types of sub-languages and domains of use. According to Trosborg, 'legal language' is an umbrella term covering different types of sub-languages, such as the language of the law, (meaning the language of legal documents), the language used in the courtroom, in textbooks, in lawyers' communication or by people (professionals and laypersons) talking about the law (cf. figure 2). In this volume, the expression 'legal language' will be used in line with Trosborg's view.

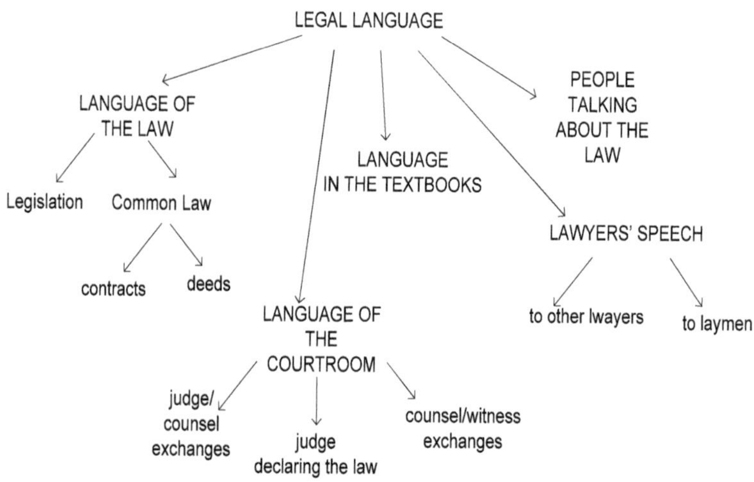

Figure 2. Legal language (Trosborg 1995: 2).

Another interesting categorization is suggested by Maley (1994: 13), who emphasizes the plurality of legal discourses and points out four main categories:

- Judicial discourse, designating the language of judicial decision, either spoken or written;
- Courtroom discourse;
- The language of legal documents;
- The discourse of legal consultation, which includes both lawyer–lawyer and lawyer–client interaction.

The basic conception for this categorization is that "[l]anguage is medium, process and product in the various arenas of the law where legal texts, spoken or written, are generated in the service of regulating social behaviour" (Maley 1994: 11).

As has been mentioned, the impossibility of treating 'legal language' as a monolithic entity is evident as the expression comprises a vast series of genres, discourse situations and communities[4]. Maley's visual representation (1994: 16) of the different discourse situations that are related to the use of legal language shows the complexity of the concept:

4 A wider discussion of the notions of 'community' would go beyond the specific goals of this section. For further details see the concepts of 'speech community' (Hymes 1972), 'discourse community' and 'place discourse community' (Swales 1991, 1998), and 'community of practice' (Lave/Wenger 1991, Wenger 1998).

DISCOURSE SITUATION	DISCOURSE SITUATION	DISCOURSE SITUATION	DISCOURSE SITUATION
Sources of law; originating points of legal process	Pre-trial processes	Trial Processes	Recording and law-making
→	→	→	→
legislature/ (legislature/ subject) regulations, by-laws (authority/subject) precedents (judges/ defendants) wills, contracts, etc. (two parties)	police/video interview (authority/ subject, witness) pleadings (lawyer/lawyer) consultation (lawyer/lawyer) (lawyer/client) subpoena, jury summons, (authority/ (subject, witness)	court examination, cross-examination, re-examination (counsel/witness) intervention, rules and procedures (judge/counsel) jury summation (judge/jury) proceedings decision (judge/defendant)	case reports -(judge/defendant, judge/other judges)
LEGAL DISCOURSES	LEGAL DISCOURSES	LEGAL DISCOURSES	LEGAL DISCOURSES

Table 1. Types of legal discourse (adapted from Maley 1994: 16).

Maley points out the circularity of the process, specifying, for instance, that once a case is reported, it may function as a precedent for following cases and become a potential source of law. At the same time, however, it is also emphasized that the sequence is not inevitable (Maley 1994: 15-17) in that certain potential originating points of legal processes may never progress to the subsequent phases. This representation succeeds in showing the plurality of discourses related to the legal sphere and attempts to emphasize the (potential) interrelation between them.

2.2.3 *Interdiscursivity*

A particularly enlightening representation of how legal discourse may be conceived is offered in Bhatia *et al.* (2004). Drawing on the concept of genre (for the purpose of this study see Bhatia 1983, 1993, Swales 1990; for a discussion of courtroom discourse as genre see Harris 1988), it is possible to "distinguish the nature of legal genres from a number of other professional genres" (Bhatia *et al.* 2004: 204). What is particularly illuminating about the conceptualization offered by Bhatia *et al.* (2004) is the clear emergence of the concepts of intertextuality and interdiscursivity. Looking at the continuum between academic and professional legal contexts, it is possible to identify genres which are typically used in legal contexts, such as legislation, judgments, legal textbooks, and legal cases. However, it may be argued that, for example, in academic contexts we may identify instances of academic genres, such as the problem-question genre and the critical essay genre, which are inevitably linked to legal practice. Similarly, other professional legal genres, such as legal memoranda and legal pleadings, derive in some way from some form of interrelation with the broadly based legal genres (for a deeper discussion see Candlin/Bhatia 1998).

Intertextuality is understood here as "the property of one text being used in another, either directly or by pragmatic implication" (Bhatia *et al.* 2004: 204). This property plays a fundamental role in legal contexts because of the inherent intertextual nature of legal texts. Interdiscursivity can be seen as an inter-exploitation of genre conventions, as "conventions associated with one genre are cleverly exploited in another genre" (Bhatia *et al.* 2004: 204). More specifically, Candlin and Maley (1997: 203) argue that "in so far as any characteristic text evokes a particular discoursal value, in that it is associated with some institutional and social meaning, such evolving discourses are at the same time interdiscursive". They suggest the following definition of interdiscursivity: "the use of elements from one discourse and social practice which carry institutional and social meanings from other discourses and other social practices" (Candlin/Maley 1997: 212). In a similar vein, therefore, when talking about legal discourse, I do not intend to infer that one single discourse of that type exists, but rather that it consists of a set of related discourses.

As has been mentioned, the interpretation of legal language adopted in this volume is in line with Trosborg's (1995) definition according to which the expression 'legal language' encompasses a series of other sub-languages and should therefore be understood as a superordinate term. Figure 3 attempts to visualize the concept of interdiscursivity in legal languages:

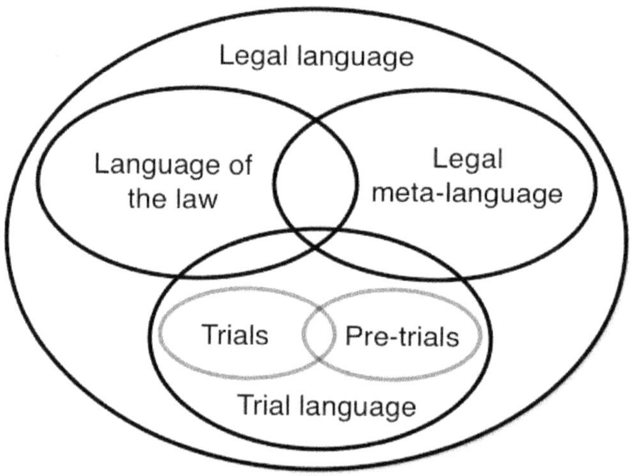

Figure 3. Interdiscursivity in legal languages.

This representation is by no means exhaustive and does not aim to unravel all the potential sub-domains of legal language. Rather, it is functional in that it shows the interconnection between some of the most clearly identifiable domains and sub-domains of legal language. Consequently, the labels I have decided to assign are to be seen as primarily heuristic (and not exhaustive and strictly exclusive) categorizations.

Legal language is seen to comprise some main categories such as *the language of the law*, *trial-related language*, and legal *meta-language*. The purest distillation of legal language may be seen as *the language of the law*, in particular the language of legislation. It is not only desirable but necessary that these domains be further delved into and expanded. For instance, the area of *the language of the law* includes a wide range of sub-categories, such as the language of legislation, statutes, regulations, by-laws, wills, contracts, etc.

The label *trial language* (for the purpose of this work, also referred to as *courtroom language*) is here intended to encompass pre-trial and trial situations, and different sub-categories may also be identified within these broader categories (ranging from police interrogations to the pronunciation of verdicts).

The term *meta-language* is here deliberately not intended in the Galdian sense (2009: 231) of a "universal descriptive language for the propositional context of legal texts", i.e. as a transitional language deriving from a technical translation process. In this study the expression *meta-language* refers to the language used to explain, interpret or discuss the law. This category includes the general notion of "language of people talking about the law" (Trosborg 1995: 2), instances of lawyer–client interactions, lawyer–to–lawyer conversations, as well the language of textbooks.

The functional character of figure 3 attempts primarily to show the complexity underlying the interrelation and the interdependence among different domains within the field of legal language, focusing on some of the prototypical situations. Indeed, the main areas that have been identified here are deeply related both intertextually and interdiscursively. For instance, as will be shown, trials and pre-trials extensively include instances of meta-language (e.g. as regards the explanation of legal concepts and processes); moreover, trial language somehow arises from the application of the language of the law and also constantly refers to it. In other words, the notion of trial language may be seen as unconceivable without taking the language of the law into account.

A more comprehensive interpretation of figure 3 could also include a variety of other contexts in which the use of legal language emerges. Such contexts may include, for example, the language of alternative dispute resolution, whose peculiarity merits separate investigation, or the translation and interpretation of legal language, among others. The picture may obviously be more deeply investigated and expanded. For instance, categorizing the role played by forensic linguistics (see McMenamin 2002, Gibbons 2003, Olsson 2004) may be particularly problematic. The discipline is related to a broad range of domains (Shuy 2007) such as the language of the law itself, the language used in the courtroom by a variety of potential participants, both in pre-trials and in trials, and the legal meta-language adopted in a variety of potential situations; rather than constituting a separate field in itself, it may therefore be seen as a cross-domain discipline.

Even though it is generally investigated in law studies, the role played by *language law* may also contribute to a more complex ramification of the visual representation suggested. *Language law* has been identified as an area of studies dealing with the legal effects and the legal rules related to the use of language (Mattila 2006: 17, Cornu 2005: 43-45); to some extent, therefore, language law may be seen as a category including the subcategory of language legislation which, in turn, according to the taxonomy presented, would be identified under the label of *language of the law*. The notion of *language law* is particularly complex in that it includes a wide variety of other sub-areas and deals with a broad variety of topics, such as language rights or language crimes (Shuy 1993).

2.3 Researching law and language

Studies in the area of legal language have grown exponentially in recent years and the importance of analyzing and reaching a deeper understanding of legal language crudely resides in the fact that "the law is such an important and influential institution, [which] is packed with language problems" (Gibbons 2006: 285).

2.3.1 Defining the field

Venturing into an identification of the origin of this field of study may be seen as an unattainable and unproductive mission. Indeed, it has often been argued that if by the study of legal language we mean a reflection upon the connection between law and language, we are confronted with an edifying past dating back to time immemorial (cf. Galdia 2009). For the purpose of this study, I will therefore adopt the modern approach to legal language studies as a discipline with a certain degree of autonomy. The term *legal linguistics* (Mattila 2006, Galdia 2009) is often used to broadly define the area and is in line with the notion of *linguistique juridique,* which goes back to Geny (1921). The aim of legal linguistics as a discipline is generally considered to be the examination of "the development, characteristics, and usage of language" (Mattila 2006: 11) in legal contexts, assuming that "the language of the law is examined, in the frame of legal linguistics, in the light of observations made by linguistics" (Mattila 2006: 11). The approach to the study of legal discourse adopted here focuses primarily on discourse dynamics in a specific legal context. Consequently, this work falls within a framework which may be defined as legal discourse analytical studies.

The study of discourse, and particularly of legal discourse, has progressively shifted from its analysis as an abstract system to a more 'integrative' (Mertz 1994: 436) approach which presupposes the creative function that language has in the construction of social dynamics and epistemologies (see *inter alia* Gumperz 1982 and Silverstein 1993)[5]. It may certainly be argued that language plays a crucial role in the creation of social and societal reality and identity, as well as in the development of different professional and vocational cultures (Gunnarsson 1995: 111). In this respect, legal language is no exception and may actually be seen as one of the most evident crystallizations of such dynamics, in that legal language is a constitutive element of a continuous process of shaping and reshaping of realities, identities and cultures. Going beyond the discussion of the (apparent) dichotomy between a reflectionist and an instrumentalist approach to discourse, this study presupposes that an attempt to investigate "the linguistic channeling and structuring of social life" seems particularly relevant in the domain of the law, if we intend it as "a key locus of institutionalized linguistic channeling of social power" (Mertz 1994: 436).

---

5 For a more in-depth conceptualization of the concept of discourse see section 3.3.

The concepts of institutionalization and, in particular, of linguistic institutionalization are of profound significance to an understanding of legal discourse. More specifically, it would be appropriate to talk about a dual process, which includes two intertwined and interdependent phenomena: on the one hand "the legal institutional regimentation and sedimentation of language" and on the other hand "the linguistic regimentation and sedimentation of legal institutions" (Mertz 1994: 447), which do not arise *sui generis* but shape (and are shaped by) a specific social context.

The reason underlying the application of some form of linguistic analysis to the legal field has often been related to "the desire to challenge the hermetic security both of substantive jurisprudence and of its meta-language, legal theory" (Goodrich 1987: 132). In this respect, one of the driving forces of these studies often derives from the desire or need to unveil the complexities of legal language and make a breach into a world which is often considered to be inaccessible and incomprehensible. However, studies in the sphere of legal discourse have gradually tended to assume a wider perspective; they generally do not originate from a purely challenging ambition towards jurisprudence or legal theory, but rather aim to explore a wider range of dynamics related to legal discourse.

2.3.2 Research perspectives

As mentioned above, legal language is pervasive in social life, and the concept of legal language is multifaceted in its very nature. Consequently, it is not surprising that research in this field includes panoplies of approaches and perspectives, and offering a complete introductory survey of the research trends related to the analysis of legal language is a task which is doomed to failure. Consequently, given the numerous and admirable sources available as a background (see in particular Danet 1980, 1985, Gibbons 1994, Levi 1994, Kurzon 1997, Tiersma 1999a, Galdia 2009), it is the aim of this section to eschew reproduction and deliberately adopt a highly selective focus.

As Stygall (1994: 6) remarks, legal language can be analyzed from a variety of perspectives (such as linguistic, sociological, and anthropological), and the author identifies three main patterns of research within the field:

- Language-as-object: works which treat language as the object of the investigation. These studies focus mainly on the description of the phenomena of legal language or on the application of theoretical linguistics to occurrences of legal language (Stygall 1994: 7).
- Language-as-process: this research trend is based on the analysis of the dynamics related to the comprehension and understanding of legal language.
- Language-as-instrument: this approach takes an instrumental perspective and analyses legal language as a tool to create and maintain dynamics of power.

Working along the same lines, but adopting a slightly different approach, and focusing on the nature of the studies, different research trends may also be categorized as follows:

- Descriptive (discourse production): the earlier work on legal language, in particular, primarily focused on the description of the most recurrent elements of legal language, mainly in comparison with what was generally placed under the heading of ordinary language. Particular attention was often devoted to written language (see Mellinkoff's seminal work, 1963).
- Experimental (discourse reception): these studies tend to focus on the reception of legal language. As will be shown, a large number of studies of this type have focused on the use of legal language in the courtroom, and, in particular, on jury trials, with the aim of understanding the processes which govern jurors' reception of specific instances of legal language. These studies are often based on experimental approaches and frequently draw on psycholinguistics (e.g. studies on the perceptions of jury instructions, such as Charrow/Charrow 1979, Elwork *et al* 1982, Sontag 1990).
- Critical (discourse interaction): the focus of these studies tends to be on the dynamics that govern the interaction between the different participants involved in the legal context, integrating

the concept of production and reception[6]. Within the same perspective, but with a more accentuated critical stance, are studies focusing on the complex relation between legal language and issues related to social dynamics of power and knowledge, often in line with Foucauldian reflections. The focus tends to be predominantly on macro-structures of discourse formations and on the reflection on how discourse is influenced and reciprocally influences social dynamics.

- Prescriptive (discourse prescription): this area assumes a more specifically legal standpoint and primarily aims to explicate the reasons (mainly related to jurisprudence and legal theory) underlying language choices in legal contexts.

This is only one of the several perspectives that may be taken in order to frame the main trends regarding the expanding sphere of legal language studies; it is by no means exhaustive, definitive or static. It simply attempts to offer a frame of reference in order to better understand the positioning of the present work.

2.3.3 Exploring courtroom language

The language of courtrooms has been extensively investigated (see *inter alia* O'Barr 1981, Danet 1985, Levi/Walker 1990, Cotterill 2003, Heffer 2005). An overview inevitably implies simplifying and excluding, and I will therefore focus solely on the most significant research areas in the field of courtroom communication for the purpose of this study.

Firstly, it is worth highlighting that a broad series of studies have been concerned with identifying and prescribing communication strategies which are successful in court. This, for instance, is the case of training manuals focusing on the most appropriate advocacy techniques to be used ('how-to' books), and they are generally based on legal scholars' experience. As will be shown, the application of these

---

6 As regards the dynamics of interaction in a jury trial, see, for instance, O'Barr (1982).

theoretical principles and recommendations can vary significantly in practical contexts. Indeed, even though courtroom language can be seen as a relatively standardized communicative event, every moment of that interaction implies a certain level of unpredictability.

Another series of studies (often, but not always, with their roots in the field of psychology) has been conducted on mock trials, often focusing on the analysis of jurors' behavior and jury decision making processes (see *inter alia* Hastie/Penrod/Pennington 1983). Mock trials can offer important insights for the understanding of a variety of courtroom dynamics; however, issues related to assessment of the ecological validity of jury simulations have often been raised (Davis *et al.* 1977, Gerbasi *et al.* 1977, Bray/Kerr 1979, 1982, Diamond 1979, 1997). Indeed, every trial is so intrinsically context-bound and situation-bound that simulations may not be revealing for the investigation of real instances of courtroom discourse; more specifically, the main issues are related to juror representativeness, the research setting, and the trial medium (Bornstein 1999: 75).

Another area of study, which is particularly relevant to the framework of this work, is based on the description, exploration and explanation of actual courtroom proceedings. Given the complexity of trial communication, an exhaustive and definite categorization is not achievable, especially when one considers that different studies have often incorporated different orientations. Some of the main areas that may be identified within courtroom language studies are based, for instance, on a conversational, a critical, or a corpus-based approach.

Among the conversationally-oriented studies we may cite Atkinson and Drew's influential work (1979) and Drew's studies (1985, 1992), which show insights into turn-taking and interactional dynamics in the courtroom, as well as Matoesian's research (1993, 1997, 1999a, 1999b, 2001). Other studies focus in particular on the processes on which the examination phase is based, and on the development of question patterns (Harris 1984, Woodbury 1984, Philips 1987, Maley/Fahey 1991). In this area particular attention has also been devoted to the analysis of styles of testimony (O'Barr 1982).

Like in other areas of legal language, the scholarly interest in language in the courtroom has progressively integrated the observation of microlinguistic details with the analysis of wider social dynamics (Conley *et al.* 1978, Bennet/Feldman 1981, Jackson 1988, Conley/O'Barr 1990, Matoesian 1993). Indeed, studies of the language of legal process have often confirmed that a courtroom represents a crucial cultural locus where dynamics of social power come into play. Critically oriented studies include, for instance, Wodak (1985), Harris (1989, 1994), Philips (1998).

The analysis of legal discourse is here not only seen as an opportunity to scrutinize fascinating language phenomena, but also as a chance to understand how legal discourse is intertwined with social dynamics, and to investigate how legal discourse production, interpretation, or co-construction has crucial consequences the participants must experience. It may certainly be argued that this assumption is applicable to all types of discourse, but it cannot be denied that the impact of legal discourse is particularly significant; indeed, it is through and within legal discourse that power may be wielded.

As has been mentioned (see section 2.2.3), another significant area of research is forensic linguistics (McMenamin 2002, Olsson 2004, Coulthard/Johnson 2007), in particular as regards the investigation of the performance of linguists as expert witnesses (Hollien 2001, Grant 2008). On a final note, it is also worth highlighting that corpus-based studies have also attracted considerable interest in recent years (see Heffer 2005).

2.3.4 Describing the language of the law

2.3.4.1 Dominant features

The study of legal language has often focused on the description of the principal features of the language of the law, interpreted primarily as the language of legal documents. Some of the main characteristics of these texts were extensively described in the pioneering study by Mellinkoff (1963). Along the same lines, Williams (2005: 31-37) identifies the following main characteristics:

- Archaic or rarely used words or expressions;
- Foreign words and expressions, especially Latinisms;

- Frequent repetition of particular words, expressions and syntactic structures;
- Long, complex sentences, with intricate patterns of coordination and subordination;
- Frequent use of passive construction;
- Highly impersonal style of writing.

At a lexical level, the language of the law has frequently been described according to its complexity, to the extent that Mellinkoff defines it as "wordy, unclear, pompous, dull" (Mellinkoff 1963: 23).

Legal language has often been associated with "the image of a context-independent lexicon of legal meanings" (Goodrich 1984: 188), but the question of stability and attribution of meaning is highly problematic even (or especially) in regard to the highly specialized nature of legal rhetoric, which is often intended as a "unitary, internally-shielded and valorized, system of communication" (Goodrich 1984: 186). Edelman writes of the language of legislation:

> The obvious approach to defining the meaning of legal language is to apply the dictionary meanings of the words, and the layman naturally assumes that this is how the experts do define its meaning. [...] But dictionary meanings are operationally close to irrelevant so far as the function of the statute or treaty in the political process is concerned. (Edelman 1972: 139)

This approach to the concept of meaning should be further problematized (see the Bakhtinian view of the appropriation of meaning mentioned above), but it does serve to highlight the potential discrepancy between what meanings laypersons may tend to attribute to certain terms and the possible interpretation of these terms in specific legal contexts.

Among the lexical features that Danet (1985) identifies as emblematic of the legal register are: technical terms and common terms with uncommon meanings; archaic expressions; formal items (see Danet 1985: 279-80). The features identified refer to the most frequently emerging traits of what is here defined as the language of the law. The most often quoted features are (see Mellinkoff 1963, Tiersma 1999a, Williams 2005):

- *The presence of archaic or rarely used words or expressions.* Lexical items of this type are, for instance, archaic deictic forms such as *hereinafter, hereafter, herein, hereof, heretofore, thereabout, thereafter, thereat, thereby, thereon, thereto, theretofore, thereupon, therewith.*
- *The use of foreign words and expressions*, especially of Latin origins. Among the Latin terms we may find[7]:
  - *ratio legis*: the reason or principle determining a law
  - *a priori*: from assumed principles
  - *bona fide*: good faith, genuine, honest
  - *in personam*: personal, personally
  - *inter se*: among themselves
  - *mens rea*: criminal state of mind
  - *mutatis mutandis*: with necessary changes
  - *obiter dictum*: part of the judgment not essential to case decision
  - *prima facie*: at first glance
- Besides Latinate forms, legal language also displays instances of terms of French origin, such as: *agreement, appeal, attorney, bailiff, bar, claim, complaint, counsel, court, covenant, damage, declaration, defendant, demurrer, evidence, indictment, judge, judgment, jury, justice, party, plaintiff, plea, plead, sentence, sue, suit, summon, verdict* and *voir dire*. Legal expressions displaying attributive adjectives placed after nouns, such as *Attorney General, court martial, fee simple absolute, letters testamentary, malice aforethought* and *Solicitor General*, also derive from the French language.
- *The use of two (or more) terms having a synonymic or similar meaning.* They are also defined as doublets (Mellinkoff 1963) or binomial expressions (Tiersma 1999a) or strings (Adams 2008: 204-207). Examples of expressions of this type would be: *of sound mind and memory; give devise and bequeath; will and testament; goods and chattels; final and conclusive; fit and proper; new and novel; save and except; peace and quiet* (Gibbons 2003: 43), as well as *annul and set aside, entirely and completely; null and void; without let or hindrance* (Mellinkoff

7 See Mellinkoff (1963: 15) for further exemplifications.

1963: 25). These practices confirm Mellinkoff's oft-quoted remark that "[l]awyers are wordy. It takes them a long time to get to the point" (Mellinkoff 1963: 24).

Other identifiable features are:

- *The use of prolix verbal constructions*, such as:
  - offer testimony → testify
  - make inquiry → ask
  - provide assistance → help
  - place a limitation upon → limit
  - make an examination of → examine
  - provide protection to → protect
  - reach a resolution → resolve
  - make mention of → mention
  - be in compliance with → comply
  - make allegations → allege
  - effect settlement → settle
- *Archaic morphological elements*, such as the morpheme *-eth* used for the third person singular in the indicative present form, deriving from the Old English. Such forms are extremely rare nowadays, but the term 'witnesseth' is still quite frequent in contracts.
- The syntactic traits that permeate legal language have been extensively investigated, particularly in a contrastive perspective in relation to more 'ordinary' uses of language. Some of the most recurrent features are above average sentence length, the pervasiveness of nominalizations and passive forms (Crystal/ Davy 1969, Shuy/Larkin 1978, Charrow/Charrow 1979). The language of the law displays a pervasive use of long, complex sentences, with intricate patterns of coordination and subordination. In particular, legal texts are often imbued with intricate syntactic patterns, and it has often been stated that these texts display relatively little punctuation, even though Crystal and Davy (1969: 200-201) observe that "[i]t is not true that legal English was always entirely punctuationless, and in fact the occasional specimens which were intended for oral presentation – proclamations, for instance – were quite fully punctuated. The idea of totally unpunctuated legal English is a later development".

- Another aspect characterizing written legal English is a highly impersonal style of writing (e.g. Šarčević 2000: 177, Williams 2005) and, in particular, the intense use of passive forms (e.g. Jackson 1995: 119-120, Williams 2004: 228), which conveys an aura of formality, impartiality and authoritativeness.

2.3.4.2 Describing the language of the law: concluding remarks

A detailed description of the features of legal language would exceed the scope of this work. Nonetheless, an outline of some common characteristics may shed some light upon the reasons behind this language's widespread reputation for intricacy and unfamiliarity. Any analysis of legal language must also take into consideration that this type of language "is a socially constructed institution in its own right" (Stygall 1994: 4) and as such develops within constraints and may to some extent be resilient to change (see *inter alia* Stygall 1994: 4). Moreover, the complexity of legal language has often been seen as a way to legitimize selective access to this variety of language, and to disempower people who are excluded. However, it should also be noted that, because of its pervasiveness and the consequent variety of contexts in which it is employed, legal language can assume surprisingly varying contours. Furthermore, although it is often considered static and immutable, legal language is, like society, inevitably in constant evolution (see the Plain English Movement, cf. Flesch 1979, Charrow/ Charrow 1979, Hathaway 1983a, 1983b, 1985, Charrow 1987).

The above-mentioned features cannot be applied *in toto* to legal language when employed as a superordinate expression, and they mainly (but not exclusively) characterize what has, for the purpose of this study, been designated as 'the language of the law'. Such features may only occasionally emerge in other areas of legal language, for instance in the language of trials.

In other words, it has been argued that the characteristics that are generally attributed to legal language (such as syntactic, lexical and semantic complexity) refer primarily to written legal language (Tiersma 2008: 22), whereas spoken legal language is "not as different from ordinary speech as one might think" (Tiersma 2008: 23). Despite the fact that legal language is clearly associated with archaic and highly formal registers, it is interesting to note that, in certain contexts, it also includes instances of informal jargon (Tiersma 2008: 16, Tiersma 1999a: 137-138), for instance in courtroom communication (as will be illustrated in chapter 5). Although a clear-cut and static distinction between the different areas of legal language is not only unachievable but also undesirable, what emerges is that these features cannot be extended indifferently to all areas of legal language use.

Put simply, law cannot be reduced to a stagnant collection of sophisms, especially when one is dealing with the multifaceted language of the courtroom.

3. Research framework

If the world is complex and messy, then at least some of the time we're going to have to give up on simplicities. (John Law)

3.1 Research interest and rationale

This study arises out of the desire to investigate the complexity underlying the interaction of different discourses within a highly institutionalized event, namely a jury trial. It may be argued that a society functions because of the interaction between experts and non-experts in different fields (Gunnarsson/Linell/Nordberg 1997: 1); consequently, an analysis of the interaction between these two broad categories is particularly crucial to any investigation of communicative events, especially those which take place in institutionalized settings.

More specifically, a trial by jury represents a typical locus of knowledge asymmetries in that the participants, by definition, display significant differences in (*inter alia*) class, status, gender, and level of education. The analysis focuses in particular on the communication process between legal experts and non-experts. Even though such categories are not self-explanatory (see section 4.4.1), in the context of a jury trial, belonging to (or being excluded from) a certain professional category is one of the fundamental criteria which determine which people may or may not assume a certain role in the event. In other words, the communicative roles assumed, for instance by lawyers and by jurors, are clearly distinct and are highly dependent on their professional membership and their personal background.

In investigating trial discourse, we are dealing with an event that is immediately associated with the legal sphere, and it may appear obvious to assume the constant emergence of a highly specialized form of language. Indeed, on the one hand the significantly standardized nature of the event determines the presence of procedural constraints and conventionalized practices; on the other hand, however, the communicative strategies and the linguistic tools employed in the interactional process display a noteworthy level of heterogeneity.

The discursive complexity of a trial calls for a series of questions: How do specialized and non-specialized discourses intermingle in a jury trial? What types of knowledge asymmetries are there? How are these asymmetries exploited communicatively? What communicative strategies and techniques are used? What are the reasons behind them?

The choice to focus on communicative processes in the courtroom derives from the consideration that trials have (potentially) fundamental consequences for the life of individuals, as well as for society as a whole; the importance of achieving a finer understanding of the dynamics that shape such a crucial event is therefore also self-evident. More specifically, the aim of this investigation is to combine a descriptive and an explanatory approach. As remarked in chapter 2, a considerable corpus of research has revealingly described the purely linguistic aspects of interactions in the courtroom, whereas another large body of work has focused on the prescription of what communicative strategies and techniques should or should not be employed. This study falls within the trend of research that aims to go beyond the descriptive-prescriptive dichotomy and attempts to merge descriptive observations with an explanatory approach.

3.2 Material and data

The main object of analysis of this study is a criminal trial by jury, namely the David Westerfield trial, which took place in San Diego, California, in 2002. This choice derives, firstly, from the desire to focus on a specific type of trial (a jury trial), because it represents a typical example of knowledge asymmetries in a communicative event (see section 4.4). The U.S. was chosen as the privileged context because it may be considered representative of jury trials, since the use of this type of trial is still relatively common there compared to other countries: indeed, it is stated that more than 90 percent of the jury trials in the world take place in the U.S. (Young 2007), even though it should be clear that exact comparative statistics are not available[8]. It should also be remembered, however, that scholars have highlighted the declining importance of the jury trial (Koski/Saks 2003), as the number of such trials is constantly decreasing even in the American system (both in criminal and civil cases), mainly because of cost and time issues, in comparison with other means of dispute resolution (Young 2007, von Mehren 2007).

In this analysis I focus on a Californian trial because of my previous knowledge of the Californian system and legislation, and the Westerfield trial in particular was selected for several reasons. Firstly, it was a relatively recent case at the time the data collection started. A considerable number of studies of trial language have been conducted, for instance, on the O.J. Simpson trials (in particular the criminal trial, 1995) because of the extraordinary media and social attention it drew, and because of its peculiarities (see Bugliosi 1996, Hunt 1999, Cotterill 2002, Felman 2002), but my intention was to focus on a more recent case; moreover, the case was concluded, which afforded me the possibility of gaining an overview of the entire case, from its initial to the conclusive stages. On a more practical note, the material was easily accessible, as the trial was televised.

Using material that has already being collected has clear methodological implications, but it proves particularly efficient in terms of time and costs; moreover, it allows researchers to select from among different cases those that are most suitable according to a series of parameters, such as the length, the place or time the trial took place, the quality and the comprehensiveness of the video material. The selection of data inevitably entails a subjective judgement, which should be

8 According to the American Bar Association "[i]t's been estimated that the United States accounts for 95% of all jury trials in the world". Available at: <http://www.abanet.org/publiced/lawday/talking/jurytalk.html.> Accessed: January 2, 2012.

acknowledged, and the different choices should be justified and explained in order to offer transparency and clarity.

When deciding to analyze the language of a jury trial, the "universe of possible texts" (Titscher *et al.* 2000: 33) is extremely varied. Given the unique particulars of every trial, a comparison of different trials would have caused a significant lack of homogeneity (on which note the inappropriateness of random sampling for qualitative-driven approaches has often been highlighted; see Bauer/Aarts 2000: 19). The choice to work on one single case certainly reduces the scope for generalizable results, but at the same time it guarantees a relatively high level of homogeneity and uniformity.

The material gathered primarily includes video-recordings of trial sessions that took place between June and September 2002. One of the most obvious yet crucial advantages recordings have over other ways of collecting data (e.g. through a single observation) is the constant availability of the material for (potentially infinite) re-examination and in-depth analyses. As Heritage remarks: "In enabling repeated and detailed examination of the events of interaction, the use of recordings extends the range and precision of the observations which can be made" (Heritage 1984: 238).

Other fundamental sources are the official transcripts carried out by the court reporter, which were constantly compared with the video recordings collected. Accurate transcripts of all the phases of the trial were available, excluding some specific moments, such as deliberations, since what happens in the jury room is not made public. The analysis of official legal transcripts represents in itself a very vast area of analysis (see *inter alia* Eades 1996), but this line of enquiry goes beyond the scope of this work.

Other important sources of information collected are media reports, press coverage, and relevant legislation. They are not treated as specific subjects of the current analysis but have nonetheless been constantly referred to and have proved invaluable in facilitating a higher familiarity with the case and the context within which it developed.

The use of video recordings would also potentially allow for an analysis of non-verbal communication. It may certainly be argued that visual signs related to proxemics, graphics, artifacts, insignia, colors, dress code (Isani 2006: 51), as well as chronemics, haptics and other areas, play a significant role in the way different dynamics develop within a trial. Without wishing to disregard the crucial functions played by other aspects, the focus of the current analysis is primarily restricted to the verbal aspects of the interaction. The importance of visual semiotics in the courtroom is by no means neglected here, but full examination in that perspective would go beyond the purpose of this study.

3.3 Theoretical background

The study of a particularly complex field of analysis such as courtroom discourse may require venturing into a variety of different theoretical approaches, with the awareness that, as Popper observes:

> [A]t any moment we are prisoners caught in the framework of our theories; our expectations; our past experiences; our language. But we are prisoners in a Pickwickian sense; if we try, we can break out of our framework at any time. Admittedly, we shall find ourselves again in a framework, but it will be a better and a roomier one, and we can at any moment break out of it again. (Popper 1970: 56)

First of all, I consider it necessary to delve into the multifaceted notion of discourse, and to clarify the approach to discourse that will be adopted here, as a specific view of language and discourse inevitably shapes the theoretical, argumentative and analytical framework.

3.3.1 The notion of discourse

Despite the limits intrinsic in any definition, it is clear that one needs to explicitly delimit the theoretical perspective that is being adopted. It is also obvious that while limiting one's perspective, one is deliberately deciding not to look at other aspects of a certain theory; however, as van Dijk remarks, that too is necessary, lest the theory employed become a 'Theory of Everything', a blunt instrument which is too broad to be incisive (van Dijk 2009: 3).

The conceptualization of 'discourse' is fundamental to the application of any form of discourse analysis and, inexorably, for any reflection upon the theme of language and the law. Therefore, some preliminary observations on the interpretation of the term 'discourse' used in this work will now be presented, though not without an awareness of the risks involved in attempting to offer any definition, and keeping in mind that the ubiquity of the word 'discourse' in different fields of analysis inevitably complicates any attempt to define it.

As has been mentioned, the core of this study is an analysis of courtroom discourses. However, defining complex concepts such as 'discourse' and 'discourse analysis' would probably be too much to ask of one work, to the extent van Dijk describes his two extensive volumes on discourse (van Dijk 1997b, 1997c) as a mere attempt to answer the basic question of what discourse is. There is little consensus as to the meaning of the term 'discourse'. While some definitions associate discourse exclusively with the notion of 'language', it is generally agreed that the concept of discourse refers broadly to 'a form of language use' (e.g. van Dijk 1997a: 2), or 'language in use' (e.g. Fairclough 2003). Obviously, a fully fledged overview of all the interpretations of the concepts of language and discourse is not feasible here. However, one of the basic assumptions I embrace is Lee's view that "language is not just to communicate information. Language is, in addition, also a device to think and feel with, as well as a device with which to signal and negotiate social identity" (Lee 1992: 78); moreover, the idea that "language has meaning only in and through practices" (Gee 1999: 8) constitutes a central theoretical postulation in this work.

De Beaugrande colorfully illustrates the complex nature of language by highlighting that "in the world of human beings, you won't find a language by itself – the Dutch language strolling by the canals, or the English language having a nice cup of tea, or the German language racing madly along the autobahn. You only find *discourse*, that is, *real communicative events*" (de Beaugrande 1997a: 36, original emphasis). The notion of 'communicative event' is also seen by van Dijk as a characterization of discourse that embodies some functional aspects, such as who uses language, why, when, where and how (van Dijk 1997a: 2).

A complementary interpretation of the concept of discourse is suggested by Tomlin *et al.* (1997: 64-65) using the concept of the 'blueprint metaphor' of discourse. From this perspective, discourse can be explained through two different metaphorical constructs. According to the idea of 'conduit metaphor' (Reddy 1979), the meaning intended by the speaker is contained within a 'textual artifact' which is then conveyed to the listener, and the latter then extracts the meaning from this artifact. Language in this view is considered a "precision instrument, which is used to craft precise meaning, fully embodied in the text" (Tomlin *et al.* 1997: 64). Conversely, the theoretical interpretation of the concept of discourse that underlies this work is akin to the idea of 'blueprint metaphor of discourse' (Tomlin *et al.* 1997: 65). That means that the listener is given a highly active role in the conceptual representation of meanings. The text itself is therefore seen as a scheme, a reference, or a guide to help the listener or the reader to construct meanings through a series of conceptual models.

As has been noted, we can take as a point of departure the idea that, as Brown and Yule note, "the analysis of discourse is, necessarily, the analysis of language in use", (Brown/Yule 1983: 1). Consequently, "it cannot be restricted to the description of linguistic forms independent of the purposes or functions which these forms are designed to serve in human affairs" (Brown/Yule 1983: 1). Some of the basic postulations shared by different approaches to discourse analysis are summarized by Johnstone (2008: 8-19):

- Discourse is shaped by the world, and discourse shapes the world
- Discourse is shaped by the possibilities and limitations of language, and discourse shapes language
- Discourse is shaped by relations among participants, and discourse shapes relations
- Discourse is shaped by prior discourse, and discourse shapes present and future discourse
- Discourse is shaped by the medium, and discourse shapes the medium
- Discourse is shaped by purpose, and discourse shapes possible purposes.

Van Dijk further explores the idea of discourse by specifying that the notion of language use is also integrated with two other dimensions, namely the communication of beliefs and social interaction, and it is highlighted that the aim of discourse studies should be to investigate these three dimensions in an integrative way (van Dijk 1997a: 2). Moreover, the crucial role played by social practice for any analysis of discourse is emphasized by Fairclough, who states that 'discourse' is "more than *just* language use: it is language use, whether speech or writing, seen as a type of social practice" (Fairclough 1992b: 28, original emphasis).

Consequently, applying this notion of discourse to the study of legal discourse, it goes without saying that legal discourse goes beyond legal vocabulary. In Cornu's terms, "le discours juridique est, par opposition au vocabulaire juridique, l'autre versant du langage du droit: c'est le langage du droit en action" [as opposed to legal vocabulary, legal discourse is the other side of the language of the law: it's the language of the law in action] (Cornu 2005: 207).

3.3.2 Analyzing discourse

The discussion of the interpretation of discourse offered here is by no means exclusive. It simply aims to foreground some of the issues related to language in use and to place its analysis within a framework that goes beyond mere linguistic description. Following van Dijk (1997a: 29-31), I will now summarize some of the main principles of discourse analysis on which the approach adopted in this study is based:

- *Naturally occurring text and talk*: unlike other approaches to language studies, discourse analysis focuses on authentic instances of discourse, and not on utterances that are artificially invented or created in order to illustrate a specific point. Indeed, the current analysis is based on authentic data drawn from a real event.
- *Context*: as I hope to have illustrated, the interdependence between text and context is one of the most crucial aspects to be considered by discourse analysts. I will therefore try to offer an

explanatory approach that is also based on the analysis of a series of contextual elements; therefore, several factors, such as the setting, the participants and the relationships between them, or the institutional constraints, will also be taken into account.

- *Discourse as talk*: the modes that characterize discourse are generally defined as written or spoken and may be seen as one of the features used to identify a typology of discourse (van Dijk 1997a: 7). The term 'text' will be used here according to the well-established conception that 'text' may be intended as a superordinate term which may refer to different modes (such as written, spoken or visual) and not exclusively to the written mode. In this study the analysis of spoken interaction will be predominant but, as discourse studies are also fashion victims, it has also been pointed out that the interest in spoken texts should not lead to a sort of 'neglect' of written ones (van Dijk 1997a: 30). It has often been stated that "everything in a trial is achieved through the spoken word" (Walter 1988: 225), even though this interpretation may be seen as an oversimplification. In this respect it is crucial to highlight that different modes constantly interrelate in trial communication, and written texts play a crucial role within a trial. It will suffice to say that, although trial proceedings are conducted orally, they are simultaneously transcribed, in order to assume the form of official records, whose importance in the context of legal proceedings is evident. Moreover, the interaction between different modes is constantly present, and there are continuous references to written texts[9]. An in-depth analysis of all the written texts produced in the course of a trial would simply be an unfeasible task and would certainly go beyond the scope of this book. It should not be forgotten, however, that a strong interrelation exists between texts characterized by different modes.
- *Discourse as social practice of society members*: discourse is to be intended as a form of social practice that is shaped by (and in

9 For instance, jury instructions may be primarily understood as written texts which are meant to be spoken, but they are also generally made available in the written mode for future reference (see section 5.3).

turns shapes) a specific context. This assumption inevitably leads to the concept of constructivity.

- *Constructivity*: the constructive aspect of discourse, in van Dijk's sense, refers to the idea that the constitutive units of discourses "may be *functionally* used, understood or analysed as elements of larger ones" (van Dijk 1997a: 30, original emphasis). Following one of the paradigms that are axiomatic in most variants of CDA (see section 3.4), discourse is not only socially constructed, but is also constructive. For instance, in the case of a trial the different discourses are socially constructed, are determined by social, cultural, institutional, professional practices, values and principles and are in turn constitutive of such practices.

Other important concepts to be highlighted in the current analysis are the fluidity of discourse boundaries and the ideas of intertextuality and interdiscursivity. Discourse may be intended according to different degrees of abstractness-concreteness and generality-specificity. From a general and abstract perspective, 'discourse' may be used to refer to language in use or to certain domains of language use. We may also use the term to refer to more concrete and specific instances of language use. More specifically, in his seminal discussion of the notion of discourse, van Dijk distinguishes between an abstract use of the term intended as a "*type* of social phenomenon in general" and a more concrete use when employed to refer to "a concrete example *token* of text or talk" (1997a: 4, original emphasis). Obviously, his distinction is not clear-cut, because the identification and establishment of boundaries of discourse is not unproblematic. For instance, if I give a five-minute speech, there may be a vast (although not unanimous) consensus in defining that communicative event as an instance of discourse, but in the case of more complex events several complications arise.

In the analysis of a trial it is unavoidable that a simplistic description may not be applicable, as we are trying to analyze an authentic instance of complex human interaction and communication. Is it possible to understand a trial as representing a single discourse? Is it to be intended as a series of micro-discourses, or as a sequence of interrelated discourses? More specifically, in van Dijk's terms, "we might have to distinguish between 'simple' and 'compound' discourses, or between discourses and 'discourse complexes'" (1997a: 4-5). The intricacy of these notions is evident if we reflect upon what parameters should be taken into consideration in order to distinguish between these potential types of discourses. What level of simplicity should we be dealing with to be able to say that we are talking about a 'simple' discourse, especially given the interdiscursive nature of all instances of discourse? Indeed, the intertextual and interdiscursive nature of discourses (see Kristeva 1970, Bakhtin 1981, 1986) is another fundamental element to be taken into consideration in their analysis. Hansen observes that the phenomenon of intertextuality allows different texts to mutually construct their legitimacy:

> As a text makes references to older texts it constructs legitimacy for its own reading, but it also simultaneously reconstructs and reproduces the classical status of the older ones. Rather than seeing new texts as depending on older ones, one should therefore see the two as interacting in an exchange where one text gains legitimacy from quoting and the other gains legitimacy from being quoted. This construction of an intertextual link produces mutual legitimacy and creates an exchange at the level of meaning. (Hansen 2005: 57)

More specifically, according to Fairclough, "intertextuality is basically the property texts have of being full of snatches of other texts, which may be explicitly demarcated or merged in, and which the text may assimilate, contradict, ironically echo, and so forth" (1992a: 84). Intertextuality is not only 'manifest', but also 'constitutive', and the idea of 'constitutive intertextuality' is defined as 'interdiscursivity' (Fairclough 1992a: 85). In this respect, Fairclough adds: "On the one hand, we have the heterogeneous constitution of texts out of specific other texts (manifest intertextuality); on the other hand, the heterogeneous constitution of texts out of elements (types of convention) of orders of discourse (interdiscursivity)" (Fairclough 1992a: 85). In Fairclough's view, interdiscursivity is defined as the phenomenon of a text's drawing upon a "particular mix of genres, of discourses, and of styles" (Fairclough 2003: 218).

The crucial constitutive role played by intertextual and interdiscursive elements is also emphasized by Candlin and Maley, who also reflect further on the evolving and dynamic character of discourse:

> Discourses are made internally variable by the incorporation of such *intertextual* and *interdiscursive* elements. Such evolving discourses are thus intertextual in that they manifest a plurality of text sources. However, insofar as any characteristic text evokes a particular discoursal value, in that it is associated with some institutional and social meaning, such evolving discourses are at the same time interdiscursive. (Candlin/Maley 1997: 203, original emphasis)

Consequently, such considerations also call for an interdiscursive analytical approach:

> What emerges is a requirement for a parallel and complex interdiscursivity of analysis, matching the interplay between the micro and the macro, the actual and the historical, the ethnographic and the ethnomethodological, the interactively sociolinguistic and the discoursal/textual and to acknowledge the need to offer explanations of *why* rather than merely descriptions of *how*. (Candlin 1997: XII, original emphasis)

3.3.3 The notion of context

3.3.3.1 Discourse in/as/and context?

The debate arising around the possibility/necessity of including 'context' in the analysis of conversation (Schegloff 1998, Wetherell 1998, Billig 1999, van Dijk 2007, Fairclough 2008) is particularly pertinent to this work. Studies in the area of Conversation Analysis (CA) tend to assume that contextual information is significant in the analysis of discourse only when it is noticeably 'oriented to' by the participants and is therefore considered 'procedurally relevant' (Schegloff 1992); however, a considerable number of studies within CA acknowledge the importance of certain aspects of context in the analysis of conversation (Boden 1994, Drew/Heritage 1992).

Crucial to this investigation is the assumption that the complex nature of discourse, the inextricability of discourse and context, and the inherent interdiscursivity of any discourse cannot be overlooked. As Fairclough and Wodak remark: "Discourse is not produced without context and cannot be understood without taking context into consideration. [...] Discourses are always connected to other discourses which were produced earlier, as well as those which are produced synchronically and subsequently" (Fairclough/Wodak 1997: 277).

All dimensions of discourse seem, therefore, to depend to some extent on what has been defined as the 'discourse relativity principle' (van Dijk 1997a: 9), the idea that any element of discourse is influenced by (and in turn influences) all the other verbal and non-verbal elements that surround (and in turn constitute) it. Indeed, the role of contextual features is fundamental because they "not only influence discourse, but also vice versa" (van Dijk 1997a: 19), and this reciprocal influence is at the heart of the interpretation of discourse and context adopted here. It is further assumed, therefore, that "discourse and its users have a 'dialectic' relation with their context: besides being subject to the social constraints of the context, they also contribute to, construe or change that context" (van Dijk 1997a: 20).

On the basis of these assumptions, any effective analysis of discourse must entail a holistic approach that considers (in a Faircloughian view) texts, discourse practices and social practices as interdependent entities. Indeed, any communicative event is not only embedded in a certain social context, but also socially situated and constructed, and in turn constructive. In other words, it is widely agreed that the meaning of any discourse cannot be alienated from the social context or situation in which it develops; moreover, beyond being socially constructed, discourses are in turn constructive, as they frame, shape and reshape the institutional and social practices they go hand-in-hand with. Discourse may therefore be seen as "a means which both reproduces and constructs afresh particular socio-discursive practices" (Candlin 1997: VIII). Put differently, discourses are understood as being inseparable from society at large.

As Merry remarks: "Discourses are aspects of culture, interconnected vocabularies and systems of meaning located in a social world" (Merry 1990: 110). The investigation of discourses in highly institutionalized contexts also calls for a reflection on the intricacy of the idea of 'systems of meanings' and on the concept of appropriation of meaning. As Wetherell observes, meaning can be seen as conventional in that it is the result of a series of conventions and practices, but it is also inevitably relational, in that discourse constantly "adds to, instantiates, extends, and transforms the cultural storehouse of meanings" (Wetherell 2001: 18). Merry's definition of discourse also emphasizes the importance of the well-established notion that a dialectic relationship exists between discourses and the specific institutions to which they are intrinsically linked:

> A discourse is not individual and idiosyncratic but part of a shared cultural world. Discourses are rooted in particular institutions and embody their culture. Actors operate within a structure of available discourses. However within that structure there is space for creativity and actors define and frame their problems within one or another discourse. (Merry 1990: 110)

What emerges, without neglecting the presence of specific structures that frame/demark the structures of possible discourses, is the enormous creative potential of the actors/participants involved. Indeed, the analysis of courtroom discourse will show instances of manifestly standardized talk which coexist with highly multifaceted and creative instances of talk.

The verbal dimension will be the privileged field of analysis; the aim is not to carry out a sterile description of words, but to understand not only what is being said (or written), but also by whom, how, when and why; this is in line with the idea that 'text' cannot be separated from 'context', intended as "the other characteristics of the social situation or the communicative event that may systematically influence text or talk" (van Dijk 1997a: 3). In other words, I will examine not only the result of the interaction, but also a number of (constituent) elements that determine it.

In operationalizing these notions of discourse, and applying them to the analysis of a communicative event, we can ask, from a primarily descriptive perspective, what is being said and how, and from a more explanatory point of view we can try to understand the reasons behind these choices, considering the immense richness of potential resources actors can choose from within a language. In doing so, it must be highlighted that context is an object of study in itself, and not just a contour to artificially isolated words and sentences: contexts not only constrain; they also create. In other words, discourse cannot be seen as an epiphenomenon of specific contexts and specific contextual dynamics.

3.3.3.2 Social context and context models

I have argued that an analysis of discourse cannot fail to take the notion of 'context'[10] into account, but the definition of this concept is highly complex. Context may generally be described as a communicative situation or environment; it may also refer to a verbal context, or co-text. However, texts, co-texts and social situations are highly interdependent and reciprocally co-construct, in a fluid and dynamic way. An attempt to visualize this interdependence is offered in figure 4:

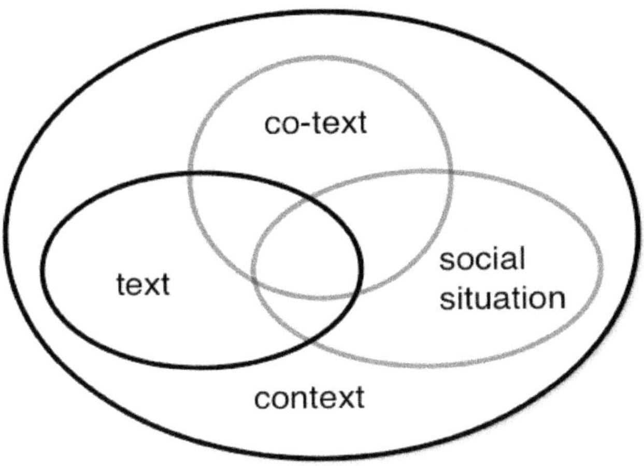

Figure 4. Interdependence of text, co-text and social situation.

Figure 4 is to be intended exclusively as a preliminary visualization which attempts to show the interrelation between contextual elements, such as text, co-text and social situation. However, a more comprehensive description of contexts must also take into account their high degree of subjectivity and relativity: contexts are subjective in that they are "embedded in a set of autobiographical representations in epi-

10 For a deeper discussion of the notion of context see *inter alia* Duranti/Goodwin 1992, van Dijk 1977, 2006, 2007, 2009.

sodic memory" (van Dijk 2009: 249) and are inevitably relative, as the participants themselves define what is relevant in the social situation (van Dijk 2009: 5).

Central to the current study are the strong bonds of interdependence and mutual construction which link the concepts of discourse and social context. It is important to highlight, however, that social contexts and their characteristics do not exercise a direct influence on discourse; indeed, "there is no direct link between situational or social structures and discourse structures" (van Dijk 2009: VII) and to assume that the existence of an inevitable causal relationship between the two would be a deterministic fallacy (van Dijk 2009: 4).

This is not to neglect the fundamental relationship between these two structures, but merely to emphasize that the link is not directly a causal one, for the very intuitive reason that, if it were, all language users sharing specific situational or social structures would therefore use language in exactly the same way (van Dijk 2009: VII). The relationship is understood here as being mediated by 'context models', which draw on the idea of 'mental models'[11] (see Johnson-Laird 1983). Context models are defined as "subjective definitions of the communicative situation as they are construed and dynamically updated by the participants" (van Dijk 2009: VII). These models determine the social, personal and situational variability of language use (van Dijk 2009: VIII). This notion is in line with the idea that "visible language is only the tip of the iceberg of invisible meaning construction" (Fauconnier 1997: 1); indeed, as van Dijk remarks, participants in a communicative event are not 'blank slates', but bring with them their socio-cultural knowledge and their personal background. The influence that social contexts have on the participants, therefore, is not au-

---

11 For a deeper discussion of mental models see *inter alia* Norman (1983) and Young (1983). In particular, Norman writes: "*Mental models* are naturally evolving models. That is, through interaction with a target system, people formulate mental models of that system. These models need not be technically accurate (and usually are not), but they must be functional. A person, through interaction with the system, will continue to modify the mental model in order to get a workable result. Mental models will be constrained by such things as the user's technical background, previous experience with similar systems, and the structure of the human information processing system" (Norman 1983: 7-8).

tomatically causal, but rather it is mediated by the individuals' 'context models' (van Dijk 2009: VIII-IX). According to van Dijk (2009: 251), context models are formed and constantly evolve, in accordance with the following elements:

- Previous context planning yielding a provisional context
- Observation and analysis of the current social and communicative situation
- Inferences from previous discourse in the situation
- Inferences from ongoing activities of participants
- Recalling previous context models
- Instantiation of general knowledge about contexts
- Application of general personal and social aims and goals (van Dijk 2009: 251).

In light of the fact that "simply getting one's hands on the shape of context is a major analytical problem" (Duranti/Goodwin 1992: 13), these reflections do not aim to offer a comprehensive definition of context; rather, they merely aim to address the complexity which underlies the concept, to stress the idea that contexts are not simple, objectively observable contours of discourse, and to point out that the strong relationship between discourse and social structures cannot be assumed to be automatic and linear. In this respect, Wodak too confirms that simplistic causal models fail to fit the complexities of most of the phenomena of modern society (Wodak 2001b: 63).

3.4 Methodological framework

This study is primarily guided by a qualitative approach, and it draws on different research orientations, in the light of the assumption that these orientations are not mutually exclusive, but can instead be seen as complementary. Indeed, they are not necessarily in conflict with one another and can be profitably combined to offer deeper insights into the same event. Social research is intrinsically sensitive to the complexity of social reality and therefore interdisciplinarity and multiple research methodologies are often adopted, in line with the idea that "different research perspectives may be combined and supplemented" (Flick 2002: 25). Discourse studies constitute no exception to this wider trend, and the application of different approaches, deriving from both qualitative and quantitative orientations, is becoming increasingly common within the discipline.

An approach based on multiple methodological standpoints might intuitively call for an association with the concept of triangulation (Denzin 1978); to some extent, this study applies the concept of 'methodological' triangulation (Denzin 1978: 295), derived from the idea that "each method reveals different aspects of empirical reality" (Denzin 1978: 28). However, I would like to point out that this approach is not naively intended as an opportunity to obtain a complete and objective picture of such a complex event. The combination of different methodological orientations can simply constitute a means of achieving a deeper understanding of the phenomenon being investigated, but it is clearly not an automatic and mechanical test of validity.

More specifically, some of the main aspects of a case study (Yin 2009) are integrated with different approaches drawing on discourse analysis, and the overall qualitative approach is also combined with instances of quantitative-based analyses. In particular, the use of computer-based analysis may be fruitfully employed for testing and corroborating purposes, and can prove revealing in investigating, for instance, specific (linguistic) features.

In the traditional dichotomy between a large-N cross-case method and a case study (or within-case) method (Gerring 2007: 1-13), this work may be seen as falling within the latter approach. However, as mentioned above, the two approaches are not necessarily mutually exclusive. Although case studies tend traditionally to be associated with qualitative research, quantitative methods are not therefore excluded *a priori* and Gerring notes that "[t]o study a single case intensively need not limit an investigator to qualitative techniques" (Gerring 2007: 10). The definition of this project as a case study is not unproblematic, as different forms of case study research may overlap with other approaches. One of the particularities of case studies is their grounding in the examination "of a single entity bounded by time and place" (Daymon/Holloway 2002: 105), but the definition of what may be labeled as a single entity may not be automatic. For instance, the case analyzed is a specific communicative and social event, i.e. a criminal trial by jury, with particular attention being devoted to some specific phases of the trial, but it is plausible to wonder whether an entire trial may be labeled as a single entity, given its compound and complex nature[12]. Case study research is, however, particularly relevant to this study, as it is guided by the intrinsic purpose of increasing "knowledge about real, contemporary communication events in their context" (Daymon/Holloway 2002: 105); moreover, concentration on one single phenomenon allows an in-depth investigation in order "to uncover the manifest interaction of significant factors characteristic of this phenomenon" (Berg 2004: 251).

3.4.1 Discourse analytical approach

The approach used in this work can be defined as primarily descriptive-explanatory. Indeed, a description of some of the linguistic features and the discursive practices that emerge in courtroom communication will be a point of departure, and it will be intertwined with the attempt to explain the linguistic, discursive, societal, and legal reasons underlying such practices.

Discourse Analysis[13] (DA) therefore plays a crucial role in this investigation. DA is not primarily concerned with language as an abstract system (Johnstone 2008: 3) and can be understood, in very general terms, as a discipline that goes beyond textual analysis and explores who uses language in certain contexts, how, why and when (van Dijk 1997a: 2). Indeed, the aim of this study is not only to describe discourse, understood as language in social practice, but also to uncover and explain some of the several complex dynamics beyond the text. In this sense discourse analysis cannot abstract from a contextual analysis

---

12 See in this respect van Dijk's (1997a) discussion of the concepts of 'simple' and 'compound' discourses, and 'discourse complexes'.

13 For an overview of discourse analysis see *inter alia* Blommaert 2005, Brown/Yule 1983, Gee 2005, Schiffrin 1994, Titscher *et al.* 2000.

that goes beyond the microtextual level. Different forms of DA tend to combine a descriptive approach (according to the idea that "describing texts and how they work is always a goal along the way", see Johnstone 2008: 27) and a more explanatory and critical goal.

It is widely agreed that DA has developed into (and according to) different approaches, and Wood and Kroger observe that "there seems to be a move toward recognizing the strengths of different approaches and the possibility of drawing on more than one approach within the same project" (Wood/Kroger 2000: 24-25).

First of all, some of the theoretical assumptions derived from Critical Discourse Analysis (CDA) will be discussed, even though the work is not purely CDA-oriented[14]. Furthermore, the fact that in courtroom communication spoken interaction plays a crucial role may call for a reflection on the potential use of Conversation Analysis (CA) in this investigation. A communicative event consists of myriad types of interaction, and studies in CA have dealt with a variety of aspects that characterize such interactions, such as turn-taking, sequence organization, repair, etc. Each of these properties of talk may prove to be particularly revealing in the comprehension of interactions. Consequently, certain concepts derived from CA will be taken into consideration; however, the study will not include their systematic methodological application. This choice is based on the idea that, as Fairclough explains, conversation analysis has generally been reluctant to make or highlight connections between the "'micro structures of conversation' and the 'macro' structures of social institutions and society" (Fairclough 2001b: 9) and the connection between these two levels constitutes one of the focal points of this study.

Furthermore, on a more practical note, the data have not been transcribed in line with the conventions which are crucial in CA studies (Jefferson 1983, 2004). Obviously, this is by no means intended to neglect the significance of their use, especially in the light of the idea that a transcription constitutes not only a way of preparing the material to be analyzed, but also a 'research activity' itself (Atkinson/

14 Given the heterogeneity of methodological and theoretical orientations included in the notion of CDA, it could certainly be argued that the definition of any work as purely CDA-oriented would be inevitably problematic.

Heritage 1984). As has often been suggested, discourse analysts generally study *records* of discourse. In the case of spoken discourse, texts are usually recorded and transcribed; their existence is therefore dependent on the analyst's choices regarding their 'entextualization' (Johnstone 2008: 20-21). As Johnstone (2008: 21) remarks, "[e]very choice about what to count as a text for analysis is a choice about what to include but also about what to exclude. Such choices about what and how much to treat as a complete unit and where to draw its boundaries have important ramifications for the conclusions we draw". Indeed, it must be underlined that the transcriber's decisions have significant theoretical and practical implications, and consequently a transcript is necessary partial (Ochs 1979a, Bucholtz 2000).

I have elsewhere (Anesa 2010: 211-212) highlighted that I share Pallotti's view that transcribed data cannot be considered as authentic data as they have inevitably undergone a process of transposition (Pallotti 2007: 41-42), and they are based on approximations that frequently depend on "the target language's alphabet" (Pallotti 2007: 41). As has often been stated, by choosing not to include certain details the transcriber is deliberately making a selection, but is not necessarily making a mistake. From this perspective, it may be misleading to assume that transcripts that do not record certain details are necessarily imperfect, especially if we admit that "[t]here cannot be a *perfect* transcript" (Silverman 1993: 124, original emphasis) and that "[n]o transcription system could possibly be ideal for all purposes" (Johnstone 2008: 23). Furthermore, in the inevitable trade-off between precision and readability that is inherent in any transcription, the latter aspect has been privileged for the purpose of this study.

3.4.2 Critical Discourse Analysis

Different approaches to discourse analysis are integrated in the current study. The perspective adopted partially draws on what Fairclough defines as "textually oriented discourse analysis" (Fairclough 2003: 2, cf. Fairclough 1992a), one of whose main assumptions is that "language is an irreducible part of social life, dialectically interconnected with other elements of social life" (Fairclough 2003: 2). Fairclough observes that this approach has its point of reference in Systemic Functional Linguistics (SFL) (see Halliday 1978, 1994, Halliday/Hasan 1976, 1989), in that "SFL is profoundly concerned with the relationship between language and other elements and aspects of social life" (Fairclough 2003: 5). However, the author also points out that the two perspectives diverge in terms of aims (Fairclough 2003: 5-6; see also Chouliaraki/Fairclough 1999).

This perspective may somehow be positioned within the broader framework of Critical Discourse Analysis (CDA). There is general consensus on the idea that CDA cannot be classified as a single method, but may be seen as an approach including different theoretical and methodological perspectives, ranging from Faircloughian approaches (Fairclough 1992b, 1995b, 1995c, 2000a, 2000b, 2001a, 2003, Fairclough/Mauranen 1997, Chouliaraki/Fairclough 1999) to more sociocognitive oriented studies (van Dijk 1993, 1997a, 1997b, 2009), from Wodak's discourse-historical line (Wodak 2001b) to Gunnarsson's applied discourse analysis (1997) or Scollon's definition of mediated-DA (Scollon 1998, 2001a, 2001b). Even though CDA does not represent the only approach adopted in this work, some of the theoretical perspectives related to it are particularly relevant.

As has been highlighted, crucial to the understanding of any discourse analytical approach are the notions of text and discourse. In Fairclough's approach to CDA (e.g. Fairclough 1993) 'text' refers to "the written or spoken language produced in a discursive event" (Fairclough 1993: 138) and the multi-semiotic value associated to the notion of text (see Fairclough 1995a) is also emphasized. 'Discourse' can be interpreted at a more abstract level referring to the "language use conceived as social practice", but it may also be described, especially when used as a countable noun, as a "way of signifying experience from a particular perspective" (Fairclough 1993: 138).

A discursive event will here be defined, following Fairclough, as an "instance of language use, analysed as text, discursive practice, social practice" (Fairclough 1993: 138), as outlined in Fairclough's oft-quoted three-dimensional model of discourse (Fairclough 1992a: 73). Even though the model may tend to mask several complexities, it nonetheless helps to show the main approach adopted to the analysis of discourse and its shifting foci. Fairclough clearly states that "text analysis is an essential part of discourse analysis, but discourse analysis is not merely the linguistic analysis of text" (Fairclough 2003: 3). Indeed, the analysis of discourse fluctuates between the investigation of textual units and discursive and social practices.

In line with the assumption that language assumes a socially constitutive function, Fairclough also affirms that "[l]anguage use is always simultaneously constitutive of (i) social identities, (ii) social relations and (iii) systems of knowledge and beliefs" (Fairclough 1993: 134). Language is simultaneously socially constitutive and socially shaped. The latter phenomenon, too, is noticeably complex, as the relationship between language use and social factors is not automatic (Fairclough 1995a), particularly in light of the fact that multiple discourses coexist within the same event.

Different variants of CDA share some of the principles of CDA highlighted in Fairclough's (e.g. 1992, 1993) and Fairclough and Wodak's (1997) seminal works. One of these fundamental principles is the focus on social problems. CDA focuses on language in use, with the aim of critically unraveling the dynamics behind social issues, and the results of such investigations have social, political, cultural and economic implications. Indeed, most variants of CDA see discourse as 'a form as social practice' (Fairclough/Wodak 1997). CDA analysts also insist on the discursive character of power relations, in that CDA aims to investigate how power dynamics are exercised and negotiated in and through discourse. More specifically, Luke remarks:

> CDA involves a principled and transparent shunting back and forth between the microanalysis of texts using varied tools of linguistic, semiotic, and literary analysis and the macroanalysis of social formations, institutions, and power relations that these texts index and construct (Luke 2002: 100)

Luke (2002: 101) also points out that "the actual power of the text, its material and discourse consequences, can only be described by reference to broader social theoretic models of the world" (Luke 2002: 102, see also Pennycook 2001), otherwise there is a tangible risk of running into 'logocentric fallacies' (Luke 2002: 102). Adopting a different but related perspective, Stubbs also emphasizes the strong interrelation between discourse and ideology and starkly highlights the danger that can spring from a conceptualization of language as clear and self-evident: "It is the view that language is natural and transparent, and that texts merely record rather than interpret, which conceals ideology and leads to indoctrination" (Stubbs 1996: 94).

Inherent in the notion of CDA is the concept of critique, which according to Wodak entails "having distance to the data, embedding the data in the social, taking a political stance explicitly, and a focus on self-reflection as scholars doing research" (Wodak 2001a: 9), often adopting an interpretative and explanatory focus (Fairclough/Wodak 1997, Wodak 1996, 2001a, 2001b). Moreover, Wodak's interpretation of the 'critical' aspect of analysis is related to the idea of "not taking things for granted, opening up complexity, challenging reductionism, dogmatism and dichotomies, being self-reflective" (Kendall 2007: 3).

3.4.2.1 Critiques of CDA

CDA has often been accused of lacking clear methodological foundations and various approaches to it have attracted criticism. From this perspective, Schegloff remarks:

> I understand that critical discourse analysts have a different project, and are addressed to different issues, and not to the local co-construction of interaction. If, however, they mean the issues of power, domination, and the like to connect up with discursive material, it should be a serious rendering of that material...Otherwise the critical analysis will not 'bind' to the data, and risks ending up merely ideological. (Schegloff 1997: 20)

Criticism along these lines primarily comes from more CA-based perspectives, but it has to be pointed out that although CA and CDA adopt considerably different orientations they are not necessarily incompatible and may potentially be adopted in a complementary way (Wetherell 1998). Indeed, as I also hope to illustrate in this work, the argument which holds that CA tools are adequate for analyzing single textual units only, while critical discourse studies are only appropriate for wider units of texts as they aim to investigate texts at a higher structural level, is misconceived. The fact that CDA is, by definition, concerned with the analysis of elements 'beyond the sentence level' does not mean that it should necessarily neglect the observation of single lexical or syntactic items (Fairclough 2003).

Exponents of CDA have often replied to criticism regarding the lack of a clear specific methodological and theoretical approach by suggesting that CDA is essentially diverse and multidisciplinary (van Dijk 2001: 95-96) in its very nature. CDA approaches have also been accused of bias in the selection of texts, and of failing to guarantee representativeness (Koller/Mautner 2004, Stubbs 1997). In this respect it has been highlighted that: "The hidden danger is that the reason why the texts concerned are singled out for analysis in the first place is that they are not typical, but in fact quite unusual instances which have aroused the analyst's attention" (Koller/Mautner 2004: 218).

A related criticism commonly leveled at CDA is that of ideological biases, with such biases impeding an objective and neutral analysis. In his well-known critiques of CDA, Widdowson (1995, 1998) argues that "CDA is, in a dual sense, a biased interpretation: in the first place it is prejudiced on the basis of some ideological commitment, and then it selects for analysis such texts as will support the preferred interpretation" (Widdowson 1995: 169). In response to such criticism, Fairclough has often highlighted the explicit position and commitment of CDA approaches: "there is no such thing as an 'objective' analysis of a text, if by that we mean an analysis which simply describes what is 'there' in the text without being 'biased' by the 'subjectivity' of the analyst" (Fairclough 2003: 15, cf. Fairclough 1996). However, as Fairclough remarks, "if we assume that our knowledge of texts is necessarily partial and incomplete […], and if we assume that we are constantly trying to extend and improve it, we have to accept that our categories are always provisional and open to change" (Fairclough 2003: 15).

3.4.2.2 CDA and courtroom discourses

By and large, CDA aims primarily at an interpretive and deconstructive reading of discourse, and one of its goals is "to investigate critically social inequality as it is expressed, signalled, constituted, legitimised and so on by language use (or in discourse)" (Wodak 2001a: 2). Indeed, the notion of social inequality plays a fundamental role in most variants of

CDA, even though investigated from different perspectives (e.g. Fairclough 2001b, 1992a, van Dijk 1993). In this respect, Gee writes:

> The fact that people have differential access to different identities and activities, connected to different sorts of status and social goods, is a root source of inequality in society. Intervening in such matters can be a contribution to social justice. Since different identities and activities are enacted in and through language, the study of language is integrally connected to matters of equity and justice. (Gee 1999: 13)

Intuitively, this holds true for every action, event, situation or phenomenon, but it is clearly essential in a trial, as it represents, *par excellence*, a context in which equity and justice must be pursued. However, applying a CDA perspective to the analysis of communicative events taking place in the courtroom is certainly complex. According to Fairclough "power in discourse is to do with powerful participants *controlling and constraining the contributions of non-powerful participants*" (Fairclough 2001b: 38-39, original emphasis), particularly in what he defines as "unequal encounters", i.e. face-to-face interactions in which the relationship between the participants is unequal in terms of the possibility of exercising power.

The identification of 'powerful' and 'non-powerful' participants calls for a deeper investigation in all contexts, and it is particularly complex within the framework of a jury trial. A dogmatic view that sees the legal experts as the ones possessing power is not in itself critical, and power dynamics developing in the courtroom display a high level of complexity. Indeed, what types of power are there? In whose hands does the power lie? Power relationships and persuasive processes are undeniably present throughout a trial and will be more deeply analyzed in the following chapters. However, deciding *a priori* that in the interaction between, for instance, lawyers and jurors, the former represent the 'powerful' participants, whereas the latter are to be intended as 'non-powerful' participants may be misleading. A dichotomy between people possessing power in discourse and people lacking such power does not seem to take into consideration the obvious fact that a fundamental type of power (the decisional power) belongs to the jurors. I am not arguing that the relationship is not unequal, but simply that the asymmetries characterizing this relationship may differ according to the variables considered. Categories such as 'powerful' and 'non-powerful' are not obvious, self-explanatory concepts, and they cannot be identified merely according to the belonging to a certain professional or social dimension, or according to the communicative role assumed in a certain event. As will be shown, in a jury trial different types of power (such as communicative or decisional power) are strictly interrelated, and identifying a definite allocation of power is highly problematic.

Nonetheless, this study places considerable emphasis upon what Fairclough (2001b: 2) describes as "'common-sense' assumptions which are implicit in the conventions according to which people interact linguistically, and of which people are generally not consciously aware". In the context of a jury trial, such assumptions would derive from the idea that, for example, the legal professionals are the participants who have a high level of legal knowledge, whereas the jurors, by definition, are not so acquainted with this kind of specialized knowledge. These are intuitively and generally accepted concepts and are fundamental to the determination of the communicative dynamics, even though they have to be placed within a broader and more problematized framework. The level of awareness that the different interactants display as regards these dynamics, the role they play, and the way in which they determine/influence the communicative process is a highly debatable matter. As these 'implicit conventions' are often perceived as natural and are automatically accepted, the possibility of interactants being consciously aware of their presence may be reduced. However, in the specific context of a jury trial, considering the crucial role these assumptions play, and the consequences they may have, it seems plausible, or at least desirable, that people may be inclined to reflect upon these issues.

3.4.3 Computer-assisted analysis

The study aims to combine a fine-grained linguistic analysis with a wider investigation of social and cultural factors, therefore ranging from a micro-textual to a macro-textual approach and vice-versa, and embedding such approaches into each other (Fairclough 2003). It is assumed here that "the specific contribution that qualitative discourse analysis can make lies in making explicit the linguistic means through which representations of reality and social relationships are enacted" (Mautner 2008: 48).

As Taylor remarks, "Discourse analysis is best understood as a field of research, rather than a single practice" (Taylor 2001a: 5). Following the interpretation that DA may include apparently divergent approaches, the orientation adopted with regard to the analysis of discourse is not presented as including an exclusive methodology. Indeed, in this work the overall qualitative approach is also integrated with approaches that are generally defined as more quantitatively oriented and, more specifically, this work also draws on computer-assisted analysis, as it is also here assumed that the harmonization of different approaches may lead to revealing complementary insights.

Data have been stored in an electronic format; consequently, beyond the obvious advantage in terms of efficiency in analyzing the data, this method allows data to be processed through concordancers and other language analysis software, such as Wmatrix or AntConc 3.2.1. Even though this approach does not represent the focus of this study, these tools may prove useful in a qualitative-based study (Stubbs 1996, 2001), as elements drawn from corpus linguistics and related disciplines may assist in adding extra information and understanding certain patterns, frequencies and tendencies. Even though the idea of eclecticism may suggest a lack of rigor in the methodological choice, combining different approaches may often lead to a fruitful 'methodological synergy' (Baker *et al.* 2008). Indeed, the merits of combining machine-based methodologies and more qualitatively oriented have often been highlighted (Hardt-Mautner 1995, Stubbs 1996, 1997, de Beaugrande 1997b, Koller/Mautner 2004). Fairclough also states that textual analysis can usefully incorporate findings offered by quantitative analysis, even though he remarks that such findings "need to be complemented by more intense and detailed qualitative textual analysis" (Fairclough 2003: 6).

In this respect, Partington clearly points out the rationale for the use of corpus linguistics in CDA studies:

> At the simplest level, corpus technology helps find other examples of a phenomenon one has already noted. At the other extreme, it reveals patterns of use previously unthought of. In between, it can reinforce, refute or revise a researcher's intuition and show them why and how much their suspicions were grounded. (Partington 2003: 12)

For the specific aims of this study the approach adopted here is not to be interpreted as a corpus-based/driven[15] analysis, and I will not refer to the data collected as constitutive of a corpus. Indeed, even though it has been stated that the term 'corpus' could be used to refer generally to "any body of discourse data" (Taylor 2001b: 313), the instances of discourse collected are not here labeled as 'corpus', as the data were not (primarily) sampled according to the basic criteria of corpus design, such as representativeness and balance. More specifically, representativeness is generally intended as "the extent to which a sample includes the full range of variability in a population" (Biber 1993c: 243) and another important aspect is that "a corpus must be 'representative' in order to be appropriately used as the basis for generalizations concerning a language as a whole" (Biber 1993c: 243). The principal aim of the current study is not to achieve generalization (even though further investigation could evolve in that direction), but to focus on one specific event and its peculiarities.

Indeed, computer-based approaches may be complementarily employed for reaching a deeper understanding of specific phenomena. For instance, the investigation may include the analysis of word frequencies: in this case the aim is not to offer a comprehensive quantitative analysis and provide wide-ranging statistical results, but to use text frequency as an additional tool to describe and understand certain processes.

As mentioned above, the computer-based approach embraced in this study primarily includes the use of two main tools, namely Wmatrix and Antcon 3.2.1 (see chapter 5). Wmatrix (Rayson 2003, Rayson 2009), developed at the University of Lancaster, is an online integrated software suite for corpus analysis and comparison. It allows analyses in terms of word frequencies, concordances, complex lexical

15 For a discussion of the distinction between the corpus-based and corpus-driven approaches see McEnery/Gabrielatos (2006).

frequency profiles, as well as statistical comparisons against standard corpus samplers. The corpora loaded are automatically tagged in terms of part-of-speech (using the CLAWS tagger, see Garside *et al.* 1997), as well as semantically (using USAS, UCREL Semantic Analysis System). In particular, the available taggers allow a keyword analysis based on key grammatical categories and semantic concepts (Rayson 2003). On a more specific note, the use of semantic tags within a Wmatrix environment is generally related to the notion of 'semantic concepts', rather than 'discourse fields' or 'category labels' (Archer *et al.* 2002: 16), and this notion is in line with the interpretation of 'concepts' intended as units of mental representation (Langacker 1987).

AntConc 3.2.1 represents another useful text analysis software, which contains the following tools:

- Concordance
- Concordance Plot
- File View
- Clusters
- N-Grams
- Collocates
- Word List
- Keyword List.

The tools applied to the analysis are described in chapter 5.

3.4.4 Methodological concluding remarks

This work is grounded in a desire to focus on real instances of interactions within a highly institutionalized communicative event, specifically a jury trial. The study is an analysis of discourse seen not as a fixed structure but as a dynamic process of spontaneous interaction. However, the word 'spontaneous' assumes particular contours within the context of a trial: it is intuitively clear that spoken language tends to assume features of spontaneity but the concept is particularly complex because of the high level of formality and the pre-structured nature of several moments of interaction within a trial.

As has been illustrated, even a single trial represents a complex and vast field of analysis; therefore, this work does not aim to describe in detail the developments of every communicative micro-event identifiable within a trial. A selection (which is inevitably a partial and subjective one) of the most salient communicative moments was carried out. In other words, given the uniqueness of this (and any) event, the focus here is on the actual use interactants make of language, without necessarily claiming generalizability, but with the awareness that a lot can be learned even from one single case, or event, or moment of interaction. The aim, therefore, is not to identify aspects that deviate from a normative conception of language or from generally accepted standards of correctness, but to observe, describe systematically, and explain actual talk.

The aim is not to replicate an entire theory but to try to understand the specific dynamics of a specific event through an interdisciplinary approach, which is fundamental to my attempts to answer the current research questions in a comprehensive way. The use of different approaches is not intended to merely provide a means of mutual corroboration of theories and data, but it brings with it issues related to the need to harmonize different epistemologies and practices. It is thanks to a multi-perspective approach that a research focus which is not only descriptive but also explanatory may fruitfully be pursued. In this respect, it has also been suggested that one of the primary goals of discourse analysis is "to achieve the *wholeness of a transdisciplinary perspective*" (de Beaugrande 1997a: 59, original emphasis).

Inherent in discourse studies is the idea of going beyond systematic descriptions and what may be defined as 'pattern seeking' (Candlin/Sarangi 2004), with the aim of integrating description, exploration, and explanation. Indeed, the intent is not to offer a universally applicable description of trial discourse, as such a goal would not only be unfeasible but also misleading and would annihilate diversity. Conversely, I aim to highlight the complex nature of courtroom discourse, and to bring forward the essential interdiscursivity that underlies any discourse.

4. Communication processes in jury trials

The Duchess: Be what you would seem to be – or, if you'd like it put more simply – never imagine yourself not to be otherwise than what it might appear to others that what you were or might have been was not otherwise than what you had been would have appeared to them to be otherwise.
Alice: I think I should understand that better, if I had it written down: but I can't quite follow it as you say it. (Lewis Carroll)

4.1 The legal system

No analysis of communication processes can be alienated from the socio-legal system within which it develops, as they are inevitably highly intertwined. Judicial systems around the world[16] are characterized by several substantial (*inter alia* procedural) variations and, consequently, the specific procedure of a trial is inextricable from a specific system. As mentioned above, the focus of this study is on one specific trial (*California vs Westerfield*), which allows us to focus exclusively on the U.S. system, and on one specific jurisdiction.

On a more specific note, even though the broader expression 'Anglo-American system' is sometimes employed, the term 'American system' (or, more specifically, 'U.S. system') will be preferred here, given the peculiarities that typify the U.S. system in relation to other Anglo-Saxon countries. A comprehensive introduction to the American legal system would go beyond the scope of this work, but some specific areas of U.S. law will be addressed, with particular reference to criminal law, and some of the most relevant aspects of the

16 For a detailed discussion of different legal systems see Kritzer's (2002) encyclopedic work.

functioning of American courts (see Baum 2001) will be touched upon, in order to provide a framework for understanding the development of communication processes in this context.

U.S. law is based on the Common Law system[17]. This system is sometimes broadly defined as 'case law', but it should be noted that a remarkable proportion of U.S. law is also codified (Lee *et al.* 2007). Moreover, it is also interesting to observe that to some extent case law "is not judge-made but also attorney-influenced law" (Lee *et al.* 2007: 11), as it is "created daily through the interaction of judges and attorneys in the courtrooms across the United States at all levels, from local courts to the U. S. Supreme Court" (Lee *et al.* 2007: 11).

The adversarial nature of the American system is one of its fundamental characteristics. The main difference between the inquisitorial and the adversarial system is concisely depicted by Cotterill as follows: "Whereas the inquisitorial system, used throughout much of the world, views the evidence elicited from witnesses with an investigative and exploratory eye, the adversarial approach prioritises argumentation and persuasion, with its primary objective a dialectic and dialogic appraisal of the evidence" (Cotterill 2003: 9).

Von Mehren and Murray also highlight the peculiarity of the adversarial system:

> American criminal justice remains adversarial to an extent that may seem extreme when compared to the standards of most other modern jurisdictions. The essential issue in any American criminal prosecution is not whether the defendant in fact committed the criminal act of which he or she is charged but rather whether the prosecution has proved, beyond a reasonable doubt, that he or she committed that act. (von Mehren/Murray 2007: 194)

Similarly, Cotterill also states that the adversarial system is "based on the adjudication of conflicting and competing versions of events presented by prosecution and defence" (Cotterill 2003: 9). Consequently, it may also be argued that it is "not primarily concerned with establishing the true facts of the case; rather, it involves attempts to per-

17 For a discussion of the main principles of the Common Law system see Arnheim 2004, and for a comparative analysis of Roman and Common Law see Buckland/McNair 2008.

suade the jury that one constructed version of reality is more plausible than another" (Cotterill 2003: 9).

The ultimate goal of a trial may be seen, from a jurisdictional point of view, as the solution of a conflict through the establishment of the factual truth. However, it is obvious that the goal pursued by some of the participants in the process is to impose a certain version of the facts upon the triers of facts. Bergman's remark, from this perspective, is self-explanatory:

> The process of reducing human events to structure, vocabulary and detail is to inevitably distort those events. As long as they will be distorted anyway, you might as well try to distort them in favor of your client. All of this may seem very far from the notion of trial as a search of truth. But your job is to advocate for your client; let the factfinder discover where the truth lies. (Bergman 1982: 227, quoted in Jacquemet 1996: 9)

4.2 The jury system

Prior to a discussion of the jury system in the U.S. it should be noted that every state has specific peculiarities. Indeed, in relation to criminal law, von Mehren and Murray observe:

> From the earliest days of the nation, criminal law has been primarily law of the individual states. Each state possesses a fully developed law of crimes. Each state also has its own prosecutorial competence and facilities as well as a complete court system to process criminal cases and a penal system to punish the offenders. (von Mehren/Murray 2007: 189)

It is also in the light of these observations that the expression 'American jury system' does not seem to take into consideration the heterogeneity of possibilities in which this system may develop, as every jurisdiction may have relatively different laws and procedures. Nevertheless, it has often been confirmed that these systems "share enough essential characteristics to make it possible to talk about the American jury system" (Jonakait 2003: 1), in particular as regards criminal trials.

Indeed, "the same constitutional standards apply to all criminal cases throughout the country" (Jonakait 2003: 2).

The jury system represents one of the key features of the American legal system and it has been observed that the highest percentage of jury trials in the world takes place in the U.S.[18] In defense of the jury system Jonakait writes:

> No matter how strong the objections to the American jury system, it is not going away. It is firmly ensconced in our state and federal constitutions, history and traditions. Juries are required for all criminal trials except those involving the most minor offenses, and no serious movement exists to amend the Sixth Amendment to the federal constitution (which commands this), to limit the reach of civil juries, or to abolish all civil jury trials. The American jury system will endure. The most important debates are the ones to discuss how to make that system better. (Jonakait 2003: XXIV)

However, even though it may be argued that in the U.S. the right to a jury trial is enshrined in legislation, it should also be noted that the percentage of cases tried by juries is constantly decreasing (Clermont/Eisenberg 2002); in this respect, Burns confirms that the trial in general as an institution is progressively disappearing[19] (Burns 2009: 2), and so are trials by jury.

As regards the possibility of introducing changes to the jury system, SunWolf reports that in 2004 Robert J. Grey Jr., the incoming President of the American Bar Association, remarked: "We've looked at and worked to improve virtually every aspect of the system – except

---

18 Indeed, it has been calculated that every year in the United States, approximately three million jurors serve in some 300,000 cases, and that 85 per cent of the world's jury trials take place in the United States (Abraham 1998).

19 More specifically, Burns writes: "The institution of the trial seems to be disappearing in one context after another, and this at a speed that has the sober social scientists who have chronicled it staring in disbelief at their own results. The percentage of federal civil cases that ended in trial declined from 11.5 percent in 1962 to an amazing 1.8 percent in 2002, *one-sixth as many*. Though the absolute number of cases 'disposed of' – to use a telling metaphor – has increased fivefold, even the absolute number of trials has declined. Similar patterns have prevailed in civil, criminal, and bankruptcy proceedings, in federal and state courts, and in both jury and bench trials. The rate of decline has rapidly accelerated in the very recent past" (Burns 2009: 2, original emphasis).

juries. No one focuses on jurors" (SunWolf 2007: 15). This remark appears debatable, considering the importance of certain reforms that have been implemented in order to improve certain aspects of the process (see, for example the reform concerning pattern jury instructions, cf. Tiersma 1999b, 2001). However, it may certainly be argued that the complexity of a jury trial seems to call for a wider reflection on the potential for achieving a better understanding underlying dynamics of this type of trial, in order that potential improvements may be implemented.

4.2.1 Jury trials: criticism

Even though the debate around the topic is not new, televised and highly publicized trials have catapulted issues related to the efficacy of a jury trial into the public conscience. On the one hand, some scholars define the jury system as one of the most fascinating aspects of American democracy (Aron *et al.* 1996), and, similarly, it has been stated that "to invest in a jury system is to invest in democracy" (Lempert 2001: 10). Convincing apologies for the American trial have often been offered, and the system has been described as one of America's "greatest cultural achievements" (Burns 2009: 1). From this perspective, juries are also seen as the guardians of the justice system, as von Mehren and Murray state: "the role of the jury in civil and criminal trials is central not only to the structure of the proceeding and functions of its participants but also to the fundamental values that the civil and criminal justice system protect and promote" (von Mehren/Murray 2007: 206).

However, there is an ongoing debate about the validity of the jury system in contemporary society. An evaluation of the system would open a series of questions which are still unanswered, and it clearly lies beyond the scope of this study. Nevertheless, some particularly problematic areas, such as fairness, impartiality, representativeness and competency, will be touched upon as they are functional to the understanding of the main communicative dynamics taking place in a jury trial.

4.2.1.1 Issues of fairness, impartiality and representativeness

The Sixth Amendment of the U.S. Constitution[20] guarantees the right to be tried by an impartial jury. However, even if it formally prevents discrimination, it has been observed that this requirement "does not guarantee that the criminal jury will in fact reflect an accurate cross-section of the community" (Fukurai 1999: 55). In 1968 the Congress laid the groundwork for the present jury selection process by passing the *Jury Selection and Service Act* which provides that juries must be "selected at random from a fair cross section of the community"[21] and that no citizen shall be excluded from this service because of "race, color, religion, sex, national origin, or economic status"[22].

The main stages of jury selection can be generally summarized as follows (Fukurai 1999: 61):

- general population defined by the court jurisdiction
- ROV (Registrar of Voters) pool
- prospective jurors identified by multiples source master lists (or wheels)
- qualified jurors
- jury eligibles
- jury panels
- trial jurors.

Today citizens who receive summons for jury service are selected randomly among registered voters or licensed drivers (King 1999: 55) or other lists, and the *venire panel*[23] (or jury pool) constitutes the entire panel selected for jury duty from which the actual jury is drawn.

---

20 "In all criminal prosecutions, the accused shall enjoy the right to a speedy and public trial, by an impartial jury of the State and district wherein the crime shall have been committed, which district shall have been previously ascertained by law, and to be informed of the nature and cause of the accusation; to be confronted with the witnesses against him; to have compulsory process for obtaining witnesses in his favor, and to have the Assistance of Counsel for his defence." (U.S. Constitution, Amendment VI)

21 Jury Selection and Service Act of 1968, 28 U.S.C., section 1861.

22 Jury Selection and Service Act of 1968, 28 U.S.C., section 1862.

23 The citizens who appear at the courthouse in response to the summons constitute the venire.

It should also be noted that the use of pre-trial juror questionnaires has increased significantly in recent years. They constitute an important tool, and according to some scholars they can lead to more honest outcomes than face-to-face questioning (Babbie 2010, cf. Lieberman/Sales 2006: 119) and are generally considered quite cost and time effective. The contents of questionnaires may vary, but they usually tend to contain general questions about demographic information (related to, for example, gender, age and ethnic origins) and more specific questions concerning personal beliefs, behaviors, etc. Their length is variable: they can range from a very limited number of pages to a large number, like in the O.J. Simpson criminal trial where the questionnaire included a total of 75 pages. In the Westerfield trial the total number of pages of the questionnaire was 22[24]. It included questions regarding, for instance, residence, family, employment and jury service; moreover, as in this case the death penalty was one of the possible sentences, an entire section of the questionnaire was devoted to 'Views on the death penalty and the penalty of life in prison without the possibility of parole'.

The *voir dire* constitutes a preliminary examination to determine whether members of the venire meet the criteria to be qualified to serve as jurors. At the same time, therefore, what takes place is the identification of any bias which may compromise the jurors' impartiality. The voir dire phase is often referred to as 'jury selection', but the term is somewhat misleading, because what happens in this phase is actually a process of 'juror exclusion' (Lieberman/Sales 2006: 21), as some prospective jurors are excluded. This can happen through challenges for cause or through peremptory challenges (see Norton/Sommers/Brauner 2007, Sommers/Norton 2007). The former constitute "an attempt to convince the judge that a prospective juror cannot be impartial", whereas the latter "allow for exclusion of individuals without explanation or evidence of potential bias" (Sommers/Norton 2007: 262)[25].

---

24 The number includes the cover page and two explanation sheets.

25 Significant variations regarding the voir dire are related to the jurisdiction taken into consideration. For instance, other jurisdictions rely significantly on case law to define the basis for granting a challenge for cause, whereas the California framework places relatively "heavy reliance on statutory provisions" (Hannaford-Agor/Waters 2004: 3).

More specifically, a challenge for cause is exercised when a juror does not meet a specific statutory requirement and there is a specific and forceful reason to believe that someone cannot be fair, unbiased or qualified to serve as a juror. These reasons include, for instance, relationships or acquaintances with the parties, the lawyers or the witnesses, inability to serve (related for example to mental or physical disability), bias and prejudice, previous felony convictions, etc. When an attorney exercises a challenge for cause, the final decision lies in the hand of the judge. In the case of peremptory challenges, each side must only inform the judge that they would like to exclude a juror, but they do not need to provide specific justification (Del Carmen 2006). In this case the number of challenges available is limited (see Hannaford-Agor/Waters 2004 for details).

As Sommers and Norton report, in the U.S. the use of peremptory challenges was "unrestricted for two centuries before the Supreme Court ruled in 1986 that prospective jurors could not be challenged solely on the basis of membership in a 'cognizable racial group' (Batson v. Kentucky)" (Sommers/Norton 2007: 262). However, the use of peremptory challenges has frequently been criticized to the extent that their abolition has been suggested (Broderick 1992, Hoffman 1997). Indeed, prospective jurors cannot be challenged on the basis of race or gender, but research shows a tendency by prosecution and defense to challenge different ethnic groups (Baldus *et al.* 2001). More generally, it has been stated that "attorneys systematically consider categories such as gender, occupation, and nation of origin in their efforts to eliminate jurors they believe to be unfavorable to their clients" (Norton/Sommers/Brauner 2007: 468; see also Zeisel/Diamond 1978, Hastie 1991, Olczak/Kaplan/Penrod 1991, Kovera *et al.* 2002).

The result of the jury selection process is often defined as the most important aspect of a criminal trial (Mogill/Nixon 1986) and it is not surprising that jury selection has always received great interest, to the extent that the importance of trial consultants specialized in this crucial process is constantly growing (Kressel/Kressel 2002); they are usually registered with the American Society of Trial Consultants, but there is no State licensure and no specific education requirements (Lieberman/Sales 2006: 91).

From a lawyer's perspective, the aim of jury selection is manifold. More specifically, Lubet identifies three main aims related to this phase:

> 1. Eliminating jurors who are biased or disposed against your case;
>
> 2. Gathering information about the eventual jurors in order to present your case effectively; and
>
> 3. Beginning to introduce yourself, your client, and certain key concepts to the jury. (Lubet 2004: 529)

Indeed, it is often argued that the voir dire phase represents an opportunity for the attorneys "to develop a rapport with venire members and ingratiate themselves in the process" (Lieberman/Sales 2006: 27).

The emphasis of the fair representation of a heterogeneous section of society seems paradoxically at odds with a process where the exclusion of potential jurors, in practical terms, aims to identify the jurors that are considered favorable to one's case, instead of aiming for the composition of a fair jury. It may also be argued, however, that the goal of defining a fair jury is unachievable in that "fairness and impartiality, like beauty, often lies in the eyes of the beholder" (Hannaford-Agor/Waters 2004: 1). On a more practical note, given the subtle nature of bias, it is not easy to define exactly and quantify the impact of the jury selection process on the final outcome of a trial. However, it is self-evident that the possibility of intervening in the process that may exclude certain people from becoming the triers of fact has some crucial implications, as all the parties clearly aim to select members that will be more likely to accept their version of the story and to give a favorable verdict.

Fairness and impartiality should be guaranteed by the concept of representativeness and, from this perspective, the fair cross-selection doctrine is at the core of the procedure. However, different issues arise as regards representativeness. For example, it has been noted that the use of registered voters or licensed drivers lists may lead to an underrepresentation of certain minorities of citizens (Piven/Cloward 1988); moreover, several states require a proficiency level of English in order to be eligible as jurors and this criterion contributes to the inadequate representation of ethnic minorities (Brown 1994).

4.2.1.2 Issues of competency

Beyond representativeness, competency has also been identified as another critical aspect of the jury system. In Knight's words, jurors are "asked to do superhuman things – things we know they cannot, and do not, do" (Knight 1996: 253-254) and they face multiple dilemmas:

> They are asked to wipe from their minds testimony they were not supposed to have heard; resolve conflicts in evidence no mortal could resolve with any confidence; identify thoughts that flickered through the consciousness of people at precise moments months and years in the past; absorb and apply pages of complex instructions concerning legal principles they have never heard of. And in reaching a verdict, they are asked to perform a feat of probably impossible schizophrenia: If they believe the defendant is guilty, they must nonetheless find that he is not if they have a reasonable doubt that he is. Each of them must find a way to agree with eleven random strangers on this elusive, difficult proposition, or their labors are in vain. (Knight 1996: 253-254)

The debate around the appropriateness of the jury trial is not new and as early as 1873 Twain noted: "We have a criminal jury system which is superior to any in the world; and its efficiency is only marred by the difficulty of finding twelve men every day who don't know anything and can't read" (Twain 1873, quoted in Shapiro 1993: 223). Similarly, Herbert Spencer colorfully depicted the nature of the jury system as depending on "twelve men of average ignorance" (quoted in Williams 1963: 271-72). Conversely, it has also been observed that such paradoxes are inevitable in that they lie in the nature of the system as "[j]urors are used in trials not for their knowledge of the law but for their knowledge of life" (Heffer 2008: 49).

As will be described, knowledge asymmetries (see Marková/Foppa 1991) are indeed at the core of trial procedures. More generally, it may be argued that asymmetries play a fundamental role in any communicative event, as remarked by Linell and Luckmann: "[I]f there were no asymmetries at all between people, i.e. if communicatively relevant inequalities of knowledge were non-existing, there would be little or no need for most kinds of communication!" (Linell/Luckmann 1991: 4).

In a jury trial different types of knowledge asymmetries emerge and are highly interdependent. For example, legal knowledge is primarily associated with the legal professionals involved; moreover, it is interesting to observe that the inevitable disparity regarding the level of legal knowledge possessed by the jurors and legal professionals is also exacerbated by the fact that in certain jurisdictions a range of professions, including attorneys and judges, are automatically exempted from jury service (Fukurai *et al.* 1993: 67). However, at the same time another crucial type of knowledge (potentially definable as 'commonsense' knowledge) is a determining factor in the outcome of the trial.

In any communication process knowing what our interlocutors know is essential (Bakhtin 1981, Nickerson 1999)[26], and this assumption clearly holds true in the communication with the jury. In this respect, it has been stated that "the better a lawyer's knowledge of the human nature of the average person, the better chance a lawyer has to communicate successfully with a lay jury" (Aron *et al.* 1996). However, defining "the human nature of the average person" is inevitably complex (if not unfeasible) in principle; moreover, the possibility of knowing the jurors involved is limited: this limitation is, first of all, procedural and is also determined by the highly constrained communicative process (see section 4.4) where a monologic mode of communication seems to prevail.

4.3 The procedure

A trial represents one of the steps in the process of doing justice. In order to position it within the broader framework, figure 5[27] shows some of the main phases that are typical of the Criminal Justice System within the U.S. context. Given the nature of the trial in question, figure 5 focuses primarily on the process concerning felonies.

---

26 As regards expert-lay communication, also see the concept of 'expert blind spot' (Nathan/Koedinger 2000).

27 Adapted from the description offered by the American Bar Association available at: <http://www.abanet.org/publiced/courts/casediagram.html> Accessed: September 2, 2010.

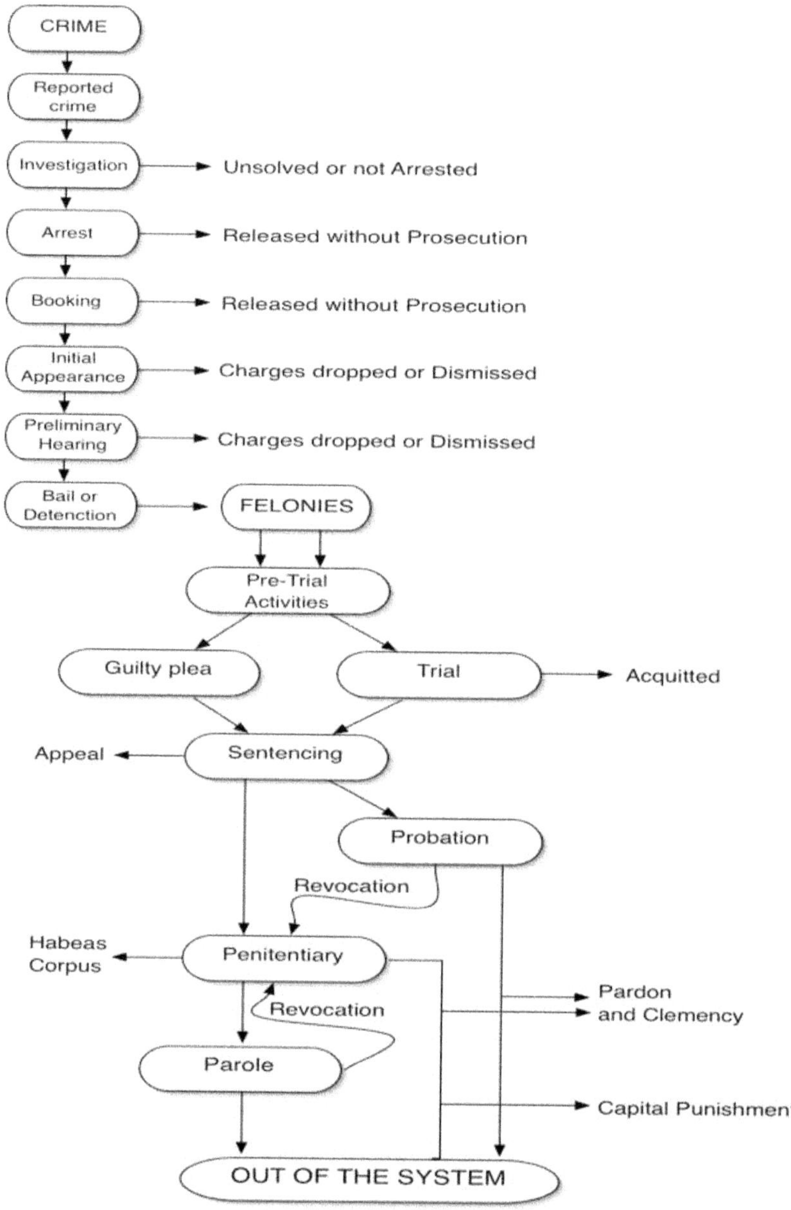

Figure 4. The sequence of events in the Criminal Justice System.

As this representation shows, a trial can be intended as one event within a longer and more complex process. A trial is then constituted of a series of macro-phases, which are themselves comprised of multiple micro-events. The different phases are also characterized by different communicative constraints and the communication develops in remarkably different ways according to the phase taken into consideration. Consequently, the communicative processes related to the development of a trial are intrinsically context-bound and situation-bound and vary significantly according to the specific phases, their aims, and their constraints.

Table 2 offers an overview of the main phases on which a jury trial is based within the U.S. legal framework and, despite the limits that are typical of any schematization, it offers a preliminary understanding of how this process may develop[28].

Trial phases[29]	*Main participants and interactional dynamics*
1. Preliminary phase Jury selection	Judge ↔ jury pool Lawyers ↔ jury pool
2. Evidential phase *Opening statements* Witness examination *Closing arguments*	 Lawyer → jury Lawyers ↔ witnesses Lawyers → jury
3. Judicial phase *Jury instructions and summing up* Jury deliberation Verdict Sentencing/release	 Judge → jury Juror ↔ juror Jury foreperson ↔ judge Judge → defendant

Table 2. Main interactional dynamics of a jury trial (adapted from Cotterill 2003: 94).

28 It should also be noted that, before the beginning of the trial, pre-trial motions are brought before the court by the prosecution and the defense. Through these documents the parties may ask the court, for example, to exclude certain physical evidence, to prevent witnesses from testifying, to change venue, etc.

29 The phases that represent the primary object of analysis of this case (chapter 5) are highlighted.

As described in section 4.2, the preliminary phase of a jury trial includes what is often defined as the jury selection process: jurors are asked questions by the court, the prosecution and the defense and may be excluded from the jury (see also section 5.2).

The second macro-phase of a trial can be defined as evidential and consists of a series of sub-phases (see chapter 5 for details). First of all, it includes opening statements, an initial presentation of the case on the part of the prosecution and the defense. They constitute a crucial phase of a trial because they provide the incipit of a story the jurors will be confronted with throughout the trial. This phase is sometimes considered to have a fundamental influence on the final result, to the extent that Aron *et al.* (1996: 21.15) remark that "[s]ome lawyers feel that as many as 80 per cent of all jurors make up their minds by the end of the opening statement." It has been suggested that opening statements contribute to creating a schema according to which jurors process and interpret the subsequent phases of the trial (Pyszczynski/Wrightsman 1981, Pyszczynski *et al.* 1994). Wells *et al.* (1985: 759) also confirm that "an opening statement can be construed as a technique of schema instantiation in that it appears to guide memory"[30].

Opening statements are generally followed by the examination phase, in which witnesses, expert witnesses and the defendant are generally examined and cross-examined by the prosecution and the defense. This phase is particularly complex, as it consists of a series of interactions involving a highly variable number of participants. The communication process taking place in this phase is also highly influenced by legal and procedural constraints: for instance, one of the main rules regarding direct examination is that leading questions (containing suggestions or prompting answers) are not allowed, except in cross-examination. More specifically, Federal Rule of Evidence 611[31], regarding the mode and order of interrogation and presentation, states

30 A schema has also been defined as "any subset of existing knowledge, based on prior experience and relevant to a limited domain, which people use as a framework to guide their observation, organisation, and retrieval from memory of perceived events" (Lingle/Ostrom 1981: 401).

31 'Federal Rules of Evidence' is available at: <http://www.uscourts.gov/rules/Evidence_Rules_2007.pdf>.

that "[l]eading questions should not be used on the direct examination of a witness except as may be necessary to develop the witness' testimony. Ordinarily leading questions should be permitted on cross-examination". Another principle applied in direct examination is that witnesses "may not testify in 'narrative' form" (Lubet 2004: 49). However, the line between narrative and non-narrative presentation can sometimes be finely drawn, and in expert examination narratives are generally allowed. Indeed, the mode in which expert witness examination is conducted varies significantly from the examination of lay witnesses (also called ordinary witnesses or percipient witnesses); moreover, "[a]n expert witness is not limited to personal knowledge and may base her testimony on information that was gathered solely for the purpose of testifying in the litigation" (Lubet 2004: 213). It has been argued that direct examination of witnesses represents a fundamental part of the trial, as it provides an opportunity to present the core evidence of a case, and to corroborate the lawyer's version of the story. In this phase establishing the credibility of a witness is fundamental, as it is mainly according to his/her level of credibility that the information presented will be accepted by the audience (Jacquemet 1996).

The evidential phase is concluded by closing arguments. Summation or closing arguments represent the phase where the attorneys can state what has been proved during the trial and argue their case, and this stage can therefore be seen as "the moment for pure advocacy" (Lubet 2004: 467).

The final macro-phase of a trial is the judicial one, which includes jury instructions[32] and summing up, jury deliberation, verdict and sentencing/release. In the event of conviction, the penalty phase, in which the sentence to be applied is determined, also takes place. Moreover, trials may naturally be followed by appeals to a higher court.

32 During jury instruction the judge explains the legal standards to be applied by the jurors in order to decide the case. It should also be noted that different types of instructions may be given at several intervals during the trial (see chapter 5).

4.4 The communicative complexity of a jury trial

Following Cotterill (2003: 93-94), it is possible to identify two main modes of interaction during a jury trial, namely a monologic and a dialogic mode. Focusing on the jurors' perspectives and on their interaction with legal experts, crucial phases such as opening statements, closing arguments and jury instructions may be definable as monologic (Cotterill 2003: 94, see table 2), as the right to speak lies exclusively in the hands of a group of participants (in this case, the lawyers or the judge), while others (the jurors) assume the role of listeners. A dialogic mode characterizes the voir dire phase, where jurors are questioned directly in order to ascertain their impartiality. If we take the plausible and often confirmed assumption (cf. e.g. Watzlawick *et al.* 1967) that a dialogic mode is more likely to facilitate understanding (as people actively participate in the conversation and may ask for clarification when needed), the prevalence of monologic events may seem to hinder understanding on the part of the jurors. Indeed, it has been argued that "[t]raditionally, the Anglo-American jury has functioned as a passive audience in its reception of information and finding of facts at trial" (von Mehren/Murray 2007: 213). The communication process may to some extent be seen as paradoxical, as "[t]he model juror is expected to sit like a sphinx and listen to the testimony and argumentation without betraying any reaction or indication of how she or he is receiving the material" (von Mehren/Murray 2007: 213).

4.4.1 Emerging asymmetries

The attribution of institutional roles (and the relations between them) is crucial in all types of human interaction and access to communication is significantly dependent on the institutional roles assumed by participants (Adelswärd *et al.* 1987). As has been shown, a trial represents a highly institutionalized setting, where roles are clearly defined and the divergence in the roles assumed by experts and laypersons emerges more evidently than in other contexts.

It may be stated that "lay participants in courtroom interaction, unlike participants in conversation, are not in full control of their verbal contributions" (Heffer 2005: 47). Indeed, their right to speak and to intervene verbally in the communication process is considerably limited by specific procedural constraints and conventions, and it is generally assumed that lawyers "control the flow of information" (O'Barr 1982: 55) in this context.

From an institutional perspective, roles are pre-established and strictly defined within a jury trial, but the complex relations between the interactants may also assume dynamic contours. It is easy to hypothesize that the status of experts and non-experts may determine asymmetrical relations between the participants, but defining (and distinguishing between) experts and non-experts is a complex (and often misleading) activity; whenever we engage ourselves in such a task, the emerging picture is always more nuanced and complex than the binary one expected. Indeed, the concept of experts has manifold ramifications whose exploration goes beyond the scope of this study.

Even though professional, institutional and social 'labels' are always simplifications, in a jury trial, the participants' roles seem to be clearly defined, and these labels cannot be disregarded, as they are at the core of the discourse developing in and through the interaction of distinctive socially constructed identities and roles. In other words, roles are fundamental in the development of discourse as, in the simplest terms, a certain perception of role influences the production and the reception of any piece of discourse, and the degree to which participants are aware of this aspect is inevitably extremely variable. On a more practical note, the items of analysis (see chapter 5) relate exclusively to subjects that prototypically represent certain communities of experts (i.e. legal experts, namely the judge and the lawyers) and laypersons (i.e. the jurors). However, it should be remembered that a wide range of categories of interactants are involved in a jury trial, and an easy identification of participants as 'experts' or 'laypersons' is often difficult, as in the case of the so-called semi-experts, such as police officers (Heffer 2005).

We all assume a variety of social identities[33]; in many situations, for example in the case of expert witnesses, the professional identity[34] is crucial and is not only presupposed but is made verbally salient and is explicitly expressed so that it can be explicitly shared with all the participants. The reasons underlying this explicit manifestation of professional identity are several, and among the main ones is the procedural necessity of having expert witnesses officially recognized as such. Moreover, the persuasive strategy of qualifying a certain witness as an expert is used in order to confirm his/her credibility in the eyes of the other participants, and in particular the jurors (see section 5.5). As previously stated, we all continuously draw on different identities, and lawyers are no exception. While presenting and construing their identity of credible professionals, they also try to convey aspects of perceived similarity in their relation with the jurors, in order not to distance themselves from laypersons and from their presumed attitudes and values.

The analysis of the complexity of the communicative dynamics that take place in the courtroom calls for a reflection on socially constructed power and power asymmetries. Even outside the courtroom setting (or any other institutionalized social setting) power is omnipresent, and so are power relationships. Drawing on a Foucauldian conceptualization of power, it can be argued that "power is co-extensive with the social body" (Foucault 1980a: 142) and any instance of social interaction, synchronous as well as asynchronous, entails phenomena of power.

As the Foucauldian ideology suggests, power in this sense is not necessarily 'evil', in that it may assume both (generally considered) negative (e.g. domination and coercion) and positive (e.g. spurring on productivity, creating healthy resistance) functions. Foucault's reflection

---

33 For a discussion of social identity theory see Tajfel 1982, Turner 1982, Tajfel /Turner 1986.

34 The theoretical approach on identity adopted here stems from van Dijk's consideration that it may be improper to talk about "one, new, ad hoc or 'hybrid' identity", as identity is not constructed afresh according to the contextual situation; rather, it would be more appropriate to talk about a "dynamic, contextually and textually controlled, activation and manipulation of various 'given' identities" (van Dijk 2009: 213).

on power goes beyond the good-evil dichotomy and the antithesis between, on the one hand, a (more sociological) conception of power as the *sine qua non* for the existence of a community and its social cohesion and, on the other hand, the interpretation of power as the expression of coercion and repression. This, in turn, leads Foucault to state that "power is not an institution, and not a structure; neither is it a certain strength we are endowed with; it is the name that one attributes to a complex strategic situation in a particular society" (Foucault 1980b: 93).

Power relations in communication are always intricate and complex and the context of a jury trial constitutes no exception. In particular, although jurors may appear to be passive spectators of a show being conducted by others, ultimately they are the sole holders of decisional power. They are not able to interact directly with the other participants and the communication process seems to be led entirely by others, but it is nonetheless entirely up to them to reach the final verdict. In other words, apparently paradoxical dynamics emerge: on the one hand, the decisional power lies in the jurors' hands, as they are the sole decision makers regarding the verdict to be reached; on the other hand, it is clear that other expressions of power determine the conduct of the trial and its development. For instance, the label 'communication power' used here indicates that the communication process is mainly guided by members of the legal profession, whereas jurors seem to be relegated to observers of the event taking place (Heffer 2005).

4.5 Narrative structures of a jury trial

The importance of narrativism in communication is essential (Bruner 1986, 1990, 1991), and it can be argued that it fundamentally allows us to frame experience (Bruner 1990: 56). The role played by narrative in a jury trial is no exception to this rule, as the decisional process is significantly based on a narrative model (Pennington/Hastie 1992, Spiecker/Worthington 2003).

More specifically, the development of a trial has often been described using the metaphor of a story or highlighting its distinctive narrative aspect (Papke 1991, Pennington/Hastie 1992, Cotterill 2003, Spiecker/Worthington 2003). The association between the trial and a story-telling process can be identified at different levels. At a macro-level the trial itself can be analyzed through Labovian structures (Labov 1966, 1972, 1981, Labov/Waletzky 1967) and, in particular, Cotterill remarks:

> [A trial] offers an introduction and background information to the case during opening statements, a presentation of the crime events in witness examination, and a final evaluative summary in the closing arguments. The trial then builds to a climax during the deliberation process, concluding with a resolution in the form of a verdict and a sentencing or release coda. (Cotterill 2003: 23)

This passage can be used to identify the Labovian narrative components, i.e. abstract, orientation, complicating action, evaluation, resolution and coda, and to observe how they develop within a trial (Cotterill 2003: 23-28). It is interesting to note that, from this perspective, the jury also assumes an active role in the narration, as the resolution (in Labovian terms) depends on the verdict issued by the jurors. Looking upon the trial as a piece of narrative allows us to see the trial's intrinsic, rudimentary narrative pattern.

At a different level, a trial is also composed of a series of micro-narratives (or sub-narratives), which are in effect embedded within the macro-narrative and may be seen as competing stories (Goodpaster 1987: 120). These narratives are to some extent divergent, but they are at the same time also closely interwoven. At this level of analysis the jurors are confronted with different narrations of stories, and they seem to assume the role of spectators. On the other hand, they cannot be seen as passive observers as they are still given the responsibility of choosing what story to accept, and they have to "construct the truth out of competing partisan presentations" (Jonakait 2003: 175). Furthermore, these observations are clearly in line with Toolan's (1988: 8) remark that the ratification of a text lies in the hands of the perceiver/addressee, and not of the teller.

4.5.1 Story framing and construction

Before analyzing what communicative and persuasive strategies are typically employed in a jury trial, it is interesting to highlight the fact that advocate training manuals often present 'script-theory' as a precious tool to be taken into consideration while planning how a story should be constructed and delivered. Schank (1986) develops script theory as the point of departure for the application of a dynamic model of memory. According to this model all new information is understood in terms of 'scripts', that could be defined as "a person's mental image or understanding of a certain context or set of events" (Lubet 2004: 32). Drawing on Lubet, it is easy to understand how script theory is applicable to the communicative processes within a jury trial. Indeed, new information is not evaluated in isolation, and fact finders (in this case the jurors) will tend to harmonize new inputs in accordance with the script they have been creating (Lubet 2004: 32-39).

The story presented by a lawyer during the trial will certainly have certain gaps, omissions or missing points – be they intentional or unintentional. This clearly happens in the everyday process of storytelling, but it may be even more evident in the development of a trial, where certain evidence may not be admitted and other information may not be presented. In this respect, Lubet writes:

> [S]cript theory informs us that many of the gaps will be filled by the fact finder's reconstruction (some would say imagination). Recall that you are telling a story whenever you present evidence or argue a case. You have, more or less, active control over the information that you choose to present. Whenever you leave out a detail, however, that void is likely to be filled – consistent with a script – by the fact finder's own supposition. This is a process where you have little or no control. (Lubet 2004: 34)

Another aspect related to the construction (and constant modification) of scripts on the part of the jurors is related to the concept of inference, which means that people tend to infer conclusions from certain information (Lubet 2004: 35). Furthermore, Lubet (2004: 37) suggests that "[t]he best way to neutralise a script is with a counterscript—provide the fact finder with a different and equally compelling context into which she can fit the trial's information".

Jurors are generally asked to accept one of the versions that have been presented and Klonoff and Colby (2007: 17) remark that "[t]he jury will generally choose either one counsel's position or that of his opponent (or a compromise between the two). Rarely will it venture beyond these bounds". It is therefore very unlikely that they would "stray from the boundaries set by the advocates" (Klonoff/Colby 2007: 17).

It is clear that in order for the story to be likely to be accepted, it generally has to comply with certain specific features. For instance, Aron *et al.* (1996: 14.29) suggest that the story presented by the lawyer should meet three fundamental requirements: it should be short, consistent and easy to understand. Most scholars suggest delivering a certain version of the story following similar criteria. Indeed, it is easy to understand that brevity can allow the jurors to concentrate on the main points the attorney wants to make and reduce the potential degree of distraction and confusion. Consistency is another crucial aspect, as one of its purposes is to make the story more readily acceptable to the jury. The fact that the story should be kept simple may seem obvious, considering that the jurors are not legal professionals. However, on the one hand it is clear that simplicity and understandability are essential features, but on the other hand showing a high level of topic-related knowledge is often considered fundamental in trial advocacy. For example, Lubet (2004: 40) highlights that "[a]n apparent command of relevant information correlates strongly with believability". Indeed, given that credibility is one of the most important features related to the acceptance of a story on the part of the fact finders, advocates consider it very important to show their level of expert knowledge to the jury.

From Tomlin *et al.*'s (1997) perspective, the interaction between speakers and listeners may also be understood as a complex process that entails a wide range of dynamics, two of which may be defined as 'knowledge integration' and 'information management'. The former refers to the listeners' need to "integrate utterances heard into a coherent representation" in order to "access or construct concepts and events that are virtually identical to those held by the speaker" (Tomlin *et al.* 1997: 65). The concept of information management in its most basic terms refers instead to the process through which the speaker tries to manage the flow of information in order to "help the listener succeed in knowledge integration" (Tomlin *et al.* 1997: 65). It is easy to understand that these processes are fundamental to any communicative interaction, and that professional communicators, such as attorneys, constantly exploit their knowledge of these processes and their dynamics. In the case of a trial, diverging representations are suggested and the jury is confronted with competing versions of a certain event; consequently, the main aim of the speaker is ultimately to lead the listeners to a representation of ideas or actions identical to the speaker's representation.

4.5.2 Narrativism

One simply cannot imagine a trial without narrative; indeed, it is through narrative that stories are presented and the use of stories allows the jurors to make sense of the process they are involved in. More specifically, it may be argued that "[i]n courtroom disputes, the raw materials for constructing stories are the pre-existing attitudes of jurors, and the arguments and evidence presented at trial" (Huntely/Costanzo 2003: 235). The term 'account' is also widely used, as "creating an account highlights the need to present messages most easily perceived as real and believable, not only in the context of the story, but also in the context of the jurors' histories" (Lisnek/Oliver 2001: 10). James Boyd White gives a very graphic description of the role played by accounts in the legal process:

> The process is at heart a narrative one because there cannot be a legal case without a real story about real people actually located in time and space and culture. Some actual person must go to a lawyer with an account of the experience upon which he or she wants the law to act, and that account will always be a narrative. The client's narrative is not simply accepted by the lawyer but subjected to questioning and elaboration, as the lawyer sees first one set of legal relevances, then another. In the formal legal process, that story is then retold, over and over by the lawyer and by the client, and by others, in developing and competing versions, until by judgment or agreement an authoritative version is achieved. (White 1985: 692)

As Gee remarks, "[n]arratives are important sense-making devices" (Gee 1999: 134). The listener has to construe his/her own narrative and has to untangle a certain story from different elements that are presented; the aim of the narrator is, therefore, to suggest and inspire his/her version of the story by presenting it as the most easily acceptable (in terms of logic, coherence, etc.). It is interesting to observe that narratives in a jury trial are also subject to complex phenomena of co-authorship, intended as the process through which a narrative is simultaneously constructed by different interactants involved in a communicative event[35]. For instance, witness and expert witness examination is a manifest realization of a narrative that develops mainly through a series of questions and answers and is evidently constructed by different interactants[36].

As previously mentioned, the interrelation between multiple narratives is at the core of a trial and its dynamics. Figure 6 attempts to visualize the complex relationship (and interdependence) between emerging narratives:

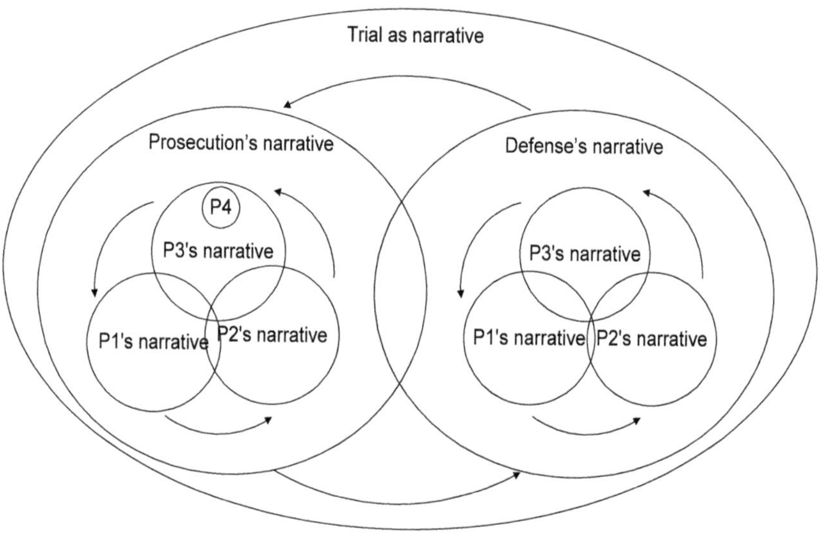

Figure 5. The circularity of narratives in a trial.

---

35 At a deeper level co-authorship may also be understood as the process of co-construction in which the active role of the receivers is emphasized. For a further discussion of this well-established concept see, *inter alia*, Goodwin (1986) and Duranti (1986).

36 Co-authorship need not necessarily be understood as a form of cooperation toward the same goals, as in several circumstances (as often happens in cross-examination), the final aims of the interactants may be divergent.

Figure 6 is by no means intended as an exhaustive representation of the totality of the narrative processes that characterize the development of a jury trial. Simply, it aims to visually show the strong interconnection of narratives and their circularity. As shown, at a macro-level the trial can be intended as a macro-narrative, which is constituted by a series of other narratives. Given the nature of the system, and for the sake of convenience in the visual representation, the two main narratives have been identified as developing within the framework suggested by defense and by prosecution. They are mainly narrated by the respective attorneys, but they consist of and draw upon multiple narratives. This multiplicity can be seen as related to the fact that the attorney's narrative derives from the combination of stories narrated in different moments and in different phases (e.g. opening statements, examination, closing); moreover, each narrative encompasses a series of micro-narratives. Indeed, narratives in a jury trial are interdependent and circular, and the stories presented by different participants[37] (e.g. P1, P2, P3, etc.) are reciprocally referred to, confirmed, denied and integrated.

The discussion of narrative frameworks emerging in a trial can be further complexified by noting that they include a series of different events which could be broadly identified as 'kernel' events and 'satellite' events (Chatman 1969), where the former are intended as the key events and the latter as secondary events. As Cohan and Shires note, "kernels advance and satellites amplify the transformation of events which a sequence lineates to produce a story" (Cohan/Shires 1988: 55). As will be shown, the complex network of narratives emerging in a trial develops not only around the main events, but also according to a series of secondary events. Following Cohan and Shire (1988), events may be 'enchained', that is, tied by a direct causal connection, where an event is presented as the direct consequence of another; events may also be

37 P1, P2, P3, P4 in figure 6 simply refer to hypothetical participants (i.e. Participant 1, Participant 2, Participant 3, Participant 4). The vast array of participants involved in the construction of a narrative is not to be seen as comprising exclusively the participants who personally narrate some events during the trial. They are rather intended as all those participants (even *in absentia*) whose narratives emerge in the trial (for example, via reference to their narrative offered by another participant).

'embedded', as they may result in a series of embedding processes where different events are concomitant and interdependent.

4.5.3 Competing stories

As has been shown, courtroom proceedings in the U.S. are based on the adversary system. It is easy to understand that according to this system "juries receive information selected, managed and controlled by the parties and their attorneys" and they have to "construct the truth out of competing partisan presentations" (Jonakait 2003: 175). In its simplest terms, the communication process underlying a jury trial is based on the idea that "[j]urors take in the information presented by lawyers and witnesses and 'decode' it into terms that fit their own experience" (Lisnek/ Oliver 2001: 4). Therefore, a jury trial represents a unique communicative situation in which a variable number of agents present (considerably) different versions of a certain event to an audience (primarily, the appointed jurors) which is in charge of making the final decision about the case. Goodpaster remarks that the adversary criminal trial tends to assume the contours of a "regulated storytelling contest between champions of competing, interpretative stories" (Goodpaster 1987: 120). The versions presented may at times overlap, supplement, contradict or be incompatible with one another. However, the final goal of this input from the various agents is to present a story that can be perceived as credible, in the sense that the story told by a particular agent (e.g. the district attorney) is presented in such a way as to be perceived as more credible than the story of another agent (e.g. the defendant's counsel).

The role played by lawyers in controlling the elements of the story displayed is self-evident. O'Barr affirms that "[l]awyers enjoy a unique freedom of movement in the courtroom; they control the flow of information; they are able simultaneously to converse with judges in the obscure language of the law and with jurors in everyday English" (O'Barr 1982: 55). Lawyers to a certain extent hold a privileged position in the communication exchange, even though the idea that one of the interactants can be in total control of the flow of information would be an overly simplistic view of the extremely complex process that is taking place. While lawyers are certainly the main agents in charge of framing, organizing and presenting the content matter dealt with in the courtroom, they are not the only direct sources of information, and one of the most complicated tasks they have to accomplish is to combine the different elements presented by different agents.

One of the principal functions attributed to courtroom communication is persuasive, as persuasion can be understood, in general terms, as "a symbolic process in which communicators try to convince other people to change their attitudes or behaviors regarding an issue through the transmission of a message in an atmosphere of free choice" (Perloff 2010: 12). In the context of a jury trial, persuasion may be broadly interpreted as the process which allows lawyers presenting their case to make their case credible and acceptable (Rieke/Stutman 1990). The narration is therefore strictly related to a constant process of persuasion, as persuading the jurors about the credibility and the acceptability of a story can be considered, to some extent, as the ultimate goal of this communicative process. Indeed, "[p]ersuasion is, in sum, the purpose of trial communication" (Aron *et al.* 1996: 1.26). In this context it is clear that the persuasive process is crucial, as "the concept of persuasion goes hand in hand with decision making" (Lubet 2004: 31).

4.6 The hybridity of courtroom language

As will be seen in more detail in chapter 5, the nature of courtroom language is highly hybrid from a variety of perspectives. Firstly, courtroom language offers a clear manifestation of the interdependence of the spoken and the written modes. Indeed, on the one hand, orality is a key feature, as remarked by Walter: "The American courtroom trial is a speech situation. Everything occurs through the spoken word" (Walter 1988: VII). In this respect, Cotterill adds: "The overwhelming primacy of the oral over the written in court also means that the verbal dexterity of the speaker becomes a significant factor in the presentation of credible testimony" (Cotterill 2003: 10). On the other hand, the relationship between the two modes is particularly complex. The significant dependence of trial procedures on orality has also often been criticized for not being conducive to a complete and clear understanding of the material being presented. In particular, von Mehren and Murray aptly remark:

> Reliance on purely oral communication limits the amount and complexity of material that can be communicated, tends to protract proceedings, and may jeopardize the retention by the jurors of complex details. For this reason, some courts have recently begun to experiment with allowing jurors to take notes during long or complex proceedings. (von Mehren/Murray 2007: 213)

With the aim of facilitating comprehension, some reforms have been introduced, and they also suggest a reflection on the relationship between the spoken and the written mode. For example, in certain cases some jurors are allowed to pose questions, and they may generally do so via a written note[38]. In this respect von Mehren and Murray write:

> Recent reforms in some jurisdictions provide juries with the ability to pose written questions to be submitted to the judge who can then determine whether they are proper to be posed to a lawyer or witness. So far, there has been little use of this procedure in practice. (von Mehren/Murray 2007: 214)

The interdependence of the written and the spoken modes often emerges during the trial; for instance, jury instructions are originally produced in a written format, but are first conveyed to the jurors orally by the judge, who may also integrate them with other oral observations; then in certain circumstances (as in the case analyzed here) the written text is also given to the jurors for reference. Moreover, the jurors have to rely primarily on what they have heard, but in this case they are also provided with notepads for taking notes, and they may refer to those notes during their jury deliberations.

At a more general level, it should also be noted that the entire trial is carried out through the spoken word, but is also transcribed.

38 Reforms in this direction are also particularly relevant for the discussion of communication processes in the courtroom in that they manifest the potential for a relatively dialogic process, and somehow controvert the claims of total passivity of the jurors, even though their use is limited and highly constrained.

Furthermore, accusations are also based on the record of what has been said before the trial, for example in the interviews carried out by the police with the defendant and in the statements made by him/her[39]. Legal/lay discourse in jury trials has been defined as "[v]erbal communication produced by legal professionals and received by lay participants – primarily the lay jury" (Heffer 2005: 10). However, it is evident that in the context of a trial verbal communication is always intertwined with non-verbal aspects. It has been shown that narrative plays a crucial role in the communicative dynamics of a jury trial. Integrating these considerations with a reflection on modality, it should also be noted that "[w]hile a narrative may be crafted through a single modality, more often narrators intertwine a multiplicity of modalities" (Ochs 1997: 186). This also happens in a trial where the narration is conducted through various means and strategies, which may be, for instance, auditory or visual. More specifically, speakers constantly point to charts, maps, diagrams, photos, other figures, or they present sound recordings (such as telephone calls) or video material[40].

Beyond modality, trial discourse may further be seen as hybrid in terms of styles and registers. Indeed, it is highly formal and technical in certain circumstances, but formality and technicality are also combined with ordinary language and even instances of oversimplification. Such variants correspond to the heterogeneity of the interactants involved in a jury trial who, by definition, have considerably different backgrounds. It is clear that attorneys adapt their talk in relation to the jurors, as "[t]he more the sender reflects the receiver's own mode of communication, the more easily will his message be understood" (Giles/Powesland 1975: 159)[41]. However, if we consider attorney/jury communicative processes, it may be difficult to establish what the jurors' 'mode of communication' is, given the predominantly

39 Other issues also emerge in relation to the fact that however accurate the transcripts may be they will never express the words pronounced in their perfect completeness. Moreover, the police are not often specifically trained in the issues related to the transcription processes.

40 As mentioned in chapter 3, a multi-modal analysis would, however, go beyond the scope of this study.

41 For a discussion of accommodation theory see Giles/Powesland 1975 and Bell 1984. Cf. section 5.4.4.

monologic nature of the process (see section 4.4, cf. Cotterill 2003). In order to define a mode of communication with such scarcity of information, advocates may work along the lines of what they may consider the prototypical juror to be, and they may also attempt to acquire a considerable amount of information about the jurors (e.g. during the voir dire phase).

Moreover, jury trials may be seen as a combination of relatively planned and relatively unplanned discourse[42] (Ochs 1979b, Tannen 1982), even though the former appears predominant. The nature of a trial is also hybrid as the context is a highly institutionalized and standardized one, but at the same time it displays a highly individual and personal character.

Courtroom discourse presents the use of legal language, characterized by a certain level of rationality and logical development, as well as a constant use of emotional language. Rationality plays an important, but not hegemonic, role. The situation is particularly complex, because rational language and emotional language are not mutually exclusive but continuously interrelated, and it is precisely this interplay that often determines the effectiveness of an interactant's speech. Merry (1990) argues that emotional language enters the courtroom when the appropriation of the terms of legal discourse is ineffective but, more generally, it may be argued that one of the factors inherent to successful legal advocacy is an ability to constantly move between emotion-laden and more aseptic words throughout the trial. Furthermore, different types of law (such as institutional or moral) are constantly contrasted and negotiated. Legislation (which shows elements of general applicability as well as specificity) may often be in conflict with the customs and values of society, and this sort of tension is fundamental within the context of a jury trial.

In sum, courtroom language is intrinsically hybrid in that it is, in turn, hypercomplex and oversimplified, extremely formal and humorous; it combines parataxis and hypotaxis, it is personal and impersonal, clear and ambiguous, precise and indeterminate, general and specific, technical and emotional.

---

42 It should, however, be observed that such distinction is not clear-cut. For a further discussion see Tannen 1982a, Ochs 1979a, Chafe 1982.

5. Analysis

The power of the lawyer is in the uncertainty of the law. (Jeremy Bentham)

Having highlighted in the previous chapter some of the main features and issues that typify courtroom communication in jury trials, the analysis based on one specific trial will now be presented. Considering the vastness of the material available related to this case, a selection had inevitably to be carried out. I will primarily focus on the communicative dynamics that characterize the interaction between legal professionals (i.e. the attorneys and the judge) and the jurors, in the attempt to show which communicative strategies and techniques are used and to examine the principles that lie behind such choices. This endeavor will be carried out by also observing the emergence of knowledge asymmetries between the interactants and how they are made 'communicatively salient' (Marková/Foppa 1991: 5), in light of the procedural standards that are to be followed in the different phases of the trial.

5.1 The Westerfield jury trial

5.1.1 The case

The case related to the death of Danielle van Dam will be briefly outlined in this section for clarifying purposes[43]. Seven-year-old Danielle disappeared from her home in Sabre Spring, San Diego, California, in

43 The case received considerable media attention, and press coverage about the case was extensive. For details about the case see, for instance, <http://articles.cnn.com/keyword/david-westerfield>.

the night between February 1 and February 2, 2002. The last person to have seen her was her father as he tucked her in, while her mother was spending the night out with some friends. David Westerfield, a 50-year-old neighbor, soon emerged as the only suspect and was questioned by the police on February 4. He was arrested on February 22 and was charged with murder, kidnapping and possession of child pornography. During the investigation, Danielle's blood, fingerprints and strands of hair were found in Westerfield's mobile home. On February 27 Danielle's corpse was found by two volunteers who were acting on a hunch in Dehsea, California, in a thicket of oaks 25 miles from Danielle's house. Paul Pfingst, the San Diego County District Attorney, affirmed that it was not possible to determine immediately the cause of death because of the body's state of decomposition; whether the girl had been sexually assaulted could not be determined either.

In June 2002 the trial started, and in opening the trial Judge William Mudd cautioned jurors to avoid news reports about the case. The defense tried to turn the spotlight away from his client and to demonstrate that Danielle's parents, Damon and Brenda van Dam, behaved coarsely the night their daughter was kidnapped. It was the parents' lifestyle to be put on trial and they were depicted as a promiscuous, immoral and irresponsible couple. Under cross-examination, Ms. van Dam testified that after spending the night in the local bar, she went home with four friends, and Danielle's parents admitted to smoking marijuana the night of her disappearance. The attempt was to lay groundwork for an alternate theory, assuming that anyone could have committed the crime. The ultimate aim was to create reasonable doubt about Westerfield's guilt, insisting on the negligence on the part of Danielle's parents instead of dwelling on forensic evidence. Indeed, predictably, during the trial forensic evidence was in turn cited to confirm the defendant's responsibility or to raise doubts about whether he could have committed the crime. On August 21 the verdict was read and David Westerfield was found guilty on all counts.

The following week the penalty phase of the trial started with the aim to decide whether Mr. Westerfield should be given life in prison without parole or death by lethal injection. On September 16 the jury recommended the death penalty, but the decision was problematic as it had initially appeared to be a deadlocked jury. Criticism arose because the jurors had originally said that they could not reach a unanimous sentence and needed further guidance; Judge Mudd had set a hearing for the afternoon, but after lunch the jury asked for more time to deliberate and ten minutes afterwards a verdict was reached. In January 2003, California Judge William Mudd sentenced David Westerfield to be executed. At the time of writing, he is detained in San Quentin State Prison.

5.1.2 The trial

This study is definable as the analysis of a single discourse event, as it is confined to one specific trial, namely *California vs Westerfield*. However, defining a trial as a single event is problematic because of its complex (albeit clearly pre-defined) structure and because it inherently consists of different sub-phases. The focus on one trial allows a more in-depth investigation and limits the risk of running into fallacious conclusions originating from the comparison of events characterized by significant differences. Indeed, every trial has a certain degree of specificity deriving from a variety of factors that determine its nature and its development, such as the specific procedures contemplated by a certain jurisdiction at a specific point in time.

Even though material was available for the entire process (from the preliminary hearings to the sentencing phase), only some phases of the trial will be analyzed, given the time, space and target constraints of this work. The analysis will focus specifically on the communication between the court and the jurors (with particular reference to the jury instruction phase) and between the attorneys and the jurors (principally during opening statements and closing arguments). The other parts of the trial will be briefly touched upon mainly for clarifying purposes and in order to position the different phases under scrutiny within a broader framework.

The Westerfield trial was conducted in 2002 and the time span that is primarily considered in this analysis goes from June 4 (starting with preliminary jury instructions and opening statements) to August 21 (verdict). Table 3 is to be intended as a merely introductory representation of the different phases of the Westerfield trial, which can be briefly outlined as follows[44]:

Dates	*Phase*
May, 2002	Jury selection
June 4	*Initial instructions by the judge*[45] *Prosecution Opening statements* *Defense Opening statements* Witness examination
June 4 - August 1[46]	Witness examination
August 6	*Jury instructions*[47] *Closing arguments*
August 7	*Closing arguments*
August 8	*Final closing arguments* *Jury instructions*[48]
August 8 - August 21	Deliberation
August 21	Verdict
August 28 - September 16	Penalty phase
January 3, 2003	Sentence[49]

Table 3. Outline of the Westerfield trial.[50]

The main participants involved in the trial are:

- Judge: William Mudd
- Defendant: David Westerfield

44 For the sake of completeness, it should be remembered that these events were also preceded by other phases, such as pre-trial hearings and pre-trial motions.

45 Identified in the analysis as 'Jury instructions, day 1'.

46 The period between opening statements (June 4) and jury instructions (August 6) also includes motions (in particular, on June 27, July 23, July 29, August 2).

47 Identified in the analysis as 'Jury instructions, day 28'.

48 Identified in the analysis as 'Jury instructions, day 30'.

49 The trial of a person charged with a capital crime also includes the sentencing phase. Once the verdict has been reached, if the defendant is found guilty, the sentencing phase leads to the selection of a sentence. As mentioned above, this analysis will not focus on this phase.

50 The phases that represent the primary object of this analysis are in italics.

- For the People of California: Jeff B. Dusek; George W. Clarke
- For the defendant: Steven E. Feldman; Robert E. Joyce; Laura G. Schaefer.

The present analysis primarily focuses on legal experts-jurors interaction, and the main agents investigated will be Judge Mudd, Mr. Dusek (prosecuting attorney) and Mr. Feldman (defense attorney).

5.2 Jury selection: who will be the audience?

The selection process[51] is a complex phase and is jurisdiction-specific (Mauet 2009: 40). In the Westerfield case, the process may be briefly summarized as follows: nearly 500 prospective jurors were randomly selected and asked to complete the 22-page juror questionnaire, which comprised 123 questions. After the review of the questionnaires, the prospective jurors (in groups of 20) were questioned by the judge, the prosecutors and the defense attorneys to determine whether they could be fair and impartial in that case. As described in section 4.2, when it is believed that a person would not render an impartial verdict based on the evidence, a challenge for cause takes place; the lawyers may also dismiss a potential juror without cause (peremptory challenge). The process continued until the twelve jurors (and six alternates) were approved by both sides and sworn in.

The jury selection aims to identify a fair and impartial jury, but attorney training manuals highlight that this phase is functional to the attorneys not only in order to attempt to select jurors that may be favorable to their side, but also to learn about jurors' attitudes and behaviors. As Mauet notes:

> The jurors also bring with them their personal experiences, deep-seated beliefs, and attitudes about life and how things work in the real world. They have expectations about how a trial should be conducted; how lawyers should

51 For details on jury selection see *inter alia* Kaye 2006, Mauet 2009.

> act; how they want witness testimony, exhibits, and visual aids to be presented; and how they want to be treated during the course of the trial. Effective lawyers recognize the jurors' needs, attitudes, and expectations and respond to them throughout the jury selection process. (Mauet 2009: 25)

Moreover, in the selection phase lawyers should also try to recognize the types of jurors involved, e.g. distinguishing between 'persuaders', 'participants', and 'non-participants' (Mauet 2009: 51) and to identify who the most influential speakers during deliberations could be.

As noted in section 4.2.2, the issue related to the impartiality of the jurors is at the core of the procedure. The case analyzed here was a high-profile case and its media coverage was extensive; under those circumstances the selection of unbiased, fair and impartial jurors is even more challenging as there is a higher potential danger that "jurors will judge the case based on pre-existing biases or media reports rather than trial evidence" (Hans 2006: XIV). The final composition of the jury included six men and six women and the alternates were five women and one man[52].

5.3 Jury instruction: what should the audience do?

Jury instructions consist of a set of legal principles and procedures that have to be applied to the case in question. More specifically, a distinction should be made between 'jury instruction' intended as a comprehensive expression for the process of instructing the jurors and 'jury instructions' intended as the specific texts delivered (see Heffer 2008: 47-52).

In *California vs Westerfield*, jurors were instructed in different moments. The analysis will primarily focus on the three main moments when jury instructions were given: pre-instructions before opening statements (June 4, day 1), instructions before closing argu-

---

52 For a description of the jury see: <http://legacy.signonsandiego.com/news/metro/danielle/images/jurors.html>. Accessed: January 7, 2009.

ments (August 6, day 28), and final instructions after closing arguments (August 8, day 30). The present analysis also takes into consideration other instances of interaction between the judge and the jurors, in which the former addresses the latter with the aim of informing and instructing them about a specific issue that has been raised or a relevant procedure that the judge deems necessary to illustrate.

The importance of the jury instruction phase cannot be overestimated in that the potential erroneous comprehension of instructions and the consequent risk of an improper application of the law raise crucial issues about the legitimacy of jury verdicts. The aim of this phase is essentially "to create a legal structure to guide juror decision making" (Lieberman/Sales 2000: 587). Its ultimate purpose appears highly challenging in that instructions have to condense considerably a vast set of intricate legal principles and trial procedures, and such instructions have to be followed by jurors who are likely to lack any legal background.

The debate around jury instructions has always been particularly vivid. As early as 1973 Friedman wrote that, generally, these texts are "stereotyped, antiseptic statements of abstract rules" and concluded that "often juries may not understand them at all" (Friedman 1973: 137). Friedman also observed that in the past, for instance in the eighteenth century, the judge explained the law to the jurors in a much more informal and accessible way, and such instructions were ultimately more informative for laypersons. Later, especially in the nineteenth century, different statutes eliminated the possibility for the judge to comment on the evidence; the use of stereotyped instructions has constantly proliferated in the last few decades. These types of instructions have often been described as confusing for the jurors, but it has been argued that, on the other hand, they may contribute to preserving the fundamental principle of the autonomy of the jury (Friedman 1973: 137).

Issues related to the drafting, the delivery and the reception of jury instructions have been addressed in a long string of cases and have been the object of a large set of empirical and non-empirical studies. In particular, problems related to the comprehensibility of jury instructions have attracted considerable attention (see *inter alia* Lieberman/Sales 1997, Tiersma 1999b, Conley 2000, Dumas 2000, Ellsworth/Reifman 2000, Heffer 2008), especially after some seminal work carried out in this direction in the seventies (Elwork *et al.* 1977, 1982, Sales *et al.* 1977, Charrow/Charrow 1979) showing the limited comprehensibility of such texts.

Much work has been done in the last few years in order to promote advancements in jurors' understanding of instructions. The State of California, where the Westerfield trial took place, carried out some pioneering work in the drafting of more accessible pattern jury instructions[53]; indeed as early as 1938 the *Book of Approved Jury Instructions* (BAJI) was published in California (Lieberman/Krauss 2009: 154). Pattern instructions, also defined as 'model, uniform, approved and standardized' instructions, can be described as "tools designed to simplify the process of issuing jury instructions and to promote consistency among judges" (Williams 2000: 123). The work aiming at improving the understandability of pattern instructions has continuously evolved (see Tiersma 1993, 2009, Tiersma/Curtis 2008). In particular, such instructions are written applying principles that may facilitate understanding, such as avoidance of an extensive use of legal jargon; avoidance of intricate syntactic patterns; clear organizational structure (e.g. including the use of numbered lists). It has also been suggested that instructions should be tailored to the individual case (e.g. including the names of parties instead of general definitions).

Jury instructions can be said to have two primary objectives: "achieving legal accuracy and effectively conveying information to jurors" (Severance/Loftus 1982: 155), and the two aims are often inevitably in contrast. Legal accuracy is indeed a fundamental aspect in that under certain circumstances a jury verdict may be the subject of appeal in a higher court on the basis of a claim of error in the instructions delivered to the jury. Pattern instructions were introduced with the aim of reducing cases of appeal based on this type of claimed error in instructing the jury, as well as with the objective of rendering the process of selecting the appropriate jury instructions quicker and simpler for judges and attorneys (Nieland 1979).

---

53 Pattern instructions are sets of standard instructions that are generally applicable; they are usually selected by the judge and the attorneys and are slightly adapted to the specific case in question.

5.3.1 Jury instruction as a multi-phase

The moment in which instructions are delivered and the amount of time jurors are exposed to them can also affect comprehension. For decades now it has been argued that it is irrational to provide jurors with instructions related to basic principles, such as the notion of 'reasonable doubt' (see section 5.6.3 for details), at the end of the trial, when significant impressions about the innocence or guilt of the defendant have already been formed and it is iniquitous to ask jurors to apply these instructions retrospectively. The use of instructions exclusively before deliberation has been described as an unreasonable practice, and has been compared to "telling jurors to watch a baseball game and decide who won without telling them what the rules are until the end of the game" (Schwarzer 1991: 583).

Conversely, pre-instructions (also called preliminary or initial instructions) are given before opening statements and generally deal with basic procedural matters and legal principles. It is often argued that giving pre-instructions on substantive legal principles and on trial procedures prior to the beginning of the trial may facilitate jurors' understanding. Indeed, initial instructions allow the jurors to organize the testimony and the evidence they are exposed to in a more meaningful legal framework and to focus more carefully on the relevant issues. Pre-instructions may also contribute to helping the jurors to frame the evidence "according to legal rather than personal criteria" (Heuer/Penrod 1989: 413). Moreover, repeated exposure to instructions may also improve recollection, even though this hypothesis has not always been confirmed (for a detailed investigation of preliminary and written instructions see Heuer/Penrod 1989).

California court rules provide that the point in the trial when instructions should be given is at the discretion of the judge. In the Westerfield case, besides preliminary instructions, the jury was instructed also before closing arguments. This practice is also generally saluted positively as it allows jurors to frame the attorneys' arguments in light of specific instructions. Finally, in *California vs Westerfield*, jurors received instructions also after closing arguments; this is a traditional practice, as it is deemed functional that the jurors hear instructions just before starting deliberating, and scholars often remark that it is also considered appropriate that the last words in the jurors' ears should be the judge's and not one of the lawyers'.

Before providing the jurors with preliminary instructions, Judge Mudd highlights that instructions will also be given at a later stage, and that no instruction is of higher importance than another, even though the task of disregarding the order of presentation of instructions may be psychologically unattainable[54]:

> THE COURT: I shall now instruct you as to your basic functions, duties, and conduct. At the conclusion of the case I will give you further instructions on the law that applies to this case. All of the court's instructions, whether they are given before, during, or after the taking of testimony, are of equal importance. (Jury instructions, day 1)

Jurors are also reminded that they will receive a written copy of the instructions, which they could refer to during deliberations:

> THE COURT: You will have these instructions in written form in the juryroom to refer to during your deliberations. (Jury instructions, day 28)

In this respect, it has been suggested that written jury instructions made available to juries are more easily understood, recalled, and applied (Elwork *et al.* 1977).

5.3.2 Humor in court

One of the elements that characterize the judge's talk is the presence of humor. However, the very definition of humor is not straightforward. For example, using consequent laughter as a defining criterion is not appropriate, as Richards notes (2006: 93), and Attardo confirms that "humor and laughter, while obviously related, are by no means coextensive" (Attardo 2003: 1288). In general terms, humor may be intended as "anything done or said, purposely or inadvertently, that is found to be comical or amusing" (Long/Graessner 1988: 37). In this specific context, given the dramatic case being tried and the (generally

---

54 In light, for example, of primacy and recency rules.

perceived) formality of a courtroom, it is implausible to expect open laughter from the juries. The judge's words are not used with an openly comic function, as that would not be appropriate, but a subtle humorous vein emerges quite frequently in his/her words. As Tannen notes, humor is a "highly distinctive aspect of a person's style" (Tannen 1984: 130), and humor is a feature that clearly typifies Judge Mudd's style. Conversely, the use of puns or punch-lines or other humorous remarks is less evident in the attorneys' words. This choice may be fundamentally related to a specific personal style, but it is also true that humor generally tends to be used more sparingly by attorneys, as it may be counterproductive. Humor serves both an inclusive and an exclusive function; if listeners are excluded, as they do not respond positively to the humorous remark, this process may be detrimental to the attempt to establish strong bonds with the juries.

At the beginning of the instruction phase, instead of starting immediately to read the jury instructions, the judge spends a few words on extra-textual references and tries to create a more familiar and relaxed atmosphere, given that a courtroom may be an unknown and untried setting to many jurors. Indeed, the judge's comments may be used to alleviate the tension the jurors may feel, given that it is the first day of the actual trial and for some of them it may be the first time they serve as jurors.

Judge Mudd starts his talk with a comment on the Padres, the San Diego Major League Baseball team. An introductory remark of this type is used both before reading the preliminary jury instructions (on day 1), but also before reading the second main set of instructions (on day 28):

> THE COURT: Good morning, ladies and gentlemen, and welcome back. I had hoped when we next met that the Padres would be on a lengthy winning streak. Unfortunately that was not to be. (Jury instructions, day 1)

> THE COURT: Good morning, ladies and gentlemen. Welcome back. About the best we can say about the Padres' performance since you left is that the football season is about ready to start. (Jury instructions, day 28)

As is often the case, the judge begins the instruction phase by offering some preliminary information about the general procedure and the unfolding of a trial:

> THE COURT: As you all know, having gone through the orientation program that was put on by the jury commissioner, trials in this state are conducted in various phases or stages. You folks have already been through the jury-selection process and are now the twelve jurors and six alternates that have been selected to hear this matter. The next phase of the trial is another orientation. This orientation, however, is a little more specific, because it now deals with some of the dos and don'ts of this new job that you have. Like everything else in this state, this has been reduced to a script for me to read. When you realize that this script was prepared by lawyers and judges, it will soon become very apparent to you that *this is not only not the most entertaining material you've ever heard*, but, in addition to that, it might sound confusing and a little convoluted. Don't worry about it. We're going to be talking about very basic concepts, and I will try to interject where all the legalese is some common-sense approach to this. As soon as I'm done with these comments, you'll hear the opening statements of counsel and the actual trial will begin. (Jury instructions, day 1)

In this passage the judge also offers a preamble announcing that the instructions are now going to be read. His attempt to introduce the instructions in a simple and somehow engaging manner is made evident; for instance, the judge refers to the contents of the instructions in a deliberately simplistic way, by defining them as 'some of the dos and don'ts of this new job that you have'. A (relatively) sarcastic remark is also made in relation to the nature of the instructions ('like everything else in this state, it has been reduced to a script for me to read').

The judge enhances his role as a facilitator of understanding. He points out the complex and tedious nature of the texts, euphemistically defined as 'not the most entertaining material you've ever heard', and he also presages that, as the authors are legal professionals, the texts may appear bewildering and tortuous. However, the judge attempts to reassure his audience by declaring his willingness to explain the instructions in a simple and understandable way which goes beyond pure 'legalese'.

Some information about basic practicalities (e.g. the use of notebooks) and procedural practices is initially presented:

> THE COURT: I want to talk to you a little bit about these notebooks. As you can see, it's basically a steno pad. Attached to that is a county of San Diego ink pen which means it has about a fifty/fifty chance of having ink in it throughout the course of this trial. But the county has spared no expense, and we have as many of these cheap pens as we need. So if yours runs out of ink or you happen to get the notebook of a prior juror who took copious notes, just let one of the staff know, and they will replenish your supply. (Jury instructions, day 1)

The judge's language in this phase of the trial appears in stark contrast with the highly formal, routinized, and conventionalized language that is generally associated with legal procedures. In particular, humor and wittiness emerge constantly; for example, jurors' badges are euphemistically presented as 'not the most stylish thing to go walking around downtown San Diego with':

> THE COURT: In that regard, I must insist that you wear your jurors' badges from the time you arrive here at the courthouse until you leave in the afternoon. Now, I also request that you wear them over the lunch hour. I know they are *not the most stylish thing to go walking around downtown San Diego with*, but by wearing those badges, others that are interested in court proceedings know you're a juror. (Jury instructions, day 1)

Humorous remarks are also integrated with personal references to the judge and his family. The judge continues to adopt a very entertaining tone, using vivid and figurative language ('my wife will have my head'):

> THE COURT: Also, if the trial is still going, and I'm not sure whether it will be, but the week of July 15th through 19th, the court is gone. I treasure my thirty-three-year marriage; and if I don't make this trip, my wife will have my head. And this was part of my agreement with everybody in taking this case. So I will not be here the 15th through the 19th. So I have no idea if the case will be over by then or whether we'll be in second phase, I have no way of knowing. But for planning purposes, for your employer purposes, you can mark this week down. You will not be in session. (Jury instructions, day 1)

The jurors are initially informed about very basic practical matters, which are introduced with a constant dose of witty humor:

> THE COURT: I'm anticipating a ninety-minute lunch break. As taxpayers I think you have a reason to know why since most of you never had lunch breaks that long. (Jury instructions, day 1)

The judge's language also presents the use of intertextual references, which are creatively and entertainingly adapted to the specific context ('Toto, we're not in San Diego anymore'):

> THE COURT: Welcome back, ladies and gentlemen. To butcher a line from the Wizard of Oz, Toto, we're not in San Diego anymore. Ladies and gentlemen, I did something in this trial that I do in every trial I have ever done for almost 20 years of doing this job, and that is, I gave you the phone number for this courtroom. And I gave you the phone number with the understanding you would use it in case of an emergency. Little did I know that every weirdo, wacko and dimestore comedian in this country was going to call my line with suggestions about my hairdo, my weight. (The Court, day 1)

It is interesting to note that in this excerpt the judge somehow establishes his credentials and reinforces his identity of expert by highlighting the length of his career ('almost 20 years'). The judge, at the same time, continues to use a particularly informal style, which includes a significant dose of colloquialisms; this approach may appear to diverge considerably from the purely 'legalistic' style that is often associated with legal professionals.

As mentioned, the judge has to use legally precise and appropriate terms in the jury instruction phase, as the delivery of understandable jury instructions has to deal with the primary concern of maintaining legal accuracy. A myopic insistence upon the use of legal jargon, without any clarifications regarding specific terminology and procedures, is more likely to fulfill the objective of preserving correctness and precision and may limit the potential danger of appeals based on improper jury instructions; however, an approach of this type may fail the other essential objective of this phase of the trial, which is to provide clear and understandable instructions for their final users, i.e. the jurors. This tension leads to an interesting blend of technical and specific definitions and ordinary language (even combined with colloquialisms).

5.3.3 Issues in instructing the jurors

The understandability and the effective applicability of instructions may be hampered by a series of factors, such as the linguistic complexity, the level of abstractness, and the mode of the delivery. Beyond comprehensibility, the correct applicability of the texts may also be highly problematic, as some of the principles mentioned appear to be in contrast with basic cognitive processes. For instance, the judge emphasizes that jurors should not be distracted by the note-taking process, but maintaining a constant level of concentration throughout the trial is obviously not possible:

> THE COURT: A word of caution. You may take notes. However, you should not permit note-taking to distract you from the ongoing proceedings. (Jury instructions, day 1)

Moreover, jurors are explicitly asked to accept and follow the law, disregarding their own opinion about it

> THE COURT: You must accept and follow the law as I state it to you, whether or not you agree with the law. (Jury instructions, day 1; Jury instructions, day 28)

Even if we assume that the law has been correctly understood, its complete acceptance may not be automatic, and it may not be feasible to ask the jurors to mechanically apply it disregarding completely their personal opinions. Another problematic principle emerges in the following instruction:

> THE COURT: Statements made by the attorneys during the trial are not evidence. However, if the attorneys stipulate or agree to a fact, you must regard that fact as proven. (Jury instructions, day 1)

Attorneys are not witnesses and their utterances do not represent evidence, but it is not possible to definitely exclude that jurors will attribute some evidential value to the attorneys' words. For example, as regards the examination phase, it can be argued that "[j]urors are unable to effectively and consistently make distinctions, during the interactive flow of examination speech, between bona fide evidence and advocate contributions." (Gaines 2006: 170).

Jurors are instructed to disregard certain type of evidence, but Wagner *et al.* (1987) show the paradox of a task that requires un-thinking of a process, as such a request actually increases thinking about the topic:

> THE COURT: Do not consider for any purpose any offer of evidence that is rejected or any evidence that is stricken by the court. Treat it as though you had never heard of it. (Jury instructions, day 1)

It has also been demonstrated that admonitions to ignore inadmissible evidence are often ineffective and may even backfire, "resulting in jurors relying more heavily on information they have been instructed to disregard" (Lieberman *et al.* 2009: 90). In a similar vein, jurors are instructed before the beginning of the actual trial that they must not be influenced by pity or prejudice towards the defendant. They are asked to mechanically apply the law that has been read to them, without letting emotions play any role in the way they process the message and evaluate it:

> THE COURT: You must not be influenced by pity for the defendant or by prejudice against him. You must not be biased against the defendant because he has been arrested for this offense, charged with a crime, or brought to trial. None of these circumstances is evidence of guilt, and you must not infer or assume from any or all of them that he is more likely to be guilty than not guilty. During this phase of the trial you must not be influenced by mere sentiment, conjecture, sympathy, passion, prejudice, public opinion or public feeling. Both the people and Mr. Westerfield have a right to expect that you will conscientiously consider and weigh the evidence, apply the law, and reach a just verdict regardless of the consequences. (Jury instructions, day 1)

A significant strain of research (e.g. Feigenson *et al.* 1997, Voss/Van Dyke 2001, Feigenson 2003) confirms the intuitive assumption that bias and emotional reactions inevitably affect jurors' evaluation of the case. In particular, different types of bias have been identified (e.g. Kramer *et al.* 1990, Kerr *et al.* 1996), such as factual (deriving from the consideration of factual information that is not legally probative in that specific case) and emotional biases. In other words, it can be argued that even though judgments inexorably derive from an inextricable combination of reason and emotion[55], the law admits only the former (Maroney 2006: 119).

5.3.4 Judge-jurors interaction and knowledge asymmetries

In a jury trial, the relationship between the legal professionals involved and the jurors is inherently asymmetrical from a variety of perspectives, e.g. in terms of communicative dynamics and level of legal knowledge.

Jurors are often described as passive spectators of an event whose communicative dynamics are predominantly seen as monologic (Cotterill 2003; see chapter 4). It has often been argued that the traditional passive role attributed to jurors is inevitably detrimental to comprehension, leads to a lack of involvement and to apathetic participation and, consequently, is cause of poor decision-making. However, involvement promoted by questions asked to the court may result in a higher degree of involvement and a higher level of comprehension.

Moreover, the jury is often depicted as holding a disadvantageous position deriving from a total or partial lack of specific legal knowledge. If we observe knowledge asymmetries between jurors and legal experts, they are sometimes made verbally explicit during the trial. Indeed, in the Californian jurisdiction jurors are generally allowed to ask for clarifications when needed by submitting a written note to the judge who will then evaluate how to clarify a certain concept in order to allow the jurors to better comprehend a specific point or a certain procedure.

In the following passage an example of knowledge asymmetry about terminological issues (related to sustained and overruled objections) is made explicit and manifested:

> THE COURT: Okay. Welcome back, ladies and gentlemen. Before we continue questioning this witness, *I have received a note from one of you* who filled out the note properly, simply wrote me the note and signed the seat number, not the name, which is the way we want you to do it. And *it basically*

55 For a wider reflection on the relation between law and emotion see Pildes 1992, Bandes 1999, Little 2001, 2002, Posner 2001.

> *asks about some terminology*. Now, *this is probably a question many of you might ask.* (The Court, June 4)

Before explaining the concept in question, the judge refers to the assumption that other jurors may have the same difficulty in understanding the same concept ("this is probably a question many of you might ask"). It can certainly be argued that this assumption is highly justified, as this issue has been brought up directly by one juror. The judge seems willing to use a very friendly tone and a style that should offer a higher level of comprehensibility:

> THE COURT: [...] and so I *'ve never personally taught any law school class, but I'm going to give you a judge's version of legalese 101.* Whenever...we are ruled, the lawyers and I are ruled by what we call objections. Basically the ground rules for how a trial is conducted. And they are rules of evidence. And from time to time a question might be asked and the one lawyer will think that the answer to that question might be objectionable for some reason. So that lawyer is going to say objection and will give me a reason why I should either sustain or overrule the objection. Now, *the reason I'm basically here is sort of the referee of this match that's going on. So my job is to make the call.* If I overrule the objection, what that means is you're going to hear the question and you will hear the answer. (The Court, June 4)

Figurative language is also used by the judge in order to facilitate the juror's understanding of the legal procedure he is explaining (*'the reason I'm basically here is sort of the referee of this match that's going on. So my job is to make the call'*). Moreover, the explanation of how objections work, and how jurors should evaluate them, is clearly presented and the concept is repeated more than once, as it is believed that repeated exposure may facilitate understanding and recollection:

> THE COURT: Remember that a question isn't evidence. Evidence is the answer to the question. So when I overrule the objection, that means the lawyer made the objection, I overruled it, you will hear the question and the answer. If I sustain the objection, what that means is you're going to hear the question, but you won't hear the answer. Again, like was covered in voir dire, remember, a question or implications or inferences in a question is not evidence. It's only the answer that is really the evidence. So overruled means that you get to hear the question and the answer. Sustained means you'll hear the question but no answer. Don't dwell on it, worry about it, or hold it against one or the

other lawyers. They're doing their jobs. In other words, that's just part of the process by which we control the trial. (The Court, June 4)

Extensive simplification efforts occur and the judge fruitfully blends specialized legal terminology with everyday language. He also openly acknowledges the difficulty the jurors may find in applying certain concepts and processes, such as disregarding questions that have been heard:

> THE COURT: Also, occasionally before I get to respond an answer has already been given. And I'll say something like the jury is to disregard the last portion of the answer. That's a very difficult concept because what I'm telling you to do basically is disregard what the person just said. Now, about the best way to do that is treat it as though you had never heard of it. I don't think that will be a problem, but those are sort of the groundrules that you are going to see played out in this courtroom in the next couple weeks. (The Court, day 1)

Sporting metaphors are often used by the judge to explain the rules of the proceedings as if they were the rules of a game. Considering the epistemic modality of his utterances, it should be notes that the judge often uses 'softeners' such as *sort of* ("sort of the referee", "sort of the groundrules"), which convey a more colloquial tone.

In another situation knowledge asymmetries between jurors and legal experts do not emerge directly, but they are dealt with on the basis of more general assumptions. In the following excerpt, the judge explains the purpose of a sidebar conference, as, thanks to his experience, he assumes that it is necessary and the jurors would benefit from it ("I think we ought to talk about that"). In this case the jurors do not explicitly ask for clarifications about the purpose of that specific event, but the judge presupposes that all or some members of the jury may be in need of such an explanation.

This can be seen, to a certain extent, as an assumed knowledge asymmetry, as it derives from the judge's assumption:

> THE COURT: Ladies and gentlemen, since this is the first of probably many of these sidebar conferences, *I think we ought to talk about that.* The purpose of a sidebar conference is very simple. I have a choice when the lawyers want to talk to me before something that doesn't directly deal with you. And that is, I can have all of you leave the courtroom or I can make Ophelia here come over here and sit on a step, and *we have a little football huddle* and we discuss

> it. Now, don't strain an ear trying to hear what it is we're talking about, because if it's meant for you to hear you're going to hear it, and if you don't hear it, you weren't going to hear it anyway. (The Court, June 4)

Interestingly, metaphorical language[56] drawing on the field of sport is also vividly used in this case to graphically describe what happens in a sidebar conference ('we have a little football huddle').

In sum, it can be argued that the highly formal and specialized form of language used in the written form of jury instructions is hybridized by conversational language which is used by the judge to clarify and complement such instructions. This hybridization process is, however, circular and there is a continuous alternation between technical and everyday language. This circularity is identifiable also from a historical perspective, as this phase of the trial originally displayed a higher level of informality which was subsequently abandoned (see Friedman 1973) and which is nowadays often introduced.

5.4 Opening statements: the story begins

The content of opening statements was traditionally limited to a presentation of what the parties expected to prove in the rest of the trial through evidence and testimonies. Instead, as Mauet notes, "[t]he modern view is broader and permits themes and the parties' positions on disputed facts and issues. The modern view recognizes the significance of opening statements in informing and orienting the jury to the facts of the case and the disputed issues" (Mauet 2009: 84). Case law identifies elements that are improper in opening statements, such as discussing inadmissible evidence, offering purely argumentative statements, asserting personal opinions, commenting about the evidence or the credibility of a witness, or discussing the law.

The opening phase is meant to offer a preview of what the evidence will show and not to be an occasion for argumentation, as ar-

56 For a further discussion of the use of metaphors in court see section 5.6.

gument cannot precede the presentation of evidence. Jurors, therefore, should not come to a decision about the case before all the evidence has been presented, but it does not seem to be cognitively possible to avoid making any sort of judgment. Consequently, as Aron *et al.* aptly note, "it is improper to argue during the opening statement, but if the lawyer can succeed in arguing without giving the impression that he or she is arguing, that will facilitate the understanding of the attorney's case on the part of the jury" (Aron *et al.* 1996: 12.17).

Opening statements represent the first moment of the trial where the jurors are confronted with a presentation of the case. Walter mentions the possibility that opening statements may determine the outcome of the trial even in 80-90% of the cases (Walter 1988: 224) and it has been confirmed that "[s]ome lawyers feel that as many as 80 per cent of all jurors make up their minds by the end of the opening statement" (Aron *et al.* 1996: 21.15). Similarly, Jeans writes that "jurors, interviewed after verdict, have confirmed that their ultimate decision corresponded with their tentative opinion after opening statements in over 80% of the cases" (Jeans 1975: 305). However, this figure has often been questioned and seen as being apocryphal, as it does not seem to be corroborated by clear evidence (Burke *et al.* 1992, Tanford 2002).

A significant area of research assigns to opening statements a remarkably important function in terms of the outcome of the trial. As Burns notes, "[t]he lawyer in opening provides an important service in trying to propose to the jury the best account, given the story expected to be told by the opponent and the anticipated evidence, of what the evidence means, what it adds up to" (Burns 2009: 24). The importance of opening statements primarily lies in the oft-cited consideration that they create a lens through which the rest of the trial will be seen and interpreted. It is also argued that it cannot be excluded *a priori* that the lens may be discarded or that its focal point may change during the course of the trial.

It has been suggested that opening statements contribute to create a schema according to which jurors process and interpret the subsequent phases of the trial (Pyszczynski/Wrightsman 1981, Pyszczynski *et al.* 1981). A schema may be broadly defined as "any subset of existing knowledge, based on prior experience and relevant to a limited domain, which people use as a framework to guide their observation, organisation, and retrieval from memory of perceived events" (Lingle/Ostrom 1981: 401). Even though the creation of a schema may develop even prior to opening statements (especially in high-profile cases), it is plausible to assume that opening statements still play a significant role in this process. In particular, two fundamental types of schemata may be identified: the role schema and the event schema. The former is used by jurors "to organise their existing knowledge about what behaviors are appropriate to what social roles" (SunWolf 2007: 188). Similarly, event schemata help the jurors to mentally organize new information that is trial-related according to their perception of the appropriateness of a certain event (SunWolf 2007: 189).

5.4.1 Narrativism in opening statements

The role of narratives as a form of social action and as an on-going constitutive element of reality is well-established (Bruner 2002, Atkinson/Delamont 2006) and in this respect Atkinson (2007) suggests:

> We are a storytelling species. Storytelling is in our blood. We think in story form, speak in story form, and bring meaning to our lives through story. Our life stories connect us to our roots, give us direction, validate our own experience, and restore value to our lives. (Atkinson 2007: 224)

In MacIntyre's words, it may be argued that if we tried to imagine human actions without a narrative framework, we would be dealing with "the disjointed parts of some possible narrative" (MacIntyre 1981: 200). It is plausible to assume that it is because of our continuing acquaintance with stories since an early age that stories help us frame the world and are constantly used as critical tools to understand different stimuli, and also to construct and express our identity. More specifically, cognitive psychology has offered precious insights into the production and processing of narrative constructs, by investigating concepts such as script theories (e.g. Schank/Abelson 1977), story schema (Mandler 1984) and narrative thought (Britton/Pellegrini 1990).

The use of stories in jury trials plays a crucial role in the decision-making process (Pennington/Hastie 1992, 1991). In its simplest terms, the 'story model' (Bennett/Feldman 1981, Pennington/Hastie 1986) suggests that while processing the information in order to reach a verdict, jurors develop a story and attempt to match it with a specific verdict category (Hans 2006: 15). Moreover, effective information management may be achieved by speakers, for example, by putting emphasis on pieces of information that the speakers share as a sort of 'prelude' (Tomlin *et al.* 1997: 65); this process allows speakers to set positive ground for the rest of their talk and to encourage in the listeners the kind of representation the speakers would like to achieve.

The use of narration also plays another crucial function within the context of a trial, which is to create solidarity (Goodwin 1994: 220). Indeed, attorneys strategically use a "universal, shared, common mode of presentation" (Goodwin 1994: 220) which may be perceived by jurors as a desire on the part of the legal experts to create solidarity and cooperation, instead of exercising power over them.

5.4.1.1 Opening your story

Opening statements often begin with formulaic expressions such as 'Good morning ladies and gentlemen', which are then followed by other micro-phases. The opening phase is often described as consisting of three principal micro-phases: an introduction where the advocate introduces himself or herself and the client; the development of the case; and a conclusion (see Aron *et al.* 1996: 12.17). Similarly, Tanford suggests that openings could be divided into five stages, namely: "(1) the introductory remarks; (2) the introduction of the witnesses, places, and instrumentalities involved in the case; (3) the identification of the major issues or contentions; (4) telling the story; and (5) the conclusion and request for a verdict" (Tanford 2002: 162).

However, the introductory remarks employed somehow depend on what was covered during voir dire, given that the scope and the procedure of the different phases may have already been mentioned in the jury selection process. As Tanford confirms, traditional introductory remarks with explanatory content may be helpful to the jurors, especially to first-time jurors, but a "more aggressive approach" is generally recommended (Tanford 2002: 163). Indeed, "[t]he modern trend is to begin directly with remarks that summarize the nature of the case, state your theme, and arouse the interest of the jury" (Tanford 2002: 163). In this respect, Mauet confirms:

> [T]he traditional way of starting an opening statement – thanking the jurors for being there, introducing the parties, analogizing the opening statement to an 'overview', comparing the evidence to 'pieces of a jigsaw puzzle', and eventually getting to 'what we expect to prove' – do not work today. Jurors will quit listening before you ever get to anything important. (Mauet 2009: 88)

This reflection confirms Coffin *et al.*'s more general consideration that "although language and indeed social conventions or norms usually develop for functional reasons, this does not mean that they remain functional or effective, particularly if there are changes in the surrounding social and cultural context" (Coffin *et al.* 2010: 10).

The opening offered by the prosecuting attorney is in line with the recommendation of a more direct approach typical of modern trials. Indeed, Mr. Dusek does not open with an introduction about himself and his client, as that may be seen as superfluous (considering, for example, that the attorney is in any case introduced by the judge when he is given the floor) and it is deemed more important to focus immediately on the core of the case.

In light of the rule of primacy[57], the first part of the opening statements is particularly crucial, and the following example shows the beginning of the prosecution's opening[58]:

> MR. DUSEK: Good morning, ladies and gentlemen. Welcome back. This trial will be about two people. Two people. David Westerfield and Danielle van Dam. More specifically, it will be about what David Westerfield did to Brenda...or Danielle van Dam. Because of that, we'll be talking about three primary time periods. The first begins, the first and primary begins February 1st and goes until Danielle's body was recovered. The two other periods will be the week before, a Friday, when Brenda van Dam and some of her friends had minor contact with the defendant. The other period of time will be in the mid-

57 For a deeper discussion of the relative effect of primacy and recency in opening statements see Linz/Penrod 1984.

58 This part corresponds more specifically to the Labovian 'abstract' (consisting of an introductory statement which has an attention-getting and a summarizing function) and 'orientation' (see Labov 1981).

> dle of that week, when Brenda van Dam and her two children went out selling girl scout cookies to the defendant. So we will be talking about the three times the van Dam family had contact with David Westerfield. (Dusek's opening)

The defense attorney opens his statements by alerting the jurors that they should not make up their mind too soon, as another version of the story will also be presented:

> MR. FELDMAN: Would that the case were so simple. Would the cases were black and white. Would that this not be a case entirely determined by circumstantial evidence. This is what the evidence will show, ladies and gentlemen. David Westerfield is a 50-year-old man. He's a design engineer. He has patents. The patents that he's been involved in, the inventions that he's been involved in relate to prosthetic devices that benefit many in our society. (Feldman's opening)

This approach is in line with Tanford's suggestion that one of the purposes of the defense opening is to warn the jurors that they should not make up their mind too soon (Tanford 2002: 147). Moreover, the introduction of the client is particularly important as the jurors' verdict often depends on their verdict on the actors involved (Tanford 2002: 164). The definition and description of actors (see also section 5.4.2.1) is a crucial element within the narrative framework, and Mr. Feldman immediately attempts to personalize his client and depict him as a respectful and considerate man; in this respect, Tanford colorfully recommends: "Imagine that you are trying to convince the jurors to go out on a blind date with your client" (Tanford 2002: 164).

5.4.1.2 Multiple narratives

The narrative presented by the attorney clearly consists of multiple narratives. In the prosecution's opening, for instance, the main narrative derives from the merger of different stories (offered by different participants) which are reconstructed, reported, or preannounced.

> MR. DUSEK: The defendant's story is that [...] (Dusek's opening)

> MR. DUSEK: Brenda will tell you that [...] (Dusek's opening)

> MR. DUSEK: The defendant told the detective Keene that [...] (Dusek's opening)

Mr. Dusek's opening statements show the presence of interrelated and circular narratives:

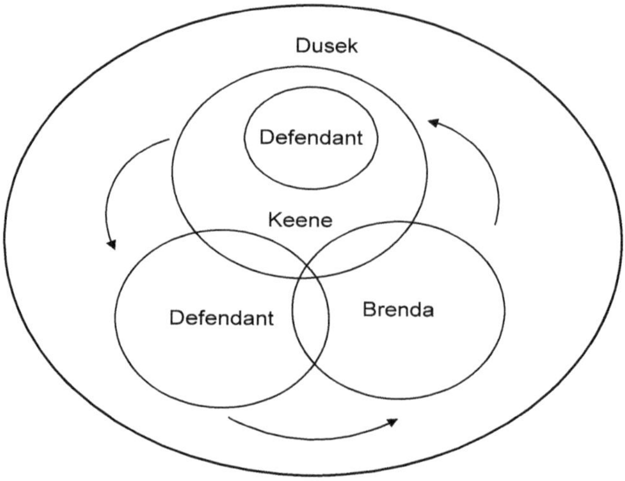

Figure 6. Example of multiple narratives in opening statements.

Figure 7 rudimentally shows that the prosecutor's narrative embeds (and consists of) multiple narratives presented by different participants. Some stories implicitly or explicitly refer, or defer, to others in a spiral of different narratives, and attorneys have to establish chronologies and relationships among the different narratives and attribute stories to the different narrators maintaining coherence and clarity.

The circularity of different accounts also emerges in the following passage, where different voices are merged within Mr. Feldman's speech which, however, seems to have a lower level of clarity:

> MR. FELDMAN: Up comes rich Brady. Up comes Keith Stone. Rich Brady, how are you? You coached my kids' soccer team. You got any drugs? Got any marijuana? Rich, you've sold me pot before. Come on. Rich Brady and Keith Stone, as Mr. Dusek told you, later are seen outside in the bar. The testimony will be that the women were dancing. (Feldman's opening)

Ability in reporting other people's testimony is fundamental in trial advocacy and this process not only has a reporting function but also a constructive one (Tannen 1986) and is functional in supporting the attorney's theory of the case. It is the aim of the attorney to present these multiple narratives within an understandable and coherent framework and it is crucial to avoid any possibility of dissonance in the events presented. The narratives offered must be acceptable in the eyes of the jurors and it can therefore be argued that they have to comply with common-sense principles and, in sum, "[a]n opening statement cannot be successful if it doesn't jibe with everyday experience" (Lubet 2004: 414).

It has been demonstrated (e.g. Bennet/Feldman 1981) that people tend to consider as genuine stories that are narrated according to traditional story format, in particular where the events determining the endpoint are noticeably emphasized, the diachronic ordering of events is clearly signaled, and the causal links are evident, explicit and abundant. In other words, narratives respecting the canons of traditional storytelling are perceived as more rational, logical and acceptable. Indeed, respecting narrative conventions can generate a sense of coherence and direction.

The ordering of events may be said to be organized according to Bakhtinian chronotopes (Bakhtin 1981) intended as space-temporal conceptions. Such conceptions are dependent on cultural ontologies, and the trial shows a tendency towards a linear presentation of events, marked by temporal references that help organize events according to the typical features of storytelling, which generally lead to a higher degree of acceptability. Deictic markers, and in particular chronological and topical references, assume important functions for the acceptability of the story being narrated. They offer cues that help to frame and position the sequence of events, and they therefore enhance clarity and contribute to the understandability of the story. Moreover, they are highly used as tools that can corroborate the veracity of a testimony.

The use of chronological markers is widespread in the trial, as "we are all used to thinking of life in chronological terms" (Lubet 2004: 432). Indeed, in his opening statements the prosecuting attorney describes the sequence of events – using the historic present typical of storytelling – by offering specific time references:

> MR. DUSEK: At about 10:00 o'clock Friday night it comes time for the van Dam children to go to bed. He scoots them upstairs. [...] And eventually goes

> off to bed, into bed by 11:00 o'clock that night. [...] He wakes up some time between 1:30 and 2:00. (Dusek's opening)

Metalinguistic references to the order of events being presented may also be offered:

> MR. FELDMAN: That's discreet period number one. We'll call that the intro. Some days go by. (Feldman's opening)

The narrative organization is strictly dependent on the need to reconstruct the sequence of events in a limited amount of time and to offer a conceptualization of the facts that is understandable to the jurors; being able to provide precise temporal and spatial references contributes to the credibility of a version of the story presented.

The conclusion of the opening statement should include an unambiguous message that leaves the jury with a clear understanding of the attorney's position and a basis for believing his side, as well as a clear recommendation of what conclusion they should reach:

> MR. DUSEK: You will find the evidence is sufficient to convict him of murdering, kidnapping, special circumstances, and possession of child pornography. Thank you. (Dusek's opening)

Opening statements can therefore be considered a sort of tool that helps the jurors (and the other parties involved) to visualize the events in a perspective that leads them to accept the attorney's theory of the case.

5.4.2 Engaging storytelling

5.4.2.1 Defining the characters

The different strategies employed in the definition of the characters involved in the story being narrated emerge clearly in the opening statements. The prosecution attorney tends to refer to Mr. Westerfield as 'the defendant', as this process of depersonalization aims to distance himself (and other participants) from the accused and suggests a form of dehumanization which is in line with the overall prosecution's strategy. Conversely, the term 'defendant' is never used by the defense attorney in his opening statements; he tries, rather, to humanize the protagonist in order to enhance sympathy towards him.

These preliminary observations are confirmed by the use of computer-based analyses, for instance by employing AntConc3.2.1[59]. The software includes a variety of tools, such as a concordancer, a word distribution plot, word and keyword frequency generators, and tools for cluster and lexical bundle analysis. For example, the concordance tool can be used to show a key word in context (KWIC) from a target text (or corpus). In this case the opening statements by defense and by prosecution were selected. Figure 8 shows the concordance lines generated for the term *defendant*:

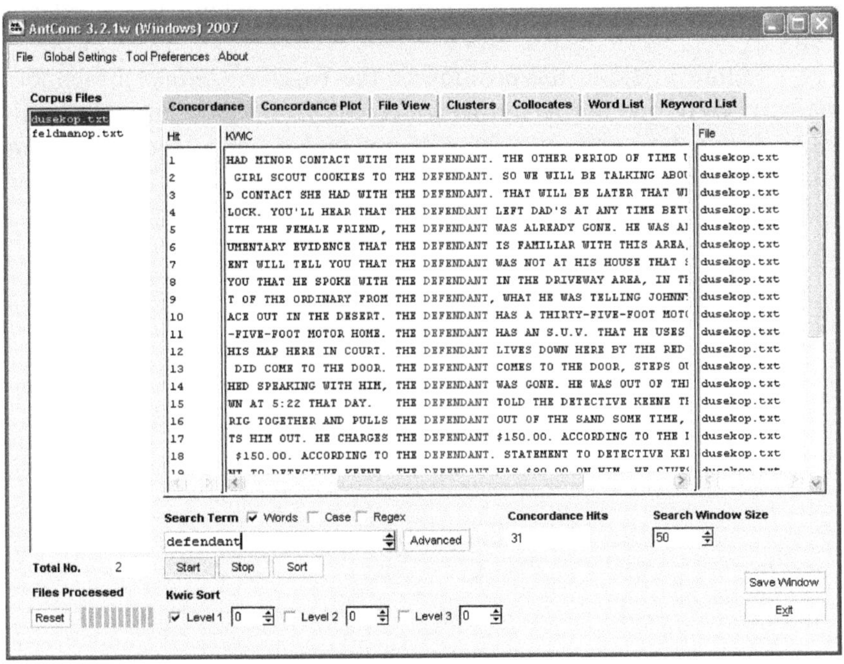

Figure 7. Concordance list for the word *defendant* in opening statements.

59 The software developed by Laurence Anthony was originally intended for applications in the classroom, but it can also offer interesting quantitative insights into a wide area of discourse analytical studies. See also <http://www.antlab.sci.waseda.ac.jp/software.html> for details.

The concordance list shows that the prosecution opening statements include 31 hits for the word 'defendant', whereas Feldman's opening shows no hit for this word. By repeatedly referring to Mr. Westerfield as 'the defendant', the prosecution creates emotional distance from him, whereas the defense uses the defendant's name (and often exclusively the first name) in order to enhance the jurors' sympathy and sense of solidarity towards Mr. Westerfield.

AntConc3.2.1 also offers the possibility of using a concordance search term plot[60], which provides a visualization of KWIC focusing on where a certain term appears in a text and its distribution pattern, and it is particularly revealing for contrastive analyses of texts. In other words, a concordancer shows how the node is used and which words accompany it, whereas the plot shows where the word appears[61].

Figure 9 shows the position of the word *defendant* throughout the text. Only one bar is shown (referring to the prosecution's opening), as the defense's opening did not include any instance of this term.

---

60 This tool is similar to, for instance, the dispersion plot tool in Wordsmith Tools.

61 Both the concordance tool and the concordance plot tool allow the user to view the search term as it appears in the target file simply by positioning the cursor over the term or over a line of the plot.

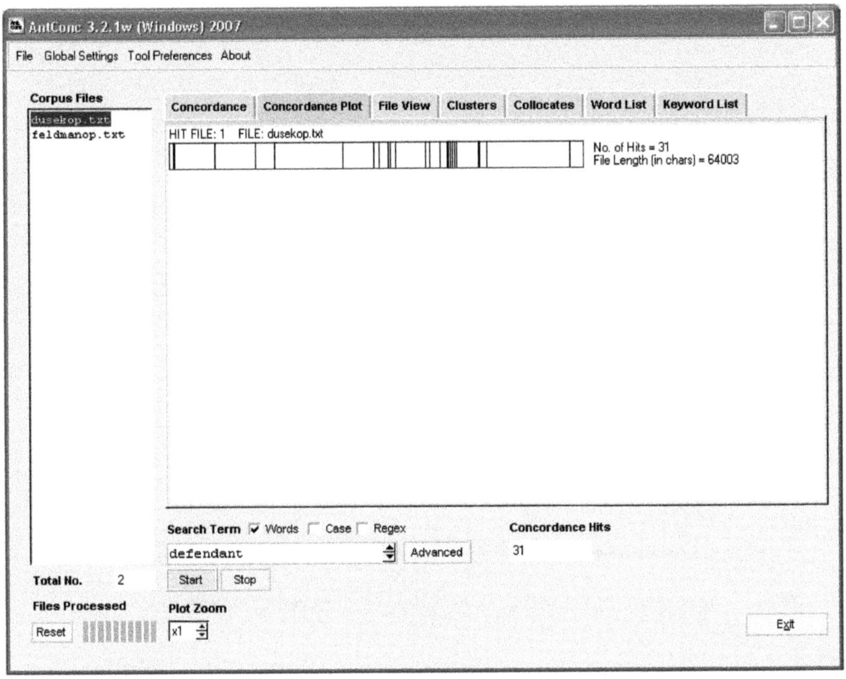

Figure 8. Concordance plot for the word 'defendant' in opening statements.

A similar approach can be used to observe the distribution of the term *Danielle*, the victim of the crime, in the texts. It is plausible to hypothesize that the prosecution, for strategic rhetorical reasons, may make use of the first name of the victim more often than the defense. This assumption is confirmed in figure 10, which presents the position of the term within the file[62].

62 The concordance plot tool also shows the total number of hits, as well as the length of each text.

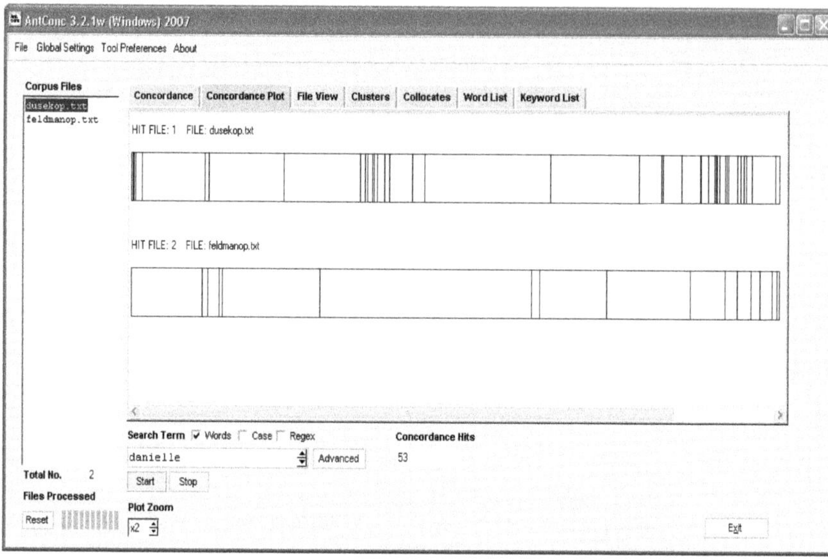

Figure 9. Concordance plot for the word *Danielle* in opening statements.

This form of visualization immediately demonstrates that prosecution's statements record a higher number of hits for the word *Danielle*[63]. The name of the victim is repeatedly mentioned, with particular emphasis at the beginning and at the end of the speech. This choice is in line with the general recommendation to "personalize your characters and depersonalize the other side's" (Mauet 2009: 93).

The prosecution's and the defense's opening can also be analyzed observing the relative frequency lists. Table 4 shows the frequency wordlist (generated in AntConc3.2.1) concerning the prosecutor's opening. For the specific purpose of the section, the frequency list was elaborated by applying a 'stoplist' excluding function words, even though this is not to say that use and frequency of function words may not lead to revealing observations.

63 This first observation has also been confirmed after the normalization of data, as well as by carrying out a 'keyness' analysis both in AntConc3.2.1 and Wmatrix. In this case the mere presentation of the data through the concordance plot is simply functional in offering a clear visualization of the position of the target word within the texts.

Rank	*Frequency*	*Word*
1	57	VAN_DAM
2	54	BRENDA
3	41	MOTOR_HOME
4	40	WESTERFIELD
5	38	DANIELLE
6	37	FRIENDS
7	36	FOUND
8	36	WENT
9	35	LITTLE
10	35	TIME
11	33	GOES
12	33	PEOPLE
13	32	NIGHT
14	31	DEFENDANT

Table 4. Wordlist (Dusek's opening).

Continuing our focus on labeling choices used to define the characters, the wordlist shows that the terms *Danielle* and *defendant* occupy a high position in Mr. Dusek's opening. However, it is also true that "[w]hile a word list highlights what is frequent in a corpus or text, it does not tell us what is important or unusually frequent" (Römer/Wulff 2010: 105). Conversely, a keyword list allows us to generate lists of words present in the file which may be ordered according to their frequency in comparison with another frequency wordlist, thus showing the 'keyness' value of the items.

In table 5 the terms *defendant* and *Danielle* have been extrapolated from the keyword list. The data confirm a higher keyness value for the two terms in the prosecution's closing in comparison with the defense's closing:

Frequency	*Keyness*	*Keyword*
38	58.843	DANIELLE
23	48.003	DEFENDANT

Table 5. Keyword list (Dusek's opening).

The linguistic choices that characterize the parties' opening statements can be further investigated thanks to another precious means for text comparison, Wmatrix[64] (Rayson 2003, 2008, 2009), the web interface to the USAS and CLAWS corpus annotation tools[65]. Wmatrix offers a variety of tools for text and corpus analysis and comparison, such as frequency lists, statistical comparisons, and KWIC concordances. In particular, the keyword cloud[66] allows us to visually identify the main differences in the use of words in different texts. Figure 11 shows the keyword cloud deriving from the comparison between Dusek's opening and Feldman's.

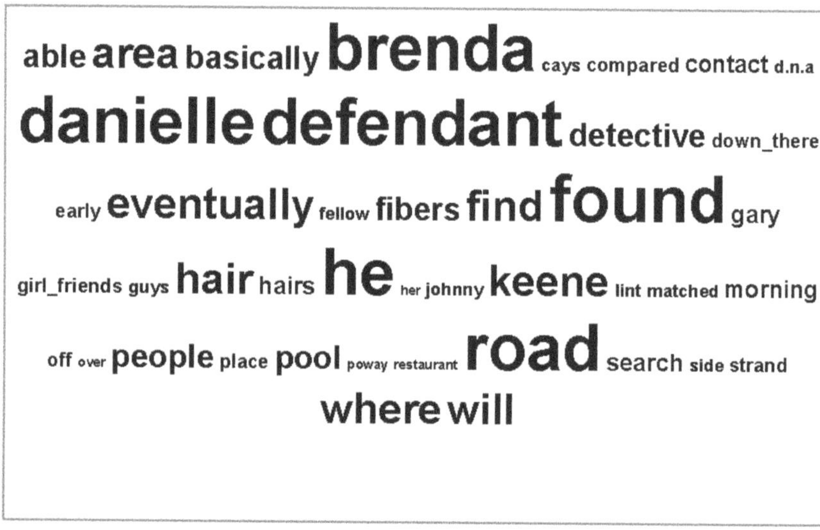

Figure 10. Keyword cloud (Dusek's opening).[67]

64 See <http://ucrel.lancs.ac.uk/wmatrix2.html>.

65 For a broader description of Wmatrix see also section 5.4.3.

66 The word cloud is calculated using log-likelihood statistics, which is automatically employed by Wmatrix. The calculation automatically takes account of the size of the two corpora or the two texts, and, therefore avoids the need to subsequently normalize the figures. For a discussion of the log-likelihood calculator see Rayson /Garside 2000.

67 Keyword cloud O1 is observed frequency in the prosecutor's opening.

As the larger items are the most significant ones in the prosecutor's opening compared to the defense's, it can be immediately seen that the strategic use of labels to define the characters (e.g. *Danielle*, *defendant*) observed by using AntConc3.2.1 is confirmed here.

5.4.2.2 Addressing the jurors

Effective advocacy is dependent on the lawyer's ability to demonstrate remarkable storytelling skills. One of the strategies attorneys adopt to achieve successful storytelling is to create a relationship with the jurors and grab their attention; in order to do so they often make use of a direct way of addressing their main audience.
It is therefore interesting to observe how and when the attorneys address directly their main audience during their narration. For example, the personal pronoun *you* is constantly used in opening statements, as figure 12 shows.

O2 is observed frequency in the defense's opening.
"%1 and %2 values show relative frequencies in the texts.
+ indicates overuse in O1 relative to O2,
- indicates underuse in O1 relative to O2
The table is sorted on log-likelihood (LL) value to show key items at the top.
This shows up to 100 significant items from the top of the LL profile.
Only items with LL > 6.63 (p < 0.01) are shown.
Larger items are more significant." See <http://ucrel.lancs.ac.uk/wmatrix/>.

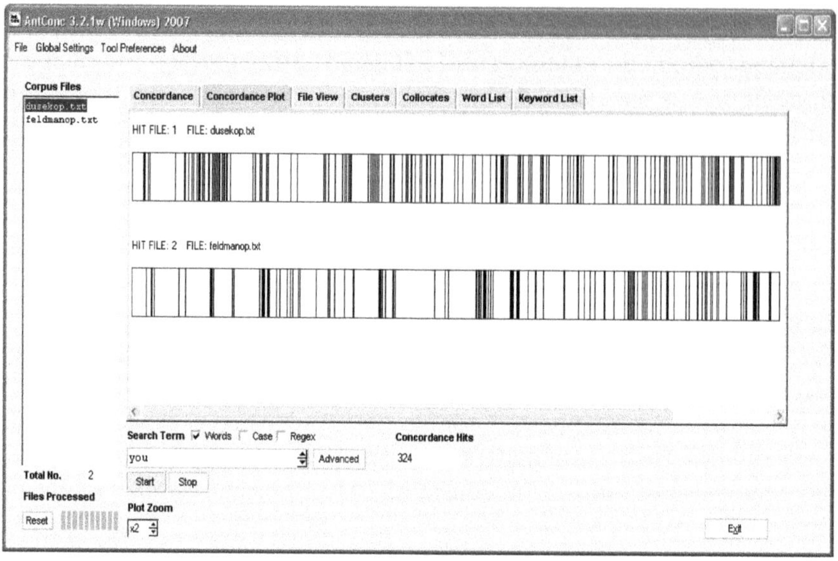

Figure 11. Concordance plot for the term *you*.

A closer analysis shows that the term *you* is predominantly used to refer exactly to the jurors. The following example is only one in the vast array of occurrences of this type of approach:

> MR. FELDMAN: And you're going to hear the results. And when you hear those results, you're going to be convinced. (Feldman's closing)

The choice of addressing the jurors directly is shared by both lawyers in order to establish a direct link with the jurors, to keep their attention, and to promote their involvement, as a juror-centered approach is vital for successful advocacy in a jury trial (Mauet 2009). The lack of a direct involvement of the jurors may instead result in an alien and distant narrative, with an inferior persuasive force.

5.4.3 Using Wmatrix for comparing stories

As briefly mentioned in section 5.4.2, the web interface Wmatrix can be fruitfully used to compare different texts (for instance, the prosecuting and the defense attorneys' speeches). The tool also offers the possibility of carrying out a computer-based semantic analysis. Before describing how the tool can be used for this purpose, it should be noted that one of the key features of Wmatrix is related to corpus annotation. Leech (1997) defines it as the practice of adding interpretative, linguistic information to an electronic corpus of spoken and/or written language data. A classic example is POS (part-of-speech) tagging (or grammatical tagging), through which lexical items are assigned a tag indicating their grammatical class in context (see Garside 1987).

Wmatrix carries out POS tagging through Claws (Constituent Likelihood Automatic Word-tagging System) (See Garside 1987, Garside/Smith 1997), which "achieved a success rate without manual intervention in the high 90s percentage accuracy" (Rayson 2003: 27)[68]. In particular, CLAWS7 operates through different stages, which, following Rayson (2003), can be summarized as follows: segmentation of text into word and sentence units; initial part-of-speech assignment (non-contextual); rule-driven part-of-speech assignment (contextual); probabilistic tag disambiguation; output (in vertical or horizontal format) (Rayson 2003: 64). Table 6 is an illustrative example and shows an instance of the tagging output in the vertical format.

68 More specifically, the accuracy of CLAWS is estimated to be around 96-97% (Rayson 2003: 63).

0000188	010	NP1	BRENDA	brenda
0000188	020	VM	WILL	will
0000188	030	VVI	TELL	tell
0000188	040	PPY	YOU	you
0000188	050	CST	THAT	that
0000188	060	PPHS2	THEY	they
0000188	070	VBDR	WERE	be
0000188	080	MC	15	15
0000188	090	NNT2	MINUTES	minute
0000188	100	II	INSIDE	inside
0000188	110	DD1	THAT	that
0000190	010	NN1	HOUSE	house

Table 6. Example of POS tagging (Feldman's opening).[69]

Besides POS tagging, Wmatrix also provides semantic tagging. The semantic tags[70] provided by USAS (see Rayson *et al.* 2004) include an upper case letter indicating the general category, followed by a digit indicating a subcategory. They may also be followed by a decimal and another digit for further subdivision and the symbols + or – to indicate a positive or negative position on a semantic scale (Rayson 2003: 66). For example:

0000036	010	JJ	unusual	A6.2-

Table 7. Example of USAS output, vertical format.[71]

In this example 'A6.2-' indicates that the term belongs to the general category of 'General and abstract words' (A), with its subcategory being 'Comparing' (A6) and, more precisely, 'Comparing:-usual/unusual' (A6.2). The minus sign shows the negative position on this semantic scale.

69 The table is obtained after running a lemmatizer and shows the result of the lemmatization process. The reference number at the start of each line indicates the number of the line of the input file where the word is located. The third column includes the tags attributed to the items. For instance, NP1 refers to a singular proper noun. See Rayson 2003 for the list of UCREL CLAWS 7 Tags.

70 See Rayson 2003 for a list of Semantic Tags.

71 For a further description see Rayson 2003.

The USAS tagger can be used to assign semantic field codes to the file related to the prosecution's opening (O1) and to the defense's opening (O2). Table 8 shows a comparison of the relative use of semantic categories in the two texts:

Item	*O1*	*%1*	*O2*	*%2*	*LL*	
M6	376	3.30	98	1.55 +	51.42	Location and direction
A10+	114	1.00	21	0.33 +	27.46	Open; Finding; Showing
O1.1	56	0.49	6	0.09 +	22.52	Substances and materials: Solid
B1	141	1.24	35	0.55 +	21.27	Anatomy and physiology
W3	49	0.43	5	0.08 +	20.37	Geographical terms
T2-	40	0.35	4	0.006+	16.85	Time: Ending
B5	35	0.31	3	0.05 +	16.19	Clothes and personal belongings
A6.1	16	0.14	0	0.00 +	14.18	Comparing: Similar/different
M7	57	0.50	11	0.17 +	12.92	Places
M1	298	2.62	113	1.78 +	12.82	Moving, coming and going
X9.1+	26	0.23	2	0.03 +	12.74	Able/intelligent
A6.2+	14	0.12	0	0.00 +	12.40	Comparing: Usual
B4	29	0.25	3	0.05 +	11.95	Cleaning and personal care
X2.4	49	0.43	9	0.14 +	11.85	Investigate, examine, test, search
N3.7	12	0.11	0	0.00 +	10.63	Measurement: Length & height

Table 8. Frequency of semantic categories in opening statements.[72]

The two opening statements can further be compared by using a Key domain cloud, which shows the keyness analysis based on the comparison of the semantic frequency lists for the two texts. Figure 13 shows the key domain cloud related to the prosecution's opening in comparison with Mr. Feldman's.

72 O1 is observed frequency in the prosecution's opening. O2 is observed frequency in the defense's opening. LL corresponds to the log-likelihood value.

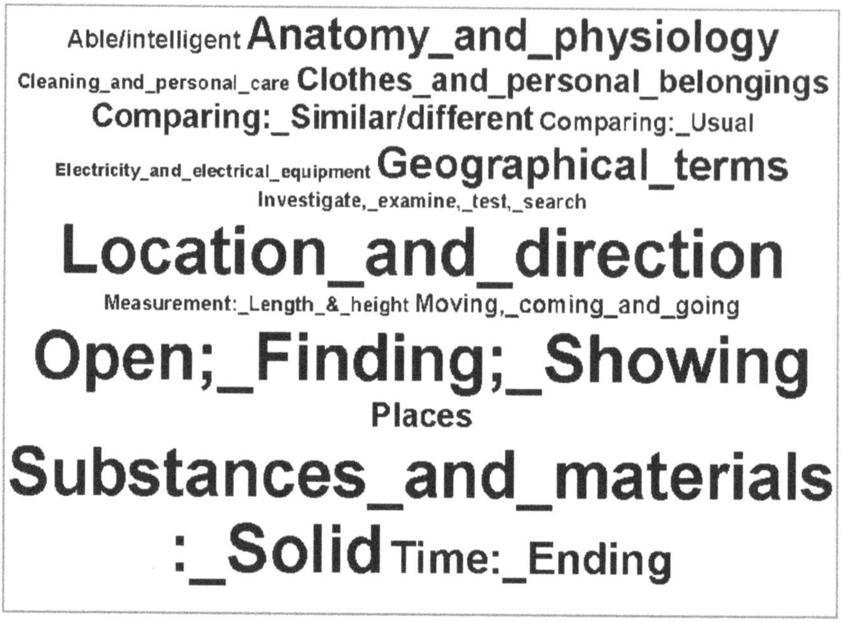

Figure 12. Key domain cloud.[73]

Table 8 and figure 13 show that the domain that is most emphasized by the prosecution is related to 'Location and direction' (LL value 51.42): Mr. Dusek, indeed, often insists on giving spatial and topical references in his account in order to convey clarity, precision and coherence. Other prominent domains are 'Open; Finding; Showing', 'Substances and materials: Solid', 'Anatomy and physiology, 'Geographical terms'. Each domain would require a separate analysis, but, for mere illustrating purposes, it can be remarked that a significant difference emerges in the domain of 'Anatomy and physiology'[74]. Prosecution highlights (at times morbidly) the details related to the state in which the victim was found in order to charge his account with in-

---

73 Only items with LL > 6.63 ($p < 0.01$) are shown.

74 Wmatrix allows us to immediately view the list of words included in every semantic domain and some of the terms included in the domain 'Anatomy and physiology' are: *hair, hairs, teeth, D.N.A., back, blood.* The user can also view the corresponding concordance lines.

volving emotional features and to emphasize the cruelty and the brutality of the crime. At the same time he also stresses the importance of the scientific evidence that will be presented in order to corroborate his theory of the case.

5.4.4 The quest for clarity and simplicity

The main features traditionally attributed to legal language rarely emerge in attorney-juror communication in a jury trial. For instance, opening statements have as their main target audience the jurors sitting in the jury box and, therefore, the convergence of the linguistic behaviors of the lawyers towards the jurors is one of the keys to successful communication. This is to some extent in line with the concept of accommodation (Giles/Powesland 1975, Thakerar *et al.* 1982), in that accommodation may be described as based on "a multiply-organized and contextually complex set of alternatives, regularly available to communicators in face-to-face talk. It can function to index and achieve solidarity with or dissociation from a conversational partner, reciprocally and dynamically" (Giles/Coupland 1991: 60-61).

However, the relationship between attorneys and jurors is not based on a typical dyadic form of interaction and it may be argued that we are dealing here with an intentional presupposed form of accommodation. From this perspective, research on the jurors and their background is generally employed in order to make the linguistic choices that are more likely to be in line with the jurors' and their expectations.

An American jury is by definition unfamiliar with the case they have to decide upon and it is the aim of the lawyer to present the case in the most comprehensible terms. For instance, from a syntactic point of view, opening statements present features that are in stark contrast with the features generally attributed to lawyers' speech. To give an example, the following excerpt does not present a high level of sentence complexity, or a significant use of other features such as passive forms, premodification, nominalization, or lexical density:

MR. DUSEK: The two ladies left first. Barbara and Denise. They got in their car and headed back to Tierrasanta. And right after that the two guys leave, Rich and Keith. They head off. They go home. And immediately Damon and Brenda van Dam go upstairs. They go to bed. (Dusek's opening)

This passage shows, instead, syntactic simplicity, sentence brevity, a high concentration of finite verbal constructions, a lack of subordination and of passive forms. It may certainly be argued that the spoken mode of interaction tends to facilitate comprehension. It should be noted, however, that the interaction between legal experts (e.g. during sidebar conferences outside the presence of the jury) is characterized by a significantly higher level of complexity (at a lexical, syntactic and textual level). Consequently, although orality certainly contributes to the simplicity of language, it cannot be seen as the only determining factor.

5.4.4.1 The use of repetition

Among the main linguistic features of opening statements, the use of repetition emerges significantly as regards both lexical items and syntactic patterns. Simplicity and clarity are often pursued by attorneys while communicating with the jurors, and repetition may also be seen as a strategy employed to reach such goals. However, the tactical use of repetition serves a variety of purposes: it contributes to both fluency of production and ease of understanding. It also helps to negotiate meanings between speakers and listeners; indeed, "[e]ach time a word or phrase is repeated, its meaning is altered. The audience reinterprets the meaning of the word or phrase in light of the accretion, juxtaposition, or expansion; thus it participates in making meaning of the utterances" (Tannen 1987b: 576).

Repetition is frequently used in both casual and planned conversation[75] (Tannen 1987a, 1987b, 2007; see also Norrick 1987). Tannen (1987b) identifies four main functions of repetition:

1) Production – repetition allows for a more efficient and fluent production of language.

75 In this work, such a distinction is not to be intended as a clear-cut dichotomy, but as developing along a continuum.

2) Comprehension – repetition allows for semantically/lexically less dense discourse, facilitating comprehension.
3) Connection – in line with Halliday and Hasan (1976), Tannen highlights the role of repetition as a cohesive device, in that "it serves a referential and tying function" (Tannen 1987b: 583).
4) Interaction – repetition serves to tie participants to the discourse and to one another and functions as a conversational management tool.

Both prosecution and defense make vast use of repetition in their openings:

> MR. DUSEK: *There were fibers found* in the motor home back by the bed of the motor home, the extreme rear of this motor home. On the driver's side they found some fibers back there that were collected and compared and found to be similar to fibers from the carpeting in Danielle's bedroom. *There were fibers found* in the hallway of the motor home. *Same result. There were fibers found* in the bath mat in the bathroom in the motor home. *Same result.* (Dusek's opening)

> MR. FELDMAN: And they're drinking and they're drinking and they're drinking. (Feldman's opening)

> MR. FELDMAN: And you're going to hear the results. And when you hear those results, you're going to be convinced *beyond any doubt* that *it was impossible, impossible* for David Westerfield to have dumped Danielle van Dam in that location. The evidence will show *beyond doubt it was impossible* for him to have placed her there. Their evidence. So *we have doubts. We have doubts* as to cause of death. *We have doubts* as to the identity of Danielle van Dam's killer. *We have doubts* as to who left her where she resided, where she remained, *and we have doubts* as to who took her. (Feldman's opening)

Repetition is a highly versatile device and it can be effectively used to highlight critical propositional content (Danet 1980: 531). In opening statements the use of repetition is strategically chosen for a variety of purposes: for instance, it contributes to clarity; a dramatic sequence of repetition also has an engaging and involving effect; it gives a particular rhythm to the speech that may lead to a mesmerizing effect; moreover, repeated items are more likely to be recalled, and therefore they assume an important function in the deliberation process.

Advocacy manuals insist on the importance of repeating the most crucial (and convincing) points. First of all, repetition plays a crucial role as it is impossible to be certain that twelve people have contemporarily paid attention to the facts being mentioned; therefore, by repeating points that are particularly favorable to the attorney's case, he increases the chance that a higher number of jurors will focus on a specific point. As with any other technique, it is also recommended that it be used carefully in order to avoid the tedium effect or the risk that the jurors may feel that they are being patronized and their abilities are being underestimated.

5.5 Examination: the plot thickens

On June 4, after opening statements, examination in the Westerfield trial began[76]. As previously mentioned, the communication process taking place in the examination phase is not the primary object of this analysis. Therefore, this chapter does not attempt to offer a detailed investigation of the complexity of the linguistic and communicative structures that characterize this phase of the trial; rather, some of the main features and functions of examination will be briefly described to functionally show the transition to the subsequent phases.

The examination phase of trials has attracted considerable scholarly attention both as regards eyewitnesses, especially since Loftus's (1975, 1979) seminal work, and expert witnesses (e.g. Jones 1994, Jasanoff 1995, Matoesian 1999a). In particular, speech and presentational style have been extensively analyzed (Conley *et al.* 1978, Erickson *et al.* 1978, O'Barr 1982) and some influential work on the complex dynamics of witness examination regards the social judgements of witnesses deriving from their style of speech on the part of the jurors (Lind/O'Barr 1979). For instance, O'Barr's oft-quoted work (O'Barr 1982) focuses on: Powerful *vs* powerless

76 It should be noted that examination gave space to motions at different stages. For a discussion of motions see *inter alia* Jorgensen 2006.

speech[77]; narrative *vs* fragmented testimony style; hypercorrect testimony style; interrupted and simultaneous speech. Moreover, it has also been shown that apparently minor variations in language use may considerably affect the way the speaker is perceived (Loftus 1975, 1979).

The examination phase consists of a series of micro-events. The examination of every witness may be interpreted as a sub-phase, which in turn consists of a series of other specific events, such as calling, swearing in, direct examination, cross-examination, (re-direct examination)[78], (cross-re-direct examination)[79], dismissal. By and large, the structure of direct examination can be said to be highly predefined, and, consequently, the communicative choices stemming from a specific strategic repertoire are easily planned. For example, it is generally recommended that "every direct examination [...] should strive to begin and end on strong points" (Lubet 2004: 57). Conversely, even though the planning of discourse is obviously still essential[80], it may be argued that cross-examination is "perhaps the most unpredictable stage of the trial" (Aron *et al.* 1996: 22.11). This phase of the trial may be defined as the clearest manifestation of the principle known as *audiatur et altera pars* (or *audi alteram partem*, let the other side be heard), and cross-examination[81] is potentially risky, as the witness is, by definition, likely to be uncooperative[82]. Indeed, in cross-examination attorneys constantly test the veracity of the testimony and this type of examina-

77 Powerless speech is seen as including, for instance, a higher frequency of disclaimers, hesitations forms, hedges, intensifiers, tag questions. It has been shown that powerful or powerless speech may in turn substantiate or hinder the witness's credibility; O'Barr (1982) shows that powerful language users among witnesses are generally perceived as more confident and credible.

78 The party who called the witness may re-examine the witness regarding evidence presented during cross-examination.

79 At the discretion of the judge, the witness may be examined again by the party who cross-examined him/her (such a possibility is limited to new subject matter brought out during the redirect examination).

80 This is apparent as the attorney's questions are obviously strategically planned in order to detect, highlight, and juxtapose possible inconsistencies within a testimony.

81 For a discussion see *inter alia* Gaines 2000.

82 This is also why it is recommended, unless in specific circumstances, that this phase be kept brief (Lubet 2004: 83).

tion can be defined as essentially hostile (Drew 1992: 470) and the credibility of witnesses is often explicitly addressed[83].

In witness examination the struggle for control over the representation of evidence is fundamental, and Pospisil aptly claims that "the secular establishment of evidence almost universally employs the questioning of witnesses" (Pospisil 1971: 236). Indeed, from a procedural point of view sworn testimony is a crucial phase, as jurors have to rely on the evidence and the testimonies that have been presented during the trial in order to make their decision.

Witness examination represents the phase where the facts and the evidence should be presented. Despite the clear need to follow the rules of evidence, lawyers inevitably tend to project moral judgements about the witnesses being examined, their character and their behavior. In this respect, Heffer highlights the presence of a sort of 'tension' that arises "between the need to conform to the evidentiary rules which prevent explicit construal of judgement and the desire to persuade a jury who might be influenced by such construals" (Heffer 2007: 145). Heffer places this phenomenon within a broader tension between two different modes of reasoning and talking, one defined as 'paradigmatic', based on objectivity and logic, and one that assumes 'narrative' contours, where what emerges is the more evident subjectivity inherent in proving an account of personal experiences (Heffer 2005, 2007).

5.5.1 The question-answer model of narration

Witness examination is clearly characterized by an asymmetrical distribution of turns (Atkinson/Drew 1979, Matoesian 1997), in the sense that the unfolding of the conversation is guided by the attorneys' choices, and witnesses can only answer the questions they have been asked[84]. But if we move beyond the simplicity of this general feature,

83 Federal Rules of Evidence, Rule 611 (b): Scope of cross-examination. –Cross-examination should be limited to the subject matter of the direct examination and matters affecting the credibility of the witness. The court may, in the exercise of discretion, permit inquiry into additional matters as if on direct examination.

84 For a discussion of the control of lawyers over witnesses' testimony see Philips 1987, Walker 1987, Ehrlich 2001.

we discover that the mechanisms of this interaction reveal a higher degree of complexity since the attorney's aim of framing the evidence in a way that is functional to his theory of the case has to follow specific procedural rules. The linguistic exchange has to develop within a clearly institutionalized environment and has to comply with specific evidentiary strictures. Procedural constraints[85] may appear to limit the creative potential of the language used in this context; however, these constraints may actually determine the use of original and ingenious linguistic choices that are "superimposed over the course of question/answer sequence" (Matoesian 1997: 140).

More specifically, the unfolding of conversation in examination assumes a very clear structure, and narration is carried out via the question-answer model. The procedural and communicative restrictions of this model endow this phase of the trial with the contours of highly controlled interaction. It is generally argued that character and eye witnesses may be especially likely to passively follow the line of questioning proposed by the attorneys. Conversely, expert or professional witnesses, because of their experience and their familiarity with court procedures, may be more resistant to following the path of reasoning paved by the attorneys. In particular, they may "resist any word choice the cross-examining lawyer appears to want to embrace" (Pozner/Dodd 1993: 22).

As regards witness examination, the general rule of competency establishes that "every person is competent to be a witness"[86], and a witness may only testify to a matter if he/she has some personal knowledge of the matter[87]. In this respect, Lubet specifies:

> Witnesses are expected to testify from personal knowledge. The most common sort of personal knowledge is direct sensory perception information gained through sight, hearing, touch, taste and smell. Witnesses may also have personal knowledge of more subjective information such as their own intentions or emotions or the reputations of another person. (Lubet 2004: 314)

85 For example, argumentative statements are not procedurally allowed.

86 Federal Rules of Evidence, Rule 601. The California Evidence Code (Section 700) also states: "Except as otherwise provided by statute, every person, irrespective of age, is qualified to be a witness and no person is disqualified to testify to any matter".

87 Federal Rules of Evidence, Rule 602.

Direct examination constitutes a fundamental part of the trial as it is a possibility of presenting the core and the evidence of a case and to corroborate a lawyer's version of the story. In particular, the choice and the preparation[88] of witnesses are clearly crucial to the success of examination. The identification of the ideal witness is a profoundly complex matter. Over 40 years ago Bailey and Rothblatt affirmed that "[w]omen, like children, are prone to exaggeration; they generally have poor memories as to previous fabrications and exaggerations. They are also stubborn. You will have difficulty trying to induce them to qualify their testimony" (Bailey/Rothblatt 1971: 190-191). It is, however, clear that prejudiced generalizations of this type are unacceptable today. More interestingly, Aron *et al.* (1996: 19.8) suggest that prospective witnesses should meet the following criteria: "competence to testify; integrity; credibility; capacity to perceive; capacity to recall; capacity to communicate; capacity to understand and follow the lawyer's instructions; attractiveness". It can also be argued that the likeability of the witness also contributes to the level of acceptability of his/her testimony, as "likeable people are more apt to be accepted as truthful" (Lubet 2004: 438).

At the crux of the matter is the allocation of credibility. In particular, establishing the credibility of a witness is fundamental, as it is according to his/her level of credibility that the information presented will be accepted by the trier of facts. Indeed, a lawyer often elicits the basis of the witness's knowledge and, on the other hand, often attempts to affect negatively the reputation of the other party's witness. Techniques of this type are crucial in jury trials as they contribute to the likeability of your witnesses and may create negative biases against your opponents' witnesses. However, biased judgments do not regard exclusively lay jurors, and it has been shown that even judges are not exempt from psychological bias about witnesses (Wagenaar *et al.* 1993).

Jacquemet (1996) defines the credibility of the participants as one of the fundamental factors that determine the allocation of aspects of truth in relation to the statements pronounced. The level of credibility assigned to different groups of "antagonistic participants" (Jacquemet 1996: 7) in the trial plays a crucial role for its outcome, as different par-

88 However, advocacy manuals (e.g. Berg 1987) often warn against overpreparation of witnesses.

ticipants try to impose their truths through authority. The main antagonistic participants are the prosecuting and the defense lawyers, whose credibility is one of the determining factors for the acceptance of one of the antagonistic narratives they present. Similarly, lay and expert witnesses undergo an equivalent process of attribution of credibility. The dichotomy between credible and non-credible is, however, not always clearly identified, and credibility is a feature that is constantly negotiated within a 'fighting arena' such as a trial (Jacquemet 1996: 10).

Unlike expert witnesses, lay witnesses are generally not allowed to testify in the form of opinions or inferences[89]. Conley and O'Barr also highlight the impossibility (from a juror's perspective) of distinguishing unerringly between facts and opinions in accounts offered in the specific context of a trial, as that is simply not in line with the standard conventions of everyday storytelling (Conley/O'Barr 1990: 177). This discrepancy is not seen here as the result of a cognitive limitation, but rather of abnormal institutional constraints.

5.5.2 Expert knowledge at trial

As previously mentioned, the nature of expert witnesses' testimony (see Wall 2009) is significantly different from that of lay witnesses (also defined as ordinary witnesses, percipient witnesses, or eyewitnesses), in that from a procedural point of view lay witnesses are not allowed to testify to their personal opinions, whereas experts may offer opinions based on their expertise[90].

---

89 Federal Rules of Evidence, Rule 701: If the witness is not testifying as an expert, the witness' testimony in the form of opinions or inferences is limited to those opinions or inferences which are (a) rationally based on the perception of the witness, and (b) helpful to a clear understanding of the witness' testimony or the determination of a fact in issue, and (c) not based on scientific, technical, or other specialized knowledge within the scope of Rule 702. (As amended Mar. 2, 1987, eff. Oct. 1, 1987; Apr. 17, 2000, eff. Dec. 1, 2000).

90 Federal Rules of Evidence, Rule 702: If scientific, technical, or other specialized knowledge will assist the trier of fact to understand the evidence or to determine a fact in issue, a witness qualified as an expert by knowledge, skill, experience, training, or education, may testify thereto in the form of an opin-

It is clear that the opinion of the expert also assumes validity and legitimacy according to the witness's credibility. Perloff (2010) remarks on the inherent dynamism of credibility, observing that "it is part of two-way interaction between communicator and message recipients" (Perloff 2010: 166). It may also be argued that credibility is a fluid concept which is shaped by and in turn shapes a series of interactions and it can be positioned within a wider process of social construction of identity.

As Gee notes, "socially situated identities are mutually constructed" (Gee 1999: 121). The construction of identities is always a dynamic and multifaceted process, and in witness examination the discursive construction of the identity of the expert derives from a series of interactions involving different participants. Instances of such processes are the testimony of the witnesses themselves, the introduction offered by the attorneys (who introduce the experts and may try, in turn, to enhance or hamper their expertise, credibility and trustworthiness), and ultimately the attribution of credibility on the part of the jurors.

Different techniques may be used in order to conduct a successful expert direct-examination (see Kuhne 2007). The ones listed by Lubet include: the humanization of the witness; the use of plain language; the use of examples and analogies; the use of the concept of consensus; and the encouragement of powerful language. It is also recommended not to stretch the witness' expertise (i.e. not to examine a witness beyond the specific scope of his/her expertise) (Lubet 2004: 229). In particular, law manuals also suggest eliciting not only the expert's professional background in order to emphasize his/her specific competence in the matter, but also "the witness's personal background of probity and honesty" (Lubet 2004: 53).

Conversely, cross-examination of the witness's credentials is based on the fact that the witness may be more or less discredited during the examination through different techniques. Lubet suggests that some of the most effective strategies are:

---

ion or otherwise, if (1) the testimony is based upon sufficient facts or data, (2) the testimony is the product of reliable principles and methods, and (3) the witness has applied the principles and methods reliably to the facts of the case.

- limiting the scope of the witness' expertise
- stressing missing credentials
- contrasting your expert's credentials (Lubet 2004: 241-245).

Indeed, as the credibility of a witness may derive from a comparison with another expert witness appointed by another party, it is often in the interest of the attorneys to severely deconstruct the trustworthiness of an expert whose position is not in line with their theory of the case. Expert witness examination is, from a historical, procedural and legal point of view, a fundamental phase. The increase in the use of science and technology in investigation determines the importance of the experts' testimony within the trial and the impact it may have on the jurors. The importance of expert witness examination in contemporary trials is crucial, as "both defense and prosecution attorneys increasingly call upon scientists and other expert witnesses to provide compelling testimony in cases ranging from patent infringement suits to murder trials" (Daemmrich 1998: 742). In other words, considering the increasing intricacy of the different types of scientific evidence presented in a trial, the use of expert testimony in court is inevitably going to increase (Jasanoff 1995, Matoesian 1999a: 491).

Expert testimony often represents a particularly lengthy, complex, and controversial phase (Jones 1994, Matoesian 1999a), and the Westerfield case is no exception. For instance, entomology was one of the disciplines that played a major role in this trial and several contradictions emerged. To give an example, the defense's entomologists testified that eggs were laid by flies in Danielle's body in mid-February, but Faulker also admitted that his research was based on the fly larvae, which does not allow the determination of a precise time spectrum. Conversely, another entomologist, N. Haskell, testified that the insect infestation must have started immediately; Dr. Hall, instead, placed the colonization between February 12 and 23, whereas Dr. Goff placed it between February 9 and 14.

Evidently, the impersonality and the objectivity of scientific truth that should be epitomized by the role of the expert are in conflict with the dynamics of a trial. An aseptic presentation of evidence on the part of the experts appointed by the parties is not the purpose of the examination, where the importance of loyalty often overcomes the need for truth (Jasanoff 1995, Matoesian 1999a). Such dynamics are inevitably related to the nature of the system, and it has been stated that "the adversarial system, in stark contrast to science, is not necessarily about truth and falsity, but about winning and losing; and that depends on which side – and which witness – can best finesse reality through the use of language" (Matoesian 1999a: 492). Moreover, Faigman revealingly remarks that "[w]hile science attempts to discover the universals hiding among the particulars, trial courts attempt to discover the particulars hiding among the universals" (Faigman 1999: 69).

The conception and, above all, the presentation of scientific evidence is obviously embedded within professional thinking and professional discourse, and the expert witness plays a crucial function in framing specialized (scientific) knowledge and often assumes the role of an expert mediator of knowledge (Jasanoff 1990). An expert should obviously present his/her theory in a clear and understandable way so that it can be more easily accepted by the jurors, who are not likely to be familiar with the specificities of a certain scientific discipline. In this respect, it is often suggested that "[t]he theory must not only state a conclusion, but almost always explain, in common-sense terms, why the expert is correct" (Lubet 2004: 217).

In a jury trial, scientific evidence is often presented as intertwined with culturally entrenched common-sense. However, it seems clear that scientific theories and data may not be in harmony with more common-sense lay values, but in order to be accepted it is important that scientific knowledge be in line with those assumed values. In other words, specialized knowledge has to be accommodated to the lay participants in order to be understood, and it has to be presented as being in accordance with what are deemed to be the common moral and ethical beliefs.

Even though similar issues also emerge in bench trials, where members of the legal profession may be confronted with highly technical scientific knowledge they are not familiar with, the crucial questions related to the presentation and the perception of specialized knowledge seem particularly salient in a jury trial.

5.6 Closing arguments: the end of the story

Different expressions, such as jury summation, closing speech, closing statement, final arguments, are used to refer to this phase (Walter 1988: 7). The use of the word 'arguments' clearly emphasizes the argumentative character of this event, which may be seen as "the moment for pure advocacy" (Lubet 2004: 467).

By and large, closing arguments represent the moment where the attorney can state what has been proved during the trial, and this phase consists of a series of sub-phases, which, following Aron *et al.* (1996) can be identified as follows:

- An introduction, where the crucial issues of the cases are emphasized.
- A development of the argument (including a review of the relevant evidence).
- A discussion of the legal principles related to the case.
- A conclusion, which mainly aims at guiding the jury through the reasoning process and towards a favorable verdict.

As Burns (2009) remarks, in their closing argument attorneys carry out a reconstruction of the story by highlighting some of its crucial elements; at the same time this phase also has a deconstructive function in that "this is the time when the advocate can point out the incoherence and implausibility of the competing account and the opponent's failure to keep his or her promise to present adequate evidence to support the story told in opening statement" (Burns 2009: 25-26). Closing statements are the last chance attorneys have to communicate directly with the jurors (Mauet 1980) and represent the final opportunity to offer a mental image of the case that will lead to a favorable verdict. In other words, the phase can be defined as "the chronological and psychological culmination of a jury trial" (Mauet 1980: 205).

5.6.1 Accommodating legal knowledge

The education of the jury is an important aspect of proficient jury trial advocacy. Complex legal issues and principles are brought up throughout the trial, and successful communication with the jury also depends on the ability to explain such issues in an accessible, involving way, emphasizing the aspects that are favorable to one's side.

Informing about legal concepts and principles is strategically important also in terms of preserving the attorney's credibility. The explanation of the law necessarily has to be precise and accurate, otherwise the presentation of a concept could easily be dismantled by the opposite party. At the same time, however, the law must be introduced in a clear and understandable way; for instance, Aron *et al.* recommend using "simply and clearly understood words" (Aron *et al.* 1996: 12.19).

The jurors are ascribed the key role of decision makers even though, by definition, they lack any legal professional expertise and competence. The reasoning processes they apply are often dependent on figurative language and analogies with personal experiences (e.g. Feigenson 2000), and that is why common exemplifications based on everyday situations are often employed. For example, Aron *et al.* (1996: 12.29) report the case of a lawyer who would explain the difference between 'simple negligence' and 'gross negligence' in the following way: "Simple negligence occurs when you are eating a plate of beans and you spill a bean on your tie. When you spill a whole knifeful of beans on your tie, that's gross negligence" (Aron *et al.* 1996: 12.29).

In attorney-juror talk the use of analogies is particularly significant and emerges clearly in closing arguments because of the nature and the scope of the phase[91]. Analogy is a common tool used by lawyers to explain abstract legal principles or elusive legal concepts. Indeed, analogies occupy a focal point in jury trial advocacy and their use is metalinguistically confirmed by Judge Mudd in a sidebar conference with the attorneys:

91 For instance, it is improper to argue about the law in opening statements (see section 5.4).

> MR. FELDMAN: There was the use of the word 'I'. When the prosecutor makes an argument, I've always understood to be improper. So I was just raising the issue because to personalize it essentially constitutes vouching. Under the federal constitution, that's not permissible. Substituting the word 'I' for 'the people' or 'the prosecution' I don't have a problem with. When it's personalized, I think it's improper.
>
> THE COURT: If he had been commenting on the evidence, you would have been correct. But he wasn't. *He was drawing an analogy. And lawyers draw analogies all the time to life experience.* When I was growing up as a boy on the farm, all the rest of that. And that's the exact context that was in. (Day 28, outside the presence of the jury)

More specifically, analogies in closing statements may assume a variety of functions, such as a rhetorical, strategic, explanatory, illustrative, epistemic, heuristic, probative, or cognitive. For instance, lawyers can use analogical explanations to stress a pivotal point and make it clearer, and they can emphasize the aspects of the analogy that are deemed to assume a particularly persuasive function in light of the party's theory of the case.

Analogies and exemplifications are powerful tools and are constantly employed to present legal concepts that would otherwise appear alien to laypersons. In particular, it is often argued that, in order to be effective, figurative language used in court should be personalized and possibly involve the jurors. For instance, the notions of 'actual possession' and 'constructive possession' are briefly explained by the prosecuting attorney in his summation by offering a clear, simple and juror-centered exemplification:

> MR. DUSEK: And you heard there was actual possession and constructive possession. You are in possession of the badge that's on you now. You have active control of that. These water bottles in front of you, you have constructive possession of them. You have control over them, but you do not have active control of them. It's not in your possession right now. (Dusek's closing-a[92])

92 'Dusek's closing-a' refers to the prosecution's closing arguments. 'Feldman's closing' refers to the defense's closing statements. 'Dusek's closing-b' refers to the prosecution's rebuttal.

The same concept had previously been described when the jury instructions were given:

> THE COURT: There are two kinds of possession: actual possession and constructive possession. Actual possession requires that a person knowingly exercise direct physical control over a thing. Constructive possession does not require actual possession but does require that a person knowingly exercise control over or the right to control a thing either directly or through another person or persons. (Jury instructions, day 28)

The comparison between the two different descriptions shows that jury instructions include the use of specific legal terminology and have a high level of formality. Conversely, the attorney succeeds in offering a highly comprehensible and juror-centered explanation. The concepts are epitomized in simple images that can be immediately visualized, and epigrammatic phrasing may also result in a more memorable, easily understood representation of a concept.

Bugliosi (1996: 199) also emphasizes the functional role of figurative language in summation and notes that it is essential in order to keep the juror's attention in such a delicate moment of the trial:

> I do not agree that it is difficult to hold a jury's attention for more than an hour or so. In fact, it is not difficult to keep their attention for one, two, or even three days if the lawyer can deliver a powerful, exciting summation that is sprinkled with example, metaphor and humour. (Bugliosi 1996: 199)

5.6.2 Metaphors in court

In their seminal work, Lakoff and Johnson argue that "[t]he essence of metaphor is understanding and experiencing one kind of thing in terms of another" (Lakoff/Johnson 1980: 5). The use of metaphor[93] in legal language has constantly attracted considerable scholarly attention. Indeed, metaphors in legal writing, reasoning or argumentation may

93 For a broader discussion of the nature and the function of metaphorical language see, among the vast array of available readings, Shibles 1971, Ortony 1979, Reddy 1979, Lakoff/Johnson 1980, 1999, Burke 1984[1954], Derrida 1986, Barlow 1994.

prove crucial for understanding and interpreting the law. Legal metaphors[94] are now considered 'constitutive of legal reasoning' and they are seen as "tools for denoting legal concepts through a shell permeable to social and economical evolutions" (Morra 2010: 387).

As Gotti notes, metaphorization offers a series of advantages, such as terminological transparency, conciseness, and "the tangible quality of images from the physical world used to represent abstract and often complex concepts that would otherwise be difficult to define" (Gotti 2011: 42). These features contribute to the use of metaphors also in courtroom communication, and the value of metaphorical imagery is particularly significant in a jury trial where metaphors may be strategically used as a persuasive tool. Indeed, the persuasive power of metaphorical language has often been underlined; in particular, Sopory and Dillard (2002) highlight that metaphors may have a greater impact when they display features of novelty (while preserving familiarity) and are introduced at an early stage in the message.

Metaphorization is often a fluid process and a novel metaphor may subsequently assume the form of an unthinking idiom[95]. In other words, it can be argued that lexicalized metaphors are not recognized as having a metaphorical meaning but, instead of a dichotomic vision between dead and living metaphors, it has often been suggested that other stages be identified, such as that of inactive metaphor[96] (Goatly 1997). The idea of intermediate stages in the life of a metaphor suggests that there may be a progressive transition from a living metaphor to a lexical item whose metaphorical origin is not generally recognized, thus highlighting the impossibility of identifying an exact demarcation between the metaphor's life and death. In a similar vein, Derrida's (1972) concept of 'usure' may also be employed to illustrate the progressive passage from living metaphor to idiomatic acceptance.

94 For a deeper discussion of legal metaphors see Winter 1989, Smith 2007, Morra 2010.

95 This process may be understood, for instance, in terms of Glucksberg's (2001) 'property attribution model'.

96 Inactive metaphors refer to items that have become lexicalized, but their original metaphorical meaning is still recognizable.

A complex web of metaphors is employed in courtroom communication, especially in closing arguments, because of their particular nature, structure and purpose. For instance, the expression 'smoking gun', which is widely used in closing arguments, shows the fluidity of metaphorization and idiomatization processes. The definition of 'smoking gun' as a metaphor is not unproblematic, as the metaphorical image may be seen as moving from the state of metaphor to that of idiom, or from 'dead' to 'living' metaphor (Billig/MacMillan 2005). The use of this expression is very common in closing statements as a way to refer to the hard evidence, the indisputable evidence or proof:

> MR. FELDMAN: Wait a minute. Where is the smoking gun? (Feldman's closing)

> MR. FELDMAN: We're still looking. That smoking gun we're trying to find. You might see the shadows of the outline of the gun, but they don't got the smoking gun. We're looking. (Feldman's closing)

In the latter example the image of a smoking gun is further elaborated from a metaphorical perspective by highlighting that 'the shadows of the outline of the gun' may be seen. The same expression is also accompanied by other figurative images that contribute to supporting the defense's theory of the case ("there's too many holes"):

> MR. FELDMAN: There's too many holes. There's no smoking gun. There's too many explanations. They can't put it together. That's the problem. It doesn't come together. (Feldman's closing)

Similarly, the defense attorney also attempts to depict the evidence shown by prosecution as irrelevant, inconsistent and insufficient to prove his client's guilt:

> MR. FELDMAN: We're trying to make a lot, a mountain, as it were, out of a mole hill. (Feldman's closing)

Metaphorical images do not emerge in isolation but are characterized by circularity. Given their representational, conceptual and ideological force, an attorney often re-employs and re-frames a metaphor used by his opponent to his advantage. Indeed, figurative representations often significantly prefigure or angle the subsequent representations suggested by the opposing attorney:

> MR. DUSEK: This is the smoking gun, right here, this jacket. This is the smoking gun. This is the smoking gun. This is the hard evidence. (Dusek's closing-b)

Other metaphors related to the field of weapons are often used; for instance one of the expert witnesses is referred to as 'a hired gun':

> MR. DUSEK: He was a hired gun. (Dusek's closing-a)

The metaphor of argument as a war (see also Lakoff/Johnson 1980) pervades closing arguments, and the image of 'war' is used repeatedly to describe the nature of the adversary system:

> MR. FELDMAN: This is part of the system. It's an adversary system. We don't fight wars in our society in the streets. This is why I used the word 'taliban' yesterday. We don't fight our wars in the streets. Literally our wars come to the courtroom. We don't have lynchings anymore. We don't have gun fights at the Okay Corral, we bring them into the courtroom. And this really is a very, very adversarial intense experience, and you can bet the other side is loading up. (Feldman's closing)

> MR. FELDMAN: I'm telling you, folks, as soon as I sit down there's going to be some fireworks. They're going to start leveling on the other side. (Feldman's closing)

Metaphors describing fighting activities show the aggressive and strategic nature of the adversarial process. The metaphorical language used to portray the antagonistic and combative nature of the system draws often on the field of war, and, in a similar vein, may extend to competitive sports. In the following examples, the conflict between the parties (and in particular the confrontational nature of cross-examination) is described as involving 'some serious punches'. Expressions of this type reinforce the competitive overtone of the process:

> MR. FELDMAN: You know, one of the things...one of the ways you can tell if a party's getting hurt by the testimony is how the cross goes. Notice that? Did you see a more aggressive cross on any witness in this case? Neil Haskell

> took some serious punches, but so too did Dave Laspisas because of what they had to say. And here again we see how the adversary system works. You're not here as casual observers. (Feldman's closing)

It should be noted that these metaphorical images not only represent a rhetorical persuasive device, but have a conceptual function. As Ullmann observes, "[b]y unthinkingly and mechanically repeating the same image, we may in the end forget that it is metaphorical," and this representation may affect our feelings for the object or idea in question, in that "our feelings for the tenor may be affected by those for the vehicle" (Ullmann 1964: 237-238). In this respect, Lakoff and Johnson suggest that "[i]f we are right in suggesting that our conceptual system is largely metaphorical, then the way we think, what we experience, and what we do every day is very much a matter of metaphor" (Lakoff/Johnson 1980).

More specifically, by applying these notions to the pervasiveness of metaphors in the courtroom, Thornburg aptly suggests that "these metaphors, while originally mythical or inspiration, become real and influence the way litigators think and behave" (Thornburg 1995: 226).

5.6.3 Concrete images for abstract principles

Some scholars discourage discussing legal principles in closing arguments as "nothing is gained by such remarks" (Klonoff/Colby 2007: 203), because they do not necessarily advance the advocate's case in the jurors' eyes. However, as previously noted, it is also in the interest of the attorney to portray the legal principles applicable to a case in the most persuasive way, by highlighting the contours of a principle that best fit his theory of the case. The description of complex legal principles cannot be based on a mere reproduction of what the law states but has to be strategically elaborated upon, paraphrased, expanded, or delimited, in order to appear understandable and acceptable.

The concept of 'reasonable doubt' is particularly important within the adversarial system, as the standard of proof beyond reasonable doubt is the highest standard that must be met by the prosecution's evidence. Given the importance of this concept for the outcome of a trial, the notion of 'reasonable' is dealt with by legal professionals on several occasions in closing arguments.

5.6.3.1 Towards a definition of reasonable doubt

As Koch and Devine remark, "[t]he term 'reasonable doubt' is not specified in the Constitution or its amendments, but it has emerged as the required standard of proof in criminal trials in the United States as a result of the way the Due Process clause has been interpreted" (Koch/Devine 1999: 654); the authors also note a "considerable variation in the language used to explain it across jurisdictions within the United States" (Koch/Devine 1999: 654).

From a legal and procedural point of view, the definition of the concept of 'reasonable doubt' is highly complex. Indeed, "[t]he difficulty for the law is that wide use of and familiarity with a phrase do not ensure accurate legal understanding and appropriate application of the standard" (Stoffelmayr/Diamond 2000: 769). Following Stoffelmayr and Diamond (2000), the criteria that the instruction on reasonable doubt should include are:

- Absolute certainty not required
- High threshold for conviction specified
- Discernibility from lower standards of proof
- Consistent application by jurors sitting on the same case encouraged
- Room for flexible tailoring of the standard to the costs of error.

The authors aptly argue that "[w]hat is reasonable depends on the consequences of the decision, and attempts to provide clear instructions should not define away the flexibility in the beyond a reasonable doubt standard in a blind drive for precision" (Stoffelmayr/Diamond 2000: 770).

The word 'reasonable' appears to display flexibility but at the same time also a high level of specificity, to the extent that it may not be possible to replace it with nearly synonymic expressions without raising interpretative issues[97]. For example, in the oft-quoted case of *Cage vs Louisiana*[98], reasonable doubt was defined as 'such doubt as would give rise to grave uncertainty' and 'an actual substantial doubt'. Unlike the Louisiana Supreme Court, the U.S. Supreme Court found that the appropriate threshold for conviction was not conveyed by this instruction, which suggested a higher level of doubt than what should be required.

In *California vs Westerfield* the jury instruction delivered regarding 'reasonable doubt' is the following:

> THE COURT: Reasonable doubt is defined as follows: it is not a mere possible doubt, because everything relating to human affairs is open to some possible or imaginary doubt. Rather, it is that state of the case which, after the entire comparison and consideration of all of the evidence, leaves the minds of the jurors in that condition that they cannot say they feel an abiding conviction of the truth of the charge. (Jury instructions, day 28)

The definition of the standard as 'not a mere possible doubt', and contrasted with 'some possible imaginary doubt' used in this case is in line with the Court's decision in *Sandoval vs California*[99], stating that this instruction does not overstate the degree of doubt required to acquit a criminal defendant.

In order to provide instructions that are as specific as possible it has also debatably been suggested that a quantitative definition should be given, stating the level of probability required to define 'reasonable doubt' (Kagehiro/Stanton 1985). However, theorists and practitioners tend to agree that the concept is qualitative in nature. Indeed, as early as 1969 Simon argues "Percentages or probabilities simply cannot encompass all the factors, tangible or intangible, in determining guilt – evidence cannot be evaluated in such terms" (Simon 1969: 113). Among the several apologies of the principle as a non-quantifiable

97 In this perspective, the word may be seen to display a monoreferential nature. Monoreferentiality is here intended according to Gotti's view that the concept does not indicate "that each term has only one referent, as words generally have several referents", but it is used "to signal that in a given context only one meaning is allowed" (Gotti 2011: 25).

98 Cage v. Louisiana, 498 U.S. 39 (1990).

99 Sandoval v. California, 511 U.S. 1 (1994).

one, Rembar also notes that "[p]roof beyond a reasonable doubt is a quantum without a number" (Rembar 1980: 412).

5.6.3.2 Defining reasonability

The definition of the word 'reasonable' is a complex matter because of its indeterminate nature. The use of vague terms is common in legal language, and the relationship between vagueness and precision in this field has often been investigated (see *inter alia* Waldron 1994, Endicott 1997, 2000, 2001, Bhatia *et al.* 2005, Cacciaguidi-Fahy/Wagner 2006). It has often been argued that "language is inherently polysemic" and "even clear expressions may appear in the absence of contextual information as indeterminate" (Charnock 2006: 66); therefore, it is through a process of contextualization that terms, and even legal terms, are interpreted and explained and acquire a more specific meaning.

In his seminal description of legal language Mellinkoff introduces the notion of 'weasel words' (Mellinkoff 1963: 21), intended as words with a highly flexible meaning. Among the several examples offered (e.g. *adequate, proper, convenient, doubtless, fair, manifest, negligence, normal, ordinary, palpable, satisfactory, safe)*, 'reasonable' is also treated as a 'weasel word'. This category of terms primarily refers to words included in written legal texts, but also the language of the courtroom shows the presence of words of this kind[100]. Weasel words also tend to appear in collocations and are particularly sensitive to the phenomenon of coselection. This process is by no means limited to these kinds of terms but is ubiquitous in human language, and Sinclair explains:

> One word can prepare the reader or listener to receive another one that comes just a little later, and to understand it in a certain way. The interconnections among words that occur close to each other are so intricate that quite often we are sure that they are not independently chosen, but COSELECTED. (Sinclair 2003: 57, original emphasis)

100 In this respect, the strong interrelation and interdependence between the written and the spoken mode in trial discourses should also be emphasized.

This coselection is often (but not necessarily) given by adjectives followed by nouns. When using expressions such as 'reasonable doubt', 'reasonable interpretation', or 'reasonable explanation', their meaning may assume very different contours and depend on a variety of factors, such as cultural, social, moral, and ethical values, and they can be associated with a particularly high level of vagueness.

Evaluative adjectives (see Fjeld 2001, 2005) such as 'reasonable' have been classified according to Fjeld's taxonomy in different categories (Fjeld 2005: 164-165)[101]:

- General quality adjectives, which moves along the line good/ bad. Adjectives of this kind are *acceptable, useful, interesting, advisable* (and their opposites).
- Modal adjectives, which regard the parameters of necessity and desirability, such as *(un)necessary* and *(un)desirable.*
- Relational adjectives, which refer to the relation between a word and some general standards (or so perceived). Examples are: *(un)suitable, (in)sufficient (in)adequate* and *(in)appropriate.*
- 'Ethic' adjectives, which denote some moral or ethical value, such as right, wrong, (in)equitable, (ir)responsible, (un)justifiable, (un)reasonable and objective.
- Consequence adjectives, which express different degrees of consequence in relation to the modified noun. The examples mentioned are: *crucial, critical, serious, considerable* and *significant.*
- Evidence adjectives, which express the relation between certain conditions and their consequences (e.g. *evident, marked, natural* and *unlikely*).
- Frequency adjectives, defined by Fjeld as the ones which "denote the evaluation of the appearance of the noun related to some kind of quantitative norm". Typical examples are: *widespread, common, normal, unusual, special,* and *deviant* (Fjeld 2005: 165).

However, the line between these categories is finely drawn, because of the intrinsic vagueness related to the nature of evaluative adjectives.

101 Even though Fjeld's research mainly focuses on written language, it is clear that evaluative adjectives play a crucial role in spoken language in the courtroom, especially if we consider the persuasive strength they may have.

For example, the term 'reasonable' is identified as an ethical adjective, but this definition appears limiting in the context of courtroom communication. The ethical aspect is certainly crucial, but the concept carries with it features that may be ascribed to general quality adjectives, evidence adjective (as the consequences of the jurors' decision are often highlighted in relation to the concept of reasonable doubt) or relational adjectives.

5.6.3.3 Reasonable doubt in closing arguments

The concept of 'reasonable' assumes a specific legal meaning within the context of a criminal trial. As shown in table 9, it tends to be used in connection with the term 'doubt' because of the specific legal meaning of the expression 'reasonable doubt'. It also accompanies other terms, as other expressions are also used in the process of explaining this legal principle (e.g. 'reasonable interpretation', 'reasonable explanation', and 'reasonable grounds'). Table 9 shows word clusters[102] including 'reasonable' that occur in closing arguments:

Frequency	*Probability*[103]	*Cluster*
65	0.374	reasonable doubt
37	0.213	reasonable interpretations
20	0.115	reasonable interpretation
8	0.046	reasonable explanation
3	0.017	reasonable grounds

Table 9. Word clusters including the adjective 'reasonable' in closing statements.

The term 'reasonable' is mentioned by both attorneys and emerges in all the three different sub-phases of closing statements: the prosecution closing, the defense closing, and the prosecution rebuttal, as shown in figure 14.

102 As Anthony notes, "[a]n alternative way to search for multi-word units is to find lexical bundles (Biber *et al.* 1999), which are equivalent to *n*-grams, where *n* can vary usually between two and five words. Few corpus analysis programs offer this feature (Coniam 2004), but AntConc3.2.1 includes lexical bundle searches as an option in the Word Clusters Tool" (Anthony 2004: 11).

103 Transitional probability between target word and other words.

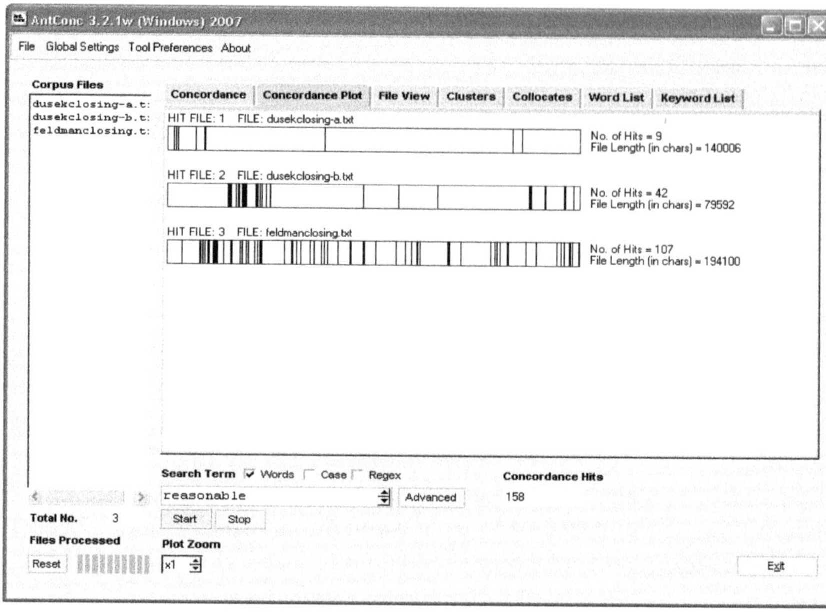

Figure 13. Reasonable: concordance plot.[104]

The notion of 'reasonable' is introduced repeatedly by the defense attorney, who attempts to exploit the concept of 'beyond reasonable doubt' to confirm his theory aiming at the defendant's acquittal. Table 10 shows the keyness of the term 'reasonable' in the defense's closing in relation to the prosecution's closing.

Frequency	*keyness*	*Word*
107	71.416	REASONABLE

Table 10. Keyness of the term 'reasonable' (defense closing arguments).

104 The file Dusekclosing-a.text corresponds to the prosecution's closing. The file Feldmanclosign.txt corresponds to the prosecution's closing. The file Dusekclosing-b.txt corresponds to the prosecution's closing.

5.6.3.4 'Do you guys play 21?': Attorney's strategies to explain reasonable doubt

Delivering indisputable explanations about the standard of proof beyond reasonable doubt is not unproblematic. The task the attorneys have to carry out is highly complex in that they have to provide definitions that are not only legally accurate but also understandable to laypersons, and at the same time functional to support one specific theory of the case.

The fact that some instructions are given to the jurors prior to closing arguments allows the lawyers to integrate the actual instructions into their arguments and the defense attorney attempts to intertextually build his definition according to the instructions that have been delivered:

> MR. FELDMAN: Reasonable doubt is defined as follows, but first remember the defendant is presumed to be innocent. Right? You know, I just took the instruction, I had it blown up. It's bold-faced. The defendant is presumed to be innocent. That's the law. And in case of a reasonable doubt, he's entitled to a verdict of not guilty. Entitled. Reasonable doubt is defined as follows: as the judge told you, it's not a mere possible doubt because everything relating to human affairs is subject to some possible or imaginary doubt. It is that state of the case which after an entire comparison, consideration of all the evidence leaves the mind of jurors in that condition that they can't say they feel an abiding conviction to a moral certainty of the truth of the charge.
>
> MR. DUSEK: Objection, Your Honor. Misstates the law.
>
> MR. FELDMAN: I'm sorry.
>
> THE COURT: There is something in there extra, Mr. Feldman.
>
> MR. FELDMAN: Abiding conviction of the truth of the charge. Judge, I'm looking for the papers. There was an easel that had papers on it. I know. I've seen it seventeen times. I'm sorry. I just don't see it now.
>
> THE BAILIFF: It's behind all that.
>
> MR. FELDMAN: Behind all that. Okay. Beyond a reasonable doubt. BDR. Okay? And an abiding conviction. (Feldman's closing)

Argumentation has to follow clear standards and, for example, counsel is not allowed to misstate the law or to offer an interpretation of the law that contradicts the court's decisions and instructions (Lubet 2004: 123). In this case the attorney fails to cite the instructions and the law accurately, but apart from being persuasive and convincing, the attorneys' words should comply with legal requirements and the rules of trial procedure. The opposing party aptly notes the law has been misstated[105] and this is detrimental to the defense attorney's credibility. Moreover, even though final arguments may often include references to jury instructions, it is generally not recommendable to dwell on them for a long time as this practice may be of little interest to the jurors (Lubet 2004: 513).

Mr. Feldman continues his explanation by offering a description of the concept of 'abiding conviction' by means of an exemplification which focuses on the jurors' feelings and beliefs and may trigger jurors' personal memories:

> MR. FELDMAN: And you have to take those words and feel whether you're so convinced that the conviction will never, never go away. It's so strong that it's the kind of belief you have that if you've got a loved one on a respirator, a terrible decision to have to make, somebody dying, it's on you to make the decision to pull the plug. Only with an abiding conviction would you do so. (Feldman's closing)

As mentioned, analogies are frequently used in courtroom communication, especially to explain concepts that have a high level of intricacy and abstractness. In his rebuttal, the prosecution attorney tackles the complex (highly specific but also multifaceted) notion of 'reason-

105 However, deciding when to object may represent a very crucial moment. In fact, in the eyes of the jurors objections are sometimes perceived as interruptions of communication or as a strategy to hide things from them. As Aron *et al.* note, "jurors do not like lawyers who make a lot of objections. They think the lawyers are trying to keep something from them" (Aron *et al.* 1996: 28.15). Moreover, when an objection is overruled, it can have particularly negative effects on the credibility of the lawyer being overruled. Conversely, a sustained objection contributes to enhancing a lawyer's reliability and competence in the eyes of the jury. Therefore, objections should be made only when they can make a point to one's case and be particularly beneficial.

able doubt' by means of vivid language, permeated by graphic exemplifications and metaphorical images:

> MR. DUSEK: And when you're making that determination of what is reasonable and what isn't, there are many ways to look at that. One might be: are there any facts to support that position? I would suggest that that is probably a good start. One other way, well, how reasonable is my position? Well, if I'm standing in a crowd of ten, 20, 30 people and I'm the only one holding my position and everyone else says I don't think so, how reasonable is my position? If everyone else sees it otherwise, maybe I'm looking at the wrong facts. Maybe I'm bringing in outside influences. Maybe I'm missing the boat somehow. (Dusek's closing-b)

As has been shown, legal language is easily associated, especially by laypeople, to legalese, intended as "that often incomprehensible verbiage found in legal documents, as well as arcane jargon used among attorneys" (Schane 2006: 2). It is the aim of the attorney to project an image of himself as a facilitator of understanding: using clear and understandable language allows him to be perceived as having the jurors' interest at heart and as being trustworthy; he strategically avoids using convoluted language, as that could potentially be processed as a sign that he is hiding something from jurors.

The attorney constantly suggests vivid visualizations in order to guide the jurors towards his interpretation of the concept, and consequently towards his perspective on the case:

> MR. DUSEK: It's kind of like…kind of like this rope…if we make like…this is the ultimate circumstantial evidence inference. The rope is made up of many, many twines, just like the ultimate conclusion in this case is made up of many, many facts. If any one of you, and you all get to make that individual assessment yourself, one fact, pick one, did he lie about the wallet? Use that one for an example. If all of you, or each individual, is convinced beyond a reasonable doubt, yes, that was a lie, that can be part of your rope. If there is a fact that I'm not convinced on that one beyond a reasonable doubt, you pull that strand out and get rid of that fact. I'm not going to consider that because it's not established beyond a reasonable doubt. Each fact leading to the inference, the final conclusion. So what you do is you put together all of the facts in this case, and then you determine whether or not the ultimate conclusion, the ultimate inference, are there two reasonable interpretations, or is one reasonable and one unreasonable? You do not do it individually. So you take all

> the facts that you are convinced beyond a reasonable doubt exist, and then you make that determination. Does that rope still hold? Is there only one reasonable inference, one reasonable interpretation, one reasonable conclusion? And you know why that's true? (Dusek's closing-b)

Prosecution continues his vivid explanation with a simple example based on card games:

> MR. DUSEK Just as an example, do you guys play 21? Blackjack, over at Vegas? If we were to get a deck of cards and go down the row here playing 21, and I've got these two guys are gonna watch and make an ultimate decision in this case, one of them I send outside the room, one of 'em I allow to sit in here while we're playing 21. He gets to watch, he doesn't. I work my way down the room here. I play one hand of 21. She pulls a 19, I get a 20. Oh, I'm pretty lucky. She's pretty unlucky. I go down to the next person, another fact. You draw an 18, I get a 19. Whoops, you're unlucky. I'm pretty lucky. Next hand, you get a 20, I get 21. And I go right down the line. Each time I beat you by one. How did I do that? Am I lucky? One inference, or did I cheat? You bring these two fellows into the room. The fellow who had to sit outside and he sits in here and watches the last hand, well, bad luck. Just a chance. The inference is I didn't cheat. No reason to think I did. He's only looking at one fact. The other individual who sat in here and watched me win every single hand by one card knows I had to cheat. That's why you have to look at all the facts before you make that ultimate decision. They don't want you to do that. They don't want you to do that. They want you to violate the law, not apply the law as it is written, as it was instructed, as you took an oath to follow. (Dusek's closing-b)

The possibility of 'characterizing' and remembering a legal principle is facilitated by connecting it to familiar or common experiences. The next step in the attorney's rebuttal is to confirm his explanation by offering another clear example. He builds his explanation around the reference to the San Diego baseball team, the Padres, which had been previously mentioned by the judge:

> MR. DUSEK: And when we start looking at circumstantial evidence, all of the evidence in this case, you kind of look at what's reasonable and what isn't. What are the possibilities of that really happening in my common sense? Perhaps the court's Padres and the local Chargers might be an example. How reasonable is it that the Padres are going to get into the World Series and win the World Series this year? And the Chargers are gonna get in the Super Bowl and win the Super Bowl this year? It's possible. It's not reasonable. Sorry, guys. The statistics of

> that, the chance of that is virtually nil. Yet the possibility of that is greater than all of these other factors coming together in one case and leading us down the path of not guilty. The Padres and the Chargers have a greater chance than all of these facts coming together at one time in one place. (Dusek's closing-b)

The circularity of figurative language emerges evidently in Mr. Dusek's words. For instance, in a subsequent moment he refers back to the exemplification based on card games that he had previously used:

> MR. DUSEK: It stings that he had to testify in a trial when his dad's on trial. That stings. They played the hand. Kind of like the guy dealing 21. It stings. (Dusek's closing-b)

In this case circular representations convey coherence and cohesion and are processed by the listeners as being more familiar. After concluding his explanation of the concept of 'reasonable doubt', Mr. Dusek clearly presents the consequences of its application:

> MR. DUSEK: If I prove this case beyond a reasonable doubt, he's guilty, he is guilty. (Dusek's closing-b)

Many adhere to the idea that closing arguments should make clear that a certain decision is necessarily a consequence of the correct application of a specific legal reasoning, and no other option is legally acceptable.

In sum, as happens in other moments of the trial such as opening statements, in closing arguments the use of easily understandable language attempts to maintain a relationship of solidarity with the jurors and, therefore, to enhance the perception of cooperation. Everyday language is more likely to be easily understood and consequently accepted; it may also be perceived as a sign of goodwill in that convoluted jargon may instead be interpreted as a way to mask something from the jurors. The hybridism of courtroom language in jury trial emerges significantly also in this phase, where formality and terminological accuracy are merged with a colloquial and informal style.

5.6.4 Explaining science

As previously mentioned, one of the main features of courtroom language could be broadly defined as the coexistence of, on the one hand, formal language permeated by specialized terminology and, on the other hand, an informal and simple style which also includes highly colloquial expressions. As the law is accommodated to the jurors' assumed needs and desires (within the framework of what is procedurally acceptable), the discussion of evidence and testimony is also tailored to what are supposed to be the jurors' capabilities to understand it and the jurors' expectations.

Lawyers attempt to position themselves as the jurors' guiding light in the labyrinth of a courtroom, its practices and its language, as well as the jurors' helpers to untangle the complex web of the scientific notions and processes presented during the trial. Science is, therefore, presented in a highly simplified manner, to the extent that its nature may even result as being somehow distorted. The scientific paradigms and the specific terminology of science are often abandoned in the pursuit of simplicity and clarity. For instance, the defense attorney tries to reduce the case to its minimal terms and neglect its inherent complexity:

> MR. FELDMAN: This case, if you step back and look at it all, is a simple case. It is not a complicated case, although there may be times when it seemed that way. Certainly some of the scientific evidence is complicated; the D.N.A. and all that type of stuff. But the facts and the reality of what this case is about is very simple. (Feldman's closing)

In particular, in their closing arguments attorneys may refer to scientific evidence and the expert witnesses' testimonies and reframe them concisely and clearly in a jurors' perspective, instead of reciting all the details of the testimony. As happens with legal principles, the scientific principles and phenomena that are particularly favorable to one's case are also often explained and discussed in closing arguments. Their explanation makes use of simplified language and clear examples, as happens in the following passage, where the Locard transfer principle (see Locard 1920) is described:

> MR. FELDMAN: The Locard transfer principle says if you go some place, you leave a portion of your physiology, and you catch a portion of somebody else's or something else. If I sit in that witness chair, we did this with the witnesses, I'm going to catch whoever's been there, and it's going to be on my jacket. And some of me is going to be left for the next person and the next and the next. (Feldman's closing)

An attempt to sound familiar and to facilitate comprehension is fundamental in communicating with jurors, but it is also crucial not to pass the limits where an excessive use of colloquialisms may be perceived as inappropriate. In his closing arguments, the defense attorney makes considerable use of colloquial expressions, which may clash with the formal setting of the courtroom:

> MR. FELDMAN: Because we all recognize there's this thing called the Locard transfer principle that messes up crime scenes, that if we put too many cops in the same spot, it's going to get things screwed up. (Feldman's closing)

Science is constantly discussed and rephrased, the multiplexed network of specialized notions is often reduced to its minimal terms, and scientific terminology is frequently replaced by ordinary words, or even by colloquial expressions. For instance, given the crucial role played by entomological evidence in the Westerfield trial, references to the field of entomology and its practices inevitably emerge in closing statements. By means of an example, discussion of larvae and their life cycle are often introduced, as they prove essential for determining Danielle's time of death. The term 'larvae' is recurrently used in the expert testimonies but is considerably underused by attorneys in their closing arguments (in total, three occurrences), where the more common term 'bugs' is preferred (in total, 27 occurrences). In particular, on one occasion the term 'larvae' is used within the expression 'those little larvae guys', which sounds more colorful and colloquial:

> MR. DUSEK: One thing you can do is you don't measure those little larvae guys. (Dusek's closing-a)

The definition of professional experts is also subject to reinterpretation and simplification. For instance, an entomologist becomes a 'bug guy' or a 'bug man', a pathologist is referred to as 'a fellow who did the autopsy', and these redefining processes are used by both parties:

> MR. DUSEK: Dr. Blackbourne, a forensic pathologist, a fellow who did the autopsy. He's the medical doctor. (Dusek's closing-a)

> MR. DUSEK: Start with the entomologists, the bug guys. (Dusek's closing-a)

> MR. FELDMAN: It's why they didn't call the bug man, their expert. Their expert is David Faulkner (Feldman's closing)

Definitions are clearly crucial for a variety of purposes. Firstly, simple labeling is often in line with attorneys' strategy to give their speech an essence of familiarity and understandability; moreover, labels of this type may also be strategically used to ultimately attack or confirm an expert's credibility.

Issues related to the credibility of a witness may also be openly remarked in summation. In their closing statements attorneys may attempt to further impugn the scientific validity of a scientist. The competence of unfavorable witnesses, their ethical values, and the reliability of their findings are constantly challenged:

> MR. DUSEK: He was a hired gun. (Dusek's closing-a)

> MR. DUSEK: We've also learned from dr. Goff and dr. Hall some of the mistakes that can be made, perhaps even cooking the books, making sure you get the results you want. Such as how can you get faulty results, unreliable results, results that are not right? One thing you can do is you don't measure those little larvae guys. You don't determine if they're beginning or end stage or the end of any of those stages. (Dusek's closing-a)

In the following example, the defense attorney also emphasizes the importance of the role of the jurors in determining the trustworthiness and reliability of the experts:

> MR. FELDMAN: It's your job to evaluate the credibility of witnesses. The jurybox is placed right here closest to you all so that you could see jugular veins going, so that you can form opinions. You know about body language. [...] If your kid says he didn't have some pie and there's pie on his face,

> you're close enough to see it. If the witness isn't telling the truth, you can see it. You can see it. That's why you're here. That's why the jury sits so close (Feldman's closing)

The interdiscursivity that underlies the judicial process is made particularly evident in the closing argument phase where discourses deriving from different domains, such as different scientific fields, are intertwined with the mechanisms of legal discourse. As Smart (1983) highlights, the processing of doing justice heavily relies on science: "A series of subsidiary authorities have achieved a stake in the penal process; psychiatrists, psychologists, doctors, educationalists, and social workers share in the judgment of formality, prescribe normalizing treatment and contribute to the process of fragmentation of the legal power to punish" (Smart 1983: 72).

In particular, the relationship between law and science is a highly complex one. The outcomes of a trial are in part dependent on scientific findings, but a trial is in turn the locus where legal supremacy reifies scientific principles, notions, and values, and establishes their admissibility and their validity. In many trials, law and science are inextricably interdependent, but, because of the nature and the goals of the two spheres, they are often in a conflicting relationship, as Haack notes:

> Science doesn't always have the final answers the law wants, or not when it wants them; and even when science has the answers, the adversarial process can seriously impede or distort communication. It's no wonder that the legal system often asks more of science than science can give, and often gets less from science than science could give; nor that strong scientific evidence some times falls on deaf legal ears, while flimsy scientific ideas sometimes become legally entrenched. (Haack 2003: 57)

5.6.5 Law, emotion and morality

It can generally be argued that "the intrinsic merits of any case are mediated by the persuasive impact of the messages which present the case and the persuasive skills of the individuals who present them" (O'Barr 1982: 16). In closing statements it is clear that every word pronounced in front of the jury assumes a persuasive function, as persuasion is the ultimate goal of every attorney arguing a case. Every moment of the interaction virtually becomes a battle that could turn out to be crucial in determining who wins or loses (Hobbs 2003: 275). A jury trial is characterized by a fundamental systemic tension: on the one hand the attorney has to convey the idea that what takes place is the objective and neutral application of the law; at the same time, because of the nature of the adversary system, his zeal has to focus also on the framing of an emotionally involving narrative. Indeed, emotion-laden words are often employed for specific persuasive purposes in a variety of contexts (Perloff 2010) and they are amply used in jury trials and in particular in closing arguments.

5.6.5.1 Comparing lexical choices in closing arguments

The comparison of the prosecution's and the defense's closing may be visualized by means of a word cloud in Wmatrix:

Figure 14. Wmatrix Word cloud – closing arguments.

Figure 15 shows significant items in the prosecution's closing in relation to the defense's closing. Some of the emerging elements are related to the sphere of crime (e.g. 'murder' and 'kidnapping'): their use pervades the prosecution's closing, which constantly emphasizes the gravity of the crimes committed.

Starting from the assumption that "[a]nyone studying a text is likely to need to know how often each different word form occurs in it" (Sinclair 1991: 30), frequency lists[106] offer interesting insights for the analysis of a text, and frequency comparison lists prove useful in identifying the most significant items in the comparison of texts. Some crime-related words have been extrapolated and their frequencies in Mr. Dusek's and Mr. Feldman's closing have been compared. Table 11 confirms the higher frequency of such terms in the prosecution's closing.

Item	*O1*	*%1*	*O2*	*%2*	*LL*
kill	21	0.08	2	0.01 +	24.36
murder	23	0.09	3	0.01 +	23.87
crime	35	0.13	13	0.04 +	17.96
kidnap	8	0.03	1	0.00+	8.44

Table 11. Frequency comparison (crime-related terms).[107]

106 In Wmatrix the comparison of two frequency lists is also based on likelihood-ratio scores (LL) in order to avoid fallacious conclusions about frequency variations between corpora which are not statically significant (Rayson 2008). The log-likelihood is also available in AntCon3.2.1 as a keyword generation method. See also Dunning 1993 for a general description of the use of the log-likelihood test for general textual analysis) and Rayson/Garside 2000 for a discussion of the use of the log-likelihood for corpora comparison.

107 O1 is observed frequency in the prosecution's closing. O2 is observed frequency in the defense's closing. %1 and %2 values show relative frequencies in the texts. + indicates overuse in O1 relative to O2 (even though developed for a different approach, a further discussion of the concept of overuse and underuse is offered by Ringbom 1998).

5.6.5.2 Emotional language

The actions attributed to the defendant are described by prosecution using hyperbolic definitions and highly connoted words, which are usually placed at one extreme end of the good/bad continuum. Negatively connoted lexical choices (such as *bad*, *evil*, *terrible*, *horrible*, etc.) are vastly used by prosecution; figures 16 and 17 show the concordance lines for the terms 'evil' and 'terrible' in Mr. Dusek's closing.

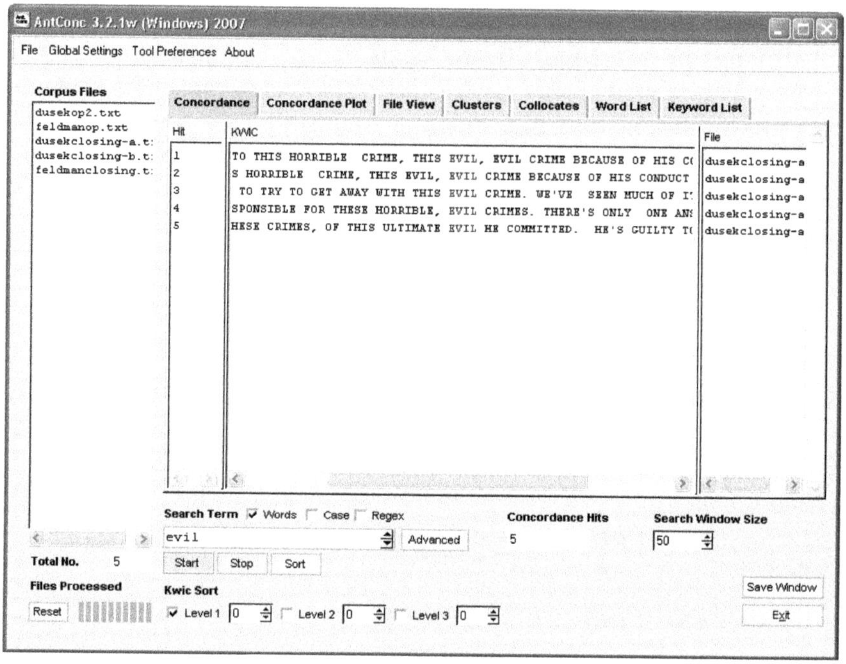

Figure 15. Concordance lines for the term 'evil'.

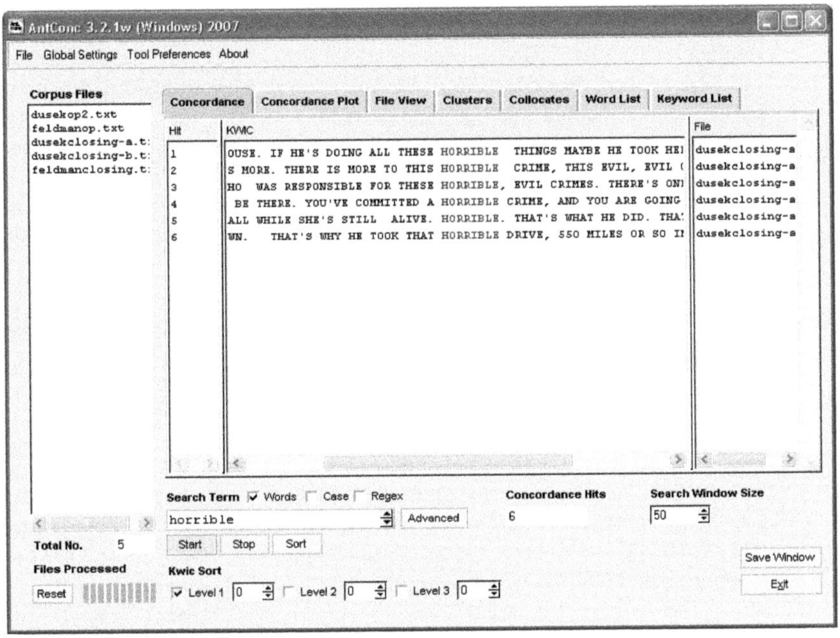

Figure 16. Concordance lines for the term 'horrible'.

Emotional language, hyperbolic definitions, and moral judgements are rhetorically used by prosecution to seek disapproval against the defendant. In the following example, the man is described according to his actions, and a sort of syllogistic line of thought is also presented to demonstrate the culpability of Mr. Westerfield:

> MR. DUSEK: If you can answer me why an individual, a normal fifty-year-old man would collect that stuff, I can tell you why a fifty-year-old man would kidnap and rape…kidnap and kill, I'm sorry, a seven-year-old child. They go hand in hand. (Dusek's closing-a)

The apparent slip of the tongue ("kidnap and rape…kidnap and kill, I'm sorry") may also cast doubts as regards a potential intentionality behind such words. Moreover, District Attorneys and prosecution attorneys are generally trained to make the victim's presence felt as much as possible in murder trials. This technique is widely used by Mr. Dusek, who frequently calls to mind Danielle's presence:

> MR. DUSEK: Murder cases are different. Certainly from a prosecution's standpoint. They are different because unlike most other cases, we are missing our best witness. We don't have our best witness here to testify. But if by chance someone could cause a miracle, create a miracle, just a little one, for a short amount of time, and bring Danielle back to life, just for a moment, just to help us out, bring her back to life, make her presentable here, ask her to come into this courtroom and help us determine the one question we need answered: who did this. Bring her into this courtroom and ask her: Danielle, please tell us; who did this to you. (Dusek's closing-b)

The attorney succeeds in evoking Danielle's presence in court, and the victim may indeed oxymoronically be defined as a participant *in absentia*:

> MR. DUSEK: In turn, I've already told you. I've already told you. I've told you with my hair. You know where you found it. I told you with the orange fiber that you found on my choker and where you found it. I told you with the blue fibers that were on my naked body and where you found them. I told you with my fingerprints. And I told you with my blood. Please listen. (Dusek's closing-b)

As Aron *et al.* remark, "vivid language creating striking mental images will help the finder of fact visualize the cases" (Aron *et al.* 1996: 12.20), and the attorney summarizes the case through highly emotional images:

> MR. DUSEK: Danielle van Dam gave us clues. She gave us the orange fiber from her necklace. She gave us the blue fibers from the blanket from her back, from her head. She gave up her hand to give us her fingerprint, the only known print we are able to get from her. She gave us her DNA, not blood because she didn't have any. We got the DNA. From her rib. That's the known source that was used. From those sources, from Danielle herself she helps us solve this case. (Dusek's closing-a)

By using the pronoun 'us', the prosecution is explicating the polarization between two groups[108] (implicitly intended as two different moral and ideological poles); the distinction between 'us' and 'him/her/them' strengthens the distance between the jurors and the defendant, minimizing therefore the possibility that the jurors may feel sympathy and em-

---

108 This process also emerged in opening statements (see section 5.4).

pathy towards him. Indeed, 'us' is intended not only as comprising prosecution and the jurors, but it is implicitly extended to the macro-level of all people sharing the same values. Expressing such a distinction emphasizes the dichotomy between 'us' and 'them', between 'good' and 'bad', therefore leading the jurors to think that only one choice is morally acceptable, and reducing their dilemma. Moreover, among the several psychological concepts that may be used to explain the processing of a message on the part of the jurors, a particularly interesting one is the creation of in-group vs out-group categorizations, as a juror identifies participants either as displaying similar features as him/herself (in-group) or not (out-group) (Fiske/Taylor 2008).

Lawyers play a leading role in the performance of a trial and what is being evaluated is not only the evidence they present but themselves as well, as they are under the constant scrutiny of the jurors. Besides professional expertise, attorneys must develop excellent rhetorical skills and master impression management in order to convey the idea of an 'attorney persona' that assumes a set of ideal features that may inspire the juror's consensus (Trenholm 1989). The optimal identity that lawyers strive to project is primarily twofold: on the one hand they have to emphasize the belonging to a certain professional category, their competence and their expertise; on the other hand, it is fundamental that the attorneys constantly construct and project a self-representation that is in line with the jurors' own identity, in order to seek alignment with them. Indeed, it is a well-assessed aspect of trial argumentation that it is easier for the jury to believe the attorney they identify most with (Mauet 1980), because they share a certain set of features (be they cultural, ethical, moral, etc.). It is the perception of a shared identity that may lead the jurors to associate with one of the participants (or a certain group of participants) and his theory of the case.

Law, common-sense and morality are presented as some of the basic values and principles that have to be applied:

> MR. DUSEK: And there are jury instructions that talk about falsehoods. If you find that before this trial the defendant made a willfully false or deliberately misleading statement concerning the crimes for which he is now being tried, you may consider that statement as a circumstance tending to prove consciousness of guilt. Basically that's what guilty people do. Certainly it's not

> enough to prove a case. But it is a factor. The law coincides with common sense. (Dusek closing-a)

In the following passage Mr. Dusek also expresses and/or constructs a specific social identity (or better a combination of identities) that goes beyond the classical categories of gender, status, race, age. This identity includes a form of professional identity that is based on features such as professionalism, credibility, competence and knowledge about the law, and at the same time a social identity construed on the sharing of widely-accepted moral and ethical values. The attorney's aim is to present a polarized vision of good/bad and he clearly positions himself as the person who deserves the juror's trust:

> MR. DUSEK: We do have a moral problem with what he did to that child. We also have a legal problem with what he did to that child. They are the same. They both violate the law, morality, all that is right in this world. Make no mistake about that. Morality and law are on the same footing here. (Dusek's closing-b)

The use of easily understandable language and the emphasis on common sense values and principles are used by the attorneys to enhance their perceived similarity in the eyes of the jurors, both in terms of membership similarity, and, in particular, of attitudinal similarity. This phenomenon is a crucial characteristic of persuasive message sources (see *inter alia* Simons *et al.* 1970, Petty/Cacioppo 1981, Bettinghaus/Cody 1987).

The courtroom is often regarded as the ultimate expression of the process of doing justice (Marry 1990) and the importance of the role assumed by the jurors is emphasized by the attorneys who also underline that the task the jurors have to accomplish is unique in its difficulty:

> MR. FELDMAN: This is the single most, I submit to you, the single most difficult decision you'll ever have to make in your lives. Never, except as jurors, do twelve people have to go into a room who don't know each other, sit down and reach an accord. Can you imagine what life would be like at home? You got four children, come on, let's go out to McDonald's. We got to vote on it. Ah, somebody wants to go to, I don't know, Carl's Jr., somebody wants pizza. Somebody wants Chinese food. Now we got to negotiate. We don't make decisions in life like that. (Feldman's closing)

Ostensibly presented as having an informative and educational value, these explanations allow the attorneys to present themselves as sympathetic assistants who try to help the jurors to understand the process; by spurning hyper-technical language and adopting ordinary language they enhance the idea that they have the jurors' interest at heart.

Following Hodge and Kress (1993), power and solidarity can be defined as on the one hand contradictory, but on the other hand complementary. As Goodwin notes, "rather than openly exerting force, then, lawyers use strategies of solidarity to entice others to accept their force" (Goodwin 1994: 218). In other words, attorneys enjoy a higher (institutionally granted) communicative power; however, it is crucial to show constant solidarity with the jurors by highlighting the importance of their role, as well as showing sympathy for the complexity of the task they are asked to carry out.

5.7 Deliberations and verdict: which story did you prefer?

As SunWolf notes, "we know little about the shadows of the deliberation room or juror misconduct" (SunWolf 2007: 14). Indeed, the deliberation phase and its communicative dynamics remain a particularly unexplored area, due to the limited access to data, as deliberations in the jury room are not transcribed and cannot be observed. As Meyer and Rosenberg point out, "researchers are forbidden to intrude upon the jury's working processes by recording and analyzing their private discussions" (Meyer/Rosenberg 1971: 105). Consequently, most research on juror deliberations is based on post-trial reports or on mock trials[109] (Hans *et al.* 2003). Indeed, once the jurors are dismissed, they may be allowed to discuss the case (Warren/Mauldin 1980), but the accuracy and the validity of post-decision recollections have often been challenged (Severance/Loftus 1982)[110].

109 For a discussion of real *vs* mock jurors studies see Reifman *et al.* (1992).

110 See also cognitive dissonance theory (Festinger 1964).

As previously mentioned, in the Westerfield trial, deliberations represent the only phase that was not recorded and not transcribed and will not specifically be the object of the analysis. During deliberations, the jurors asked to review some of the testimony concerning Danielle's time of death, the child pornography evidence, and Westerfield's audiotaped statement to police. Deliberations lasted more than 40 hours over ten days, prompting speculation that the jurors were deadlocked. The jury was entering its tenth day of deliberations when Judge William D. Mudd was notified that the verdict had been reached.

Von Mehren and Murray describe the deliberation phase from a historical perspective:

> For centuries, trial or petit juries acted only by unanimous consensus of the members. A single 'holdout' could result in a 'hung jury' and prevent the rendition of a verdict. This requirement of unanimity has been regarded by many as an important safeguard for criminal defendants. A single juror maintaining a reasonable doubt can prevent a criminal conviction. Although unanimity continues to be the rule for criminal trials, in many states civil juries may speak based on super-majorities such as 9–3 or 5–1. In a criminal case, a 'hung jury' is not the equivalent of an acquittal but rather leads to a retrial of the case before a different jury. (von Mehren/Murray 2007: 221)

Within deliberations, jurors collectively have to choose which narrative to accept, in light of the instructions they have been provided with. In other words, "deliberating a verdict involves weighing the relative merits of different storytellers and their tales, but juries do so guided by the judge's charge to them" (Goodwin 1994: 215).

Once deliberations terminate, the verdict is read. Within the macro-structure of a trial as a macro-narrative (see section 4.5) the reading of the verdict represents the verbalization of the final collective judgment about the narratives the jurors have been confronted with. In this case the verdict was read on August 21 and Mr. Westerfield was found guilty of fist-degree murder, kidnapping and misdemeanor possession of child pornography. The reading of the verdict also represents a phase that consists of a series of specific subphases. The verdict is firstly read by the court clerk:

> THE COURT: Good morning, ladies and gentlemen, and welcome back. Juror number 10, I understand the panel's made a decision. Is that correct?
>
> THE FOREMAN: That's correct.
>
> THE COURT: If you would kindly hand the verdict forms to my bailiff. All right. Each of the forms has been properly executed. Please recite the verdicts for the record.
>
> THE CLERK: The people of the state of California, plaintiff, versus David Alan Westerfield, defendant. Case number scd165805. Verdict. we, the jury in the above-entitled cause, find the defendant David Alan Westerfield, guilty of the crime of murder, in violation of penal code section 187(a), as charged in count one of the information, and fix the degree thereof as murder in the first degree. Dated August 21st, 2002. Signed juror number 10, foreperson.

This sub-phase is followed by the reading of the verdict in relation to the other crimes the defendant is charged with, and afterwards the jurors are collectively asked to confirm that those are their verdicts. In the Westerfield trial the panel was also polled individually for each verdict. Pronouncing the verdict is one of the activities where the power of the jurors emerges more clearly. First of all, it is the expression of their exclusive decisional power; secondly, in terms of communicative dynamics in this phase the jurors are entitled to express their opinion verbally. In particular, in the case examined, as the jury were also polled individually, every single juror had to confirm their verdict. Besides voir dire, this is the only phase where the voice of the jurors is heard in court, recorded, and transcribed.

6. Conclusions

Law is an ongoing project in the development of mankind. One of the most impressive achievements in its long history is the strengthening of its discursive nature.
(Galdia 2009: 331)

The dynamics of courtroom interaction develop within a clear institutional framework where setting, topic, and participants are, to some extent, pre-established; on the other hand, the specific contingencies of a single case have to be acknowledged in order to avoid making straightforward assumptions that ignore the complexity and the subtlety of some courtroom dynamics. This work has analyzed specific moments of interaction and some of the emerging linguistic and communicative features of a jury trial, and it has offered some explicative considerations that also take into account, for instance, whether the speakers' choices are in line with the behavior recommended in attorney's legal manuals. Legislation and doctrine have also been identified as legitimate analytical resources.

Instead of positioning my work within the wide debate on the validity of generalizations in research (see e.g. Williams 2002), I have followed Richards' observation that "the researcher must somehow establish a working compromise between a desire to draw general conclusions and the responsibility to do justice to the uniqueness of the particular" (Richards 2006: 2). Consequently, this investigation did not aspire to draw some generalizable considerations, to establish a definite characterization of courtroom language, or to provide a key to the unveiling of all the complex dynamics that are at play in the course of trial proceedings. However, it has identified some coordinates to explain some of the linguistic and communicative choices that emerge in different phases of a jury trial, with the hope that such observations will contribute to a better understanding of these dynamics and might prove useful in informing interventions aimed at improving some aspects of expert-lay interaction in jury trials.

It can certainly be argued that the highly constrained and institutionalized nature of courtroom interaction may lead to clear interactional structures and predictable ways of phrasing, but this work emphasizes the unique nature of every jury trial. Indeed, courtroom language, by virtue of its heterogeneity and versatility and because of the multiplicity of factors involved, cannot be treated as a monolithic entity. Consequently, the aim of the analysis was not to offer a generalizable and always applicable interpretation of social dynamics and communication processes in a jury trial, as that would be unachievable, especially in the light of the assumption that "[m]eanings are situated in the specific contexts we are building here and now in our interactions with others" (Gee 1999: 134).

This work also takes into account Mertz's view that a profound understanding of the dynamics and the power of legal language can best be achieved through a systematic analysis of language as structure-in-use, combined with a wider observation of the social dynamics with which it is inexorably intertwined, as "legal language crystallizes the interplay of pragmatics, poetics, and social power" (Mertz 1994: 448).

The attempt was to place the description and analysis of the significance of aspects such as the syntax and semantics of utterance forms within the broad framework of the social and institutional order of discourse. Indeed, on the one hand the observation of linguistic details is crucial because, as Conley and O'Barr note, "the details of legal discourse matter because language is the essential mechanism through which the power of the law is realized, exercised, reproduced, and occasionally challenged and subverted" (Conley/O'Barr 1998: 129). On the other hand, the approach adopted in this work also tries to go beyond an atomistic description of different aspects of the language of the courtroom as if it developed in a vacuum; rather, this analysis constantly looks at how discursive social practices are shaped and reshaped *in situ* and emphasizes that courtroom discourses are not scissile from their wider contexts.

From a methodological perspective, I hope to have shown the practical possibility of working within a qualitative approach without excluding the use of quantitative tools. Moreover, I have argued that different approaches to discourse analysis may be positively and coherently integrated since, as has often been stated, discourse analysis is not necessarily to be understood as one theory and one methodology, but as a set of possible theories and methods that can be exploited in a complementary way. In short, while the fulfillment of the methodological requirements of proponents of different approaches to the analysis of legal discourse inevitably remains an open matter, the combined use of such approaches has enormous potential for fruitful investigation, both on the micro and macro levels of analysis.

6.1 Courtroom dynamics

The communication process in jury trials certainly assumes a special character. In very general terms, it is often described as a series of separate monologues (Aron *et al.* 1996: 16.1), and it is often argued that "[t]he jurors are thus almost totally passive participants in a one-way communication process" (Aron *et al.* 1996: 16.3). Indeed, in a jury trial, jurors may be perceived to be passive spectators of acts being performed in front of them. On the other hand, the complexity of the function performed by the jurors has to be emphasized; indeed, they are involved in a constant process of construction and de-construction of meanings, and, within the multifaceted communicative situation of a trial, they play a crucial decisional role in choosing which meanings are to be accepted.

From an interactional point of view, the jury apparently "talk openly in court only at the close of the trial when the jury foreperson reads the final verdict" (Goodwin 1994: 217-218). However, there are several moments in which jurors can assume a more active role. First of all, in the voir dire phase prior to the beginning of the actual trial, jurors reveal a lot of information about themselves and interact with both the judge and the attorneys. Moreover, most jurisdictions allow jurors to submit written notes to the judge to ask for clarifications and explanations, or to bring up issues they are concerned about. These are forms of active interaction, even though they are characterized by certain peculiarities: for example, they are initially carried out through the written mode and, after they have been approved, they are presented orally in court by another participant. Moreover, jurors can request, for example, to re-examine certain testimony during deliberations or to have access to specific material. Finally, after the reading of the verdict, the jury may also be polled individually.

A jury trial offers a fascinating instance of a scenario involving people displaying significantly varying levels of (specialized) knowledge. By definition, in a jury trial the triers of facts are ordinary people, who should represent a varied section of society and are unlikely to display the same degree of legal knowledge as the legal experts. The issues of impartiality and competence are obviously particularly crucial as the triers of fact are asked to base their decisions exclusively on the relevant evidence presented in the court proceedings, and not to be influenced by any other factors in their decision-making process; jurors also have to follow all the jury instructions thoroughly and accurately. However, cognitive studies demonstrate the difficulty of applying such processes. For instance, information cannot be automatically disregarded on command, and the complexity of some jury instructions may lead to difficulty in their application. As Fiske and Taylor note, "[e]ven the smallest interference or judgement begins with the process of deciding what information is relevant and sampling the information that is available. According to normative models, the social perceiver should take in all relevant information, but in fact efficiency pressure often precludes such thoroughness" (Fiske/Taylor 2008: 178).

It may certainly be argued that "in the courtroom, signs of institutional power abound" (Goodwin 1994: 217), from the physical layout of the court, to dress, gestures and verbal formulas (Goodwin 1994: 217). The institution of the law is inevitably "powerful, authoritative and hierarchical", which may lead one to assume that "as invited participants, jurors should regard themselves, naturally and properly, at the bottom of this hierarchical structure" (Goodwin 1994: 217). However, the dynamics of a jury trial are highly complex, and the identification of the jurors as the least powerful participants should not lead us to overlook the crucial fact that the ultimate decisional power lies exclusively in their hands.

In other words, from an interactional and communicative perspective, the asymmetrical allocation of opportunities to talk and the length and type of these opportunities are highly constrained (Matoesian 1993: 99). However, this apparently disadvantageous position is combined with a privileged position in terms of decisional force.

6.2 The hybridity of expert-lay talk

The nature of courtroom proceedings is highly institutionalized, standardized and constrained, but at the same time it also displays traits of unpredictability. On the one hand, the courtroom language used by members of the legal profession displays some convergent traits, due to the fact that they share analogous professional backgrounds. For instance, attention to verbal correctness is a characteristic element of legal experts' talk, and it may simply be interpreted as an aspect of their *forma mentis*. Moreover, legal experts are also particularly aware that the words they pronounce during the trial are not only heard in court but become part of an official transcript, and may potentially appear in the report of an appellate opinion. Consequently, it comes as no surprise that their speech is characterized by stylistic correctness and precision.

At the same time, however, courtroom language has proven to be extremely heterogeneous, as speakers draw on different lexical, syntactic and textual features, as well as different registers and styles. This investigation has shown that linguistic and communicative choices cannot be understood in isolation from the institutional context and its constraints, from the legal system in which the trial takes place or from the social contexts that shape and are shaped by discursive dynamics. In other words, communicative and linguistic preferences emerge as a result of a complex nexus of different factors, such as procedural constraints, rhetorical strategies and individual choices.

The danger of erroneously assuming that a particular type of behavior is extendible to an entire professional category is generally acute. It is natural to equate the language of legal experts to 'legalese', and to assume that professionals make a pervasive use of specialized terminology and convoluted syntactic patterns. However, the general features that are often associated with legal language predominantly derive from 'the language of the law'. The language employed by the judge and the attorneys in their interaction with the jurors is unique within the sphere of legal language and involves the use of an informal style, figurative language, ordinary and colloquial lexical choices. The hybridity of courtroom discourse emerges evidently in the case observed in this work, the analysis of which has shown a hiatus between the features that are generally attributed to legal language and the characteristics emerging in the interaction between experts and laypersons in court. From this perspective, Tiersma confirms that "many lawyers continue to sprinkle their written work with archaic expressions", but he also points out that the situation of spoken legal language is certainly different (Tiersma 2005: 5). Moreover, if it can be argued that even the language of the law may occasionally assume dynamic and innovative contours, this is much more evident in the language of the courtroom.

Legal discourse has traditionally tended to be impervious to attempts at reform, but the language of the courtroom shows a distinctive level of versatility and heterogeneity, to the extent that it should not be considered a form of legal language *stricto sensu*. This analysis has shown that, while on the one hand some communicative moments are organized around preformulated textual patterns, on the other, courtroom interaction is also characterized by significant versatility of linguistic devices and communicative strategies.

6.2.1 The tension between formality and informality

Given the multiple potential dimensions of analysis that may be applied to courtroom communication, the focus has been restricted to the analysis of the interaction between legal experts and laypersons[111]. The judge's interaction with the jurors has been investigated, in particular, by observing the jury instruction phase. Jury instructions are complex texts: indeed, on the one hand, their target audience is represented by superior courts and therefore the texts have to maintain a faultless level of legal accuracy. On the other hand, their immediate users are the jurors, who are definable as outsiders in relation to the legal world.

The issues related to the presentation of specific instructions and the description of legal concepts and procedures to laypersons are not limited to the maintenance of accuracy and precision, but also include finding an adaptation of such concepts that may be understood by people who, by definition, generally lack any specific legal knowledge in that they are a representative cross-section of society. Crafting specific instructions to jurors' exigencies may be particularly problematic and Judge Mudd, in his interaction with the jurors, constantly alternates the reading of the instructions with comments that elaborate, paraphrase, simplify and summarize such instructions. Indeed, the jury instruction phase is characterized by an alternation between the reading of the actual instructions, which are originally in a written form, and the other pieces of information provided by the judge in his speech. This alternation is reflected in the judge's talk, which displays several examples of register mixing and shows a constant fluctuation between formality and informality.

In his comments, the judge tends to use a familiar and colloquial tone, which is permeated by instances of witty humor. It can certainly be argued that these aspects may simply be a peculiarity of his personal style, but they are also functional insofar as they maintain the juror's attention and facilitate the understanding of the instructions. Moreover, a familiar approach can also be used to maintain a more relaxed atmosphere and to limit the risk that the courtroom be perceived as "a strange and alien setting" (Gibbons 1994: 32).

111 The impossibility of defining such categories as self-explanatory has also been addressed (see chapter 4).

6.2.2 The multifaceted nature of attorneys' talk

Lawyers' speech is generally portrayed as hypercorrect (see *inter alia* Walker 1986), lacking ungrammatical features or dialect markers, avoiding false starts and hesitations, and with a tendency to include features that are related to the idea of 'powerful speech' (in O'Barr's terms). This analysis also shows that hypercorrectness sometimes gives way to informal utterances and colloquialisms, in a delicate process of constant balance between apparently divergent approaches. In other words, as Aron *et al.* note, it may be argued that "[t]rial advocacy is both a science and an art; the trial lawyer must have a systematic, 'scientific' knowledge of the principles and methods and must apply these with artistry and creativity in the courtroom" (Aron *et al.* 1996: 1.26).

The two principal moments of attorney-juror interaction investigated in this study are the opening and closing statements. The attorneys' opening statements serve the main functions that are generally assigned to this phase (see Tanford 2002: 147). First of all, attorneys strive to offer a clear picture of the case; secondly, they attempt to grab the jurors' attention and stimulate their interest in listening carefully to the evidence that will be introduced. Another crucial purpose of opening remarks is to establish a relationship with the jurors (building on the process that was initiated in the voir dire phase). During opening statements, a specific theory of the case is presented through narrative processes, and attorneys have to present a story that is not only epistemically plausible, but its acceptance must also be cogent.

This phase helps to create schemata according to which the jurors will process the rest of the story; for example, characters and events are introduced in a clear and coherent framework, as their presentation is functional to the creation of specific role schemata and event schemata (SunWolf 2007). In particular, a clear depiction of the characters contributes to bringing the story to life. A character can be seen as a 'construct', i.e. a 'network of character-traits' (Rimmon-Kenan 1983: 59), and in their narratives the attorneys incorporate a variety of 'character-indicators' (Rimmon-Kenan 1983: 59) which are functional in that they offer a characterization of the participants that can corroborate a specific theory of the case.

Opening statements present a chronological order of events, which is often defined as "the safest, easiest, and most natural way to tell a story" (Tanford 2002: 167), as it assumes clear and understandable contours. Time references are also plainly pointed out: by explaining the clear sequence of events the story is easy to follow and appears more plausible, in that the emphasis on the precise time the events occurred can be functional to corroborating one's version of the story. This analysis also shows that facts are not simply listed or recited, but they are narrated by combining a vast network of micro-narratives within a wider framework.

This study emphasizes the importance of narrativization strategies used by legal professionals. In particular, the persuasiveness of the attorneys' narratives is also related to their ability to blend canonical legalese with extralegal narratives (see Maynard 1990). Attorneys have to work within the constraints of legal conventions, but at the same time they have to move away from abstract terminology and fossilized conceptualizations of the law. Their narrative has to be placed within a framework that is perceived as going beyond purely legal principles and in line with more 'down-to-earth' concepts; indeed, realism and concreteness play a crucial role in the attorneys' speech (for a discussion of legal realism see Sarat/Felsiner 1990). This apparent process of distancing themselves from the most abstract features of the legal order allows the attorneys to place themselves closer to the lines along which the reasoning of lay people presumably takes place.

As Goodwin points out, abandoning "signs of distance", such as "legalese, complex sentence, formal appellations", somehow corresponds to abandoning signs of power (Goodwin 1994: 219) and also enhancing perceived similarity with the jurors. Even though stemming from a different perspective, the strategies that are often adopted by attorneys in their interaction with the jurors may also be interpreted in the light of Bourdieu's (1991) concept of 'condescension' in that it could be argued that, "by virtue of his position", an attorney "is able to negate symbolically the hierarchy without disrupting it" (Thompson 1991: 19). The avoidance of pure legalese on the part of the attorneys may be considered as a process that is related to the 'strategies of condescension', intended as "symbolic transgressions of limits which provide, at one and the same time, the benefits that result from conformity to a social definition and the benefits that result from transgression" (Bourdieu 1991: 124).

In a different but related vein, Goodwin states that the use of everyday language may have two 'profits': "The first profit: by merely knowing the acceptable, superior legal language, the lawyer is superior in verbal, and therefore institutional, power over the jury. The second profit: by speaking the conversational, inferior language, the lawyer defers her power to accommodate the jury" (Goodwin 1994: 219). Even though the use of labeling such as 'inferior' and 'superior' calls for a deeper analysis, as does the correlation between verbal and institutional power, it is evident that a conversational style may be used strategically to show that the speaker has the jurors' interests at heart and to gain trust in the jurors' eyes.

It is often stated that "[p]ersuasion is, in sum, the purpose of trial communication" (Aron *et al.* 1996: 1.26) and, therefore, concentrating on the jurors is even more important than concentrating on the case. The intricate relation of 'power and solidarity' which characterizes different settings (see Tannen 1987c) emerges evidently between legal experts and laypersons in courtroom communication. The relationship between the attorneys and the jurors is particularly complex and there is a constant tension between the need to exercise control over the jurors and, at the same time, to express solidarity towards them. Moreover, it may also be argued that even instances of solidarity can be seen as an indirect form of power, in that the prerogative of displaying solidarity lies predominantly in the hands of the experts (Tannen 1987c: 9). The complexity and the subtlety of the strategies used by the attorneys to establish a rapport with the jurors emerge throughout the trial. For instance, the importance of the role of the jurors is often stressed for deliberative epideictic purposes, and their action is treated as praiseworthy in that it is fundamental for the process of justice. Laudatory remarks have a variety of functions, one of which is clearly that of ingratiating the jurors.

It has been shown that courtroom discourse encompasses a wide range of styles and registers that are significantly different, and even apparently incompatible. For instance, attorneys constantly merge specialized terminology with ordinary and simplified definitions. The use or abuse of jargon throughout the trial plays a crucial role. Indeed, there is sometimes a sort of hope “that the difficult word has enough of an aura of brilliance to dazzle the jury” (Aron *et al.* 1996: 10.11), but it is also remarked that “jargon can be a useful weapon or a hindrance in court depending on how it is used” (Aron *et al.* 1996: 10.12). Specific technical terms may be used by lawyers in order to provide their speeches with an aura of erudition or to embellish their style, but they must be used sparingly in order to avoid creating a counterproductive distance between them and the jurors.

In certain phases of the trial, and in particular in closing arguments, attorneys adopt an explanatory stance. This approach aims to provide the jurors with the tools to apply the law correctly, but primarily assumes the overarching function of creating a sense of collaboration with the jurors, fostering consensus and solidarity, and strengthening bonds with the jurors.

Moreover, by mentioning, describing and explaining the law, the lawyers enhance their credentials as experts, and showing their knowledge of the law contributes to boosting their credibility in the eyes of the jurors. Flaunting a high level of topic-related knowledge is often considered fundamental in trial advocacy because, as Lubet notes, “[a]n apparent command of relevant information correlates strongly with believability” (Lubet 2004: 40). Given that credibility is one of the most important aspects in the acceptance of a story on the part of the fact finders, it is clear that advocates consider it very important to confirm their expert knowledge in front of the jurors. In other words, the explanation of legal concepts, principles and procedures is obviously not primarily aimed at extending the jurors’ understanding of theories and practices that the attorneys deem worth explaining; rather, it contributes to building or maintaining the experts’ credibility and reputation and it allows them to craft those principles according to the version of the story they want jurors to accept.

Speakers gain their listeners’ acceptance by indirectly emphasizing their epistemic authority and by presenting themselves as facilitators of understanding. In order to do so, they make considerable use of easily comprehensible and memorable terms, and often explicate complex legal concepts through figurative language and epigrammatic phrasing. This analysis has shown that attorneys skillfully use epitomizing images to describe complex legal topics and employ striking figures of speech that are recurrent during the trial. Figurative language serves a vast array of concurrent goals; for example, it may perform a clarifying function and is also extensively used for persuasive purposes in order to enhance the acceptance of a specific theory of the case.

Certain legal concepts are particularly complex and have to undergo processes of condensation, limitation and simplification. For instance, the concept of 'reasonable doubt' often seems to assume the contours of a monoreferential expression and its explanation has to comply with specific legal standards; however, given the indeterminate nature of the term 'reasonable', it may be difficult to position it into a neat scheme of discrete categories which allow one to clearly establish which meaning is acceptable. The word 'reasonable' as used in the expression 'reasonable doubt' has a precise legal meaning, and its definition is of crucial importance for the outcome of the trial: the concept is central to the adversarial process and the presumption of innocence has to be guaranteed until the defendant is proven guilty beyond reasonable doubt. Consequently, different aspects of its definition are highlighted, in turn, by the defense and the prosecuting attorney and, despite the inherent indeterminacy of this concept, attorneys strive to present an interpretation that, according to the law, should be perceived as unequivocal. In other words, a tension exists between the need to maintain legal accuracy and precision and the need to bring forward a specific interpretation which perfectly fits within a broader theory of the case.

Even though attorneys do enjoy a certain freedom in court (O'Barr 1982), what they say is constantly monitored and scrutinized, especially by the opposing party, and a sustained objection by their opponent may have serious consequences on a lawyer's credibility. Consequently, the attorneys wish to discuss the law with great precision, as their words may be subject to objections, and therefore they state claims with the appropriate caution. Moreover, the presentation of their statements in an apparently complete, accurate and precise manner contributes to the maintenance of their epistemic authority and the establishment of their credibility. Such an approach also has to be combined with a style that is easily understood and grabs the listeners' attention; adopting a style that meets the jurors' desires and needs has a clear persuasive function, as establishing credibility is a complex process that is achieved through the affirmation of different factors, such as goodwill, perceived similarity and trustworthiness.

This analysis shows that both law and science undergo a constant process of accommodation in the courtroom. Technical jargon is often replaced by informal or even colloquial terms; specific concepts are defined, simplified and paraphrased, specialized terminology is juxtaposed to figurative language and often described through simple exemplifications or memorable metaphors. Accommodation, however, has to preserve the essence of legal concepts, as law cannot be misstated. What emerges is a transition between the technical terms that the law requires and a simple, and at times even simplistic, way of phrasing, describing and explaining them.

6.3 Concluding remarks

This work has attempted to bridge a linguistic description with the observation of a wider dimension of social interaction in the courtroom. This approach has also been combined with a legal focus, in particular with insights into advocacy theory and practice, as the analysis has attempted to take into account new developments in 'modern trial advocacy' (Mauet 2009) throughout. The study was not conceived as an omni-comprehensive analysis, but it is to be considered as part of a wider ongoing process (especially in light of the continuous changes in legislation and doctrine).

The future of discourse analytical studies related to courtroom communication is not easily predictable, but one can expect a growing need for transdisciplinary integration. Indeed, on a practical note, different disciplines may be drawn into the milieu of law: entomologists, chemists, biologists, IT analysts, coroners, psychiatrists, psychologists and a potentially infinite series of other professionals may be involved in the trial process; science and technology have increasingly penetrated proceedings and have often proved crucial for their development and outcomes. From a wider perspective, this work also argues for an interdisciplinary approach to language study with a critical perspective (see Wodak/Chilton 2005), where "in bringing disciplines and theories together to address research issues, [transdisciplinary research] sees dialogue between them as a source for the theoretical and methodological development of each of them" (Wodak/Meyer 2007: 163).

As has been shown, some considerations drawing on Critical Discourse Analysis (CDA) have also shaped the nature of this work. CDA has often attempted to show and expose issues of inequality and injustice in society by discussing complex issues such as the relation between language and power. The aim of this study was not primarily to investigate such disparities, but to show which dynamics take place and observe the role played by different asymmetries in courtroom communication, starting from the assumption that all human relations are necessarily asymmetrical to some extent. However, a more 'critical' impetus, intended as aiming at achieving "enlightenment and emancipation" (Wodak/Meyer 2007: 7), constitutes a productive avenue for further research in this field, especially in the light of possible miscarriages of justice and the high number of cases involving people who feel they have been wrongly convicted of criminal offences or unfairly sentenced.

Legal language is often seen as the language of the legal community, endogenously created, developed and exploited by its members. However, legal language permeates everybody's life. As Merry (1990: 9) notes, "[l]egal words and practices are cultural constructs which carry powerful meanings not just to those trained in the law or to those who routinely use it to manage their business transactions but to the ordinary people as well." The court provides a useful locus for the analysis of expert-lay interaction in legal settings, and the pervasive presence and significance of the law and its intrinsic linguistic nature call for a deeper investigation in the area of language and law. Gaining a deeper understanding of courtroom dynamics is not only a fascinating and interesting process, but is also imperative in that the courtroom is by definition the locus of justice, and it is therefore one of the most basic aspects of democracy.

References

Abraham, Henry J. [7]1998. *The Judicial Process*. New York: Oxford University Press.

Adams, Kenneth A. 2008. *A Manual of Style for Contract Drafting*. Chicago: American Bar Association.

Adelswärd, Viveka / Aronsson, Karin / Jönsson, Linda / Linell, Per 1987. The Unequal Distribution of Interactional Space: Dominance and Control in Courtroom Interaction. *Text – Interdisciplinary Journal for the Study of Discourse*, 7/4. 313-346.

Anesa, Patrizia 2010. Spoken Interaction in Arbitration: An Analysis of Italian Arbitration Proceedings. In Bhatia, Vijay K. / Candlin, Christopher N. / Gotti, Maurizio (eds) *The Discourses of Dispute Resolution*. Bern: Peter Lang. 207-230.

Anthony, Laurence 2004. AntConc: A Learner and Classroom Friendly, Multi-Platform Corpus Analysis Toolkit. *IWLeL 2004: An Interactive Workshop on Language e-Learning*. 7-13. Available at: <http://www.antlab.sci.waseda.ac.jp/research/iwlel_2004_anthony_antconc.pdf>. Accessed: January 2, 2010.

Archer, Dawn / Wilson, Andrew / Rayson, Paul 2002. *Introduction to the USAS Category System*. Available at: <http://ucrel.lancs.ac.uk/usas/usas%20guide.pdf>. Accessed: January 10, 2010.

Arnheim, Michael 2004. *Principles of the Common Law*. London: Gerald Duckworth & Co Ltd.

Aron, Roberto / Fast, Julius / Klein, Richard B. 1996. *Trial Communication Skills*. Deerfield, Ill.: Clark Boardman Callaghan.

Atkinson, John M. / Drew, Paul 1979. *Order in Court: The Organisation of Verbal Interaction in Judicial Settings*. London: Macmillan.

Atkinson, John M. / Heritage, John (eds) 1984. *Structures of Social Actions*. Cambridge: Cambridge University Press.

Atkinson, Paul / Delamont, Sara 2006. Rescuing Narrative from Qualitative Research. *Narrative Inquiry*, 16. 164-172.

Atkinson, Robert 2007. The Life Story Interview as a Bridge in Narrative Inquiry. In Clandinin, D. Jean (ed.) *Handbook of Narrative Inquiry, Mapping a Methodology*. London: Sage. 224-246.

Attardo, Salvatore 2003. Introduction: The Pragmatics of Humor. *Journal of Pragmatics*, 35. 1287-1294.

Babbie, Earl R. 2010. *The Practice of Social Research*. Belmont: Wadsworth Publishing.

Bailey, Lee F. / Rothblatt, Henry B. 1971. *Successful Techniques for Criminal Trials*. Rochester, N.Y.: Lawyers Co-operative Pub. Co.

Baldus, David C. / Woodworth, George / Zuckerman, David / Weiner, Neil Alan / Broffitt, Barbara 2001. The Use of Peremptory Challenges in Capital Murder Trials: A Legal and Empirical Analysis. *University of Pennsylvania Journal of Constitutional Law*, 3/1. 3-172.

Baker, Paul / Gabrielatos, Costas / Khosravinik, Majid / Krzyzanowski, Michal / McEnery, Tony / Wodak, Ruth 2008. A Useful Methodological Synergy? Combining Critical Discourse Analysis and Corpus Linguistics to Examine Discourses of Refugees and Asylum Seekers in the UK Press. *Discourse & Society*, 19/3. 273-305.

Bakhtin, Mikhail 1981. *The Dialogic imagination: Four Essays by M.M. Bakhtin*. Edited by Michael Holquist. Austin: University of Texas Press.

Bakhtin, Mikhail 1986. *Speech Genres and Other Late Essays*. Edited by Cary Emerson / Michael Holquist. Austin: University of Texas Press.

Bandes, Susan A. (ed.) 1999. *The Passions of Law*. New York: New York University Press.

Banister, Peter / Burman, Erica / Parker, Ian / Taylor, Maye / Tindall, Carol 1994. *Qualitative Methods in Psychology: A Research Guide*. Buckingham: Open University Press.

Barlett, Tom 2010. Towards Intervention in Positive Discourse Analysis. In Coffin, Caroline / Lillis, Theresa / O'Halloran Kieran. *Applied Linguistics Methods: A Reader*. New York: Routlege. 133-147.

Bauer, Martin W. / Aarts, Bas 2000. Corpus Construction: A Principle for Qualitative Data Collection. In Bauer, Martin / Gaskell, George (eds) *Qualitative Researching with Text, Image and Sound: A Practical Handbook*. London: Sage. 19-37.

Baum, Lawrence [5]2001. *American Courts: Process and Policy*. Boston, MA: Houghton Mifflin.
Bell, Allan 1984. Language Style as Audience Design. *Language and Society*, 13. 145-204.
Bennet, W. Lance / Feldman, Martha S. 1981. *Reconstructing Reality in the Courtroom*. New Brunswick, NJ: Rutgers University Press.
Berg, Bruce L. [5]2004. *Qualitative Research Methods for the Social Sciences*. Boston, MA: Allyn and Bacon.
Berg, David 1987. Preparing Witnesses. *Litigation*, 13/2. 13-58.
Bergman, Paul 1982. *Trial Advocacy*. St. Paul, Minn.: West.
Bettinghaus, Erwin P. / Cody, Michael J. [4]1987. *Persuasive Communication*. New York, NY: Holt Rinehart and Winston.
Bhatia, Vijay K. 1983. *An Applied Discourse Analysis of English LegislativeWriting*. Birmingham: University of Aston.
Bhatia, Vijay K. 1993. *Analyzing Genre. Language Use in Professional Settings*. New York: Longman.
Bhatia, Vijay K. / Engberg, Jan / Gotti, Maurizio / Heller, Dorothee (eds) 2005. *Vagueness in Normative Texts*. Bern: Peter Lang.
Bhatia, Vijay K. / Langton, Nicola M. / Lung, Jane W. Y. 2004. Legal Discourse: Opportunities and Threats for Corpus Linguistics. In Connor, Ulla / Upton, Thomas (eds) *Discourse in the Professions: Perspectives from Corpus Linguistics*. Amsterdam: John Benjamins. 203-234.
Biber, Douglas 1993. Representativeness in Corpus Design. *Literary and Linguistic Computing*, 8/4. Oxford: Oxford University Press. 243-257.
Biber, Douglas / Johansson, Stig / Leech, Geoffrey / Conrad, Susan / Finegan, Edward 1999. *Longman Grammar of Spoken and Written English*. London: Longman.
Billig, Michael 1999. Conversation Analysis and the Claims of Naivety. *Discourse & Society*, 10/4. 572-576.
Billig, Michael / MacMillan, Katie 2005. Metaphor, Idiom and Ideology: The Search for 'No Smoking Guns' across Time. *Discourse & Society*, 16/4. 459-480.
Blommaert, Jan 2005. *Discourse*. Cambridge: Cambridge University Press.

Boden, Deirdre 1994. *The Business of Talk: Organizations in Action*. Cambridge, Mass.: Polity Press.

Bogoch, Bryna 1999. Courtroom Discourse and the Gendered Construction of Professional Identity. *Law & Social Inquiry*, 24/2. 329-375.

Bornstein Brian H. 1999. The Ecological Validity of Jury Simulations: Is the Jury Still Out? *Law and Human Behavior*, 23/1. 75-91.

Bray, Robert M. / Kerr, Norbert L. 1979. Use of the Simulation Method in the Study of Jury Behavior: Some Methodological Considerations. *Law and Human Behavior*, 3. 107-119.

Bray, Robert M. / Kerr, Norbert L. 1982. Methodological Considerations in the Study of the Psychology of the Courtroom. In Kerr, Norbert L. / Bray, Robert M. (eds) *The Psychology of the Courtroom*. New York: Academic Press. 287-323.

Britton, Bruce K. / Pellegrini, Anthony D. 1990. *Narrative Thought and Narrative Language*. Hillsdale, NJ: Erlbaum.

Broderick, Raymond 1992. Why the Peremptory Challenge should be Abolished. *Temple Law Review*, 65. 369-423.

Brown, Cynthia 1994. A Challenge to the English-Language Requirement of the Jurors Qualification Provision of New York's Judiciary Law. *New York Law School Review*, 39. 479-510.

Brown, Gillian / Yule, George 1983. *Discourse Analysis*. Cambridge: Cambridge University Press.

Bruner, Jerome 1986. *Actual Minds, Possible Worlds*. Cambridge, MA: Harvard University Press.

Bruner, Jerome 1990. *Acts of Meaning*. Cambridge, MA: Harvard University Press.

Bruner, Jerome 1991. The Narrative Construction of Reality. *Critical Inquiry*, 18/1. 1-21.

Bruner, Jerome 2002. *Making Stories: Law, Literature, Life*. New York: Farrar, Straus and Giroux.

Bucholtz, Mary 2000. The Politics of Transcription. *Journal of Pragmatics*, 32. 1439-1465.

Buckland, William Warwick / McNair, Arnold D. ^{2}2008. *Roman Law and Common Law: A Comparison in Outline*. Cambridge: Cambridge University Press.

Bugliosi, Vincent 1996. *Outrage: The Five Reasons Why O.J. Simpson Got away with Murder*. New York: Island Books.
Burke, William L. / Poulson, Ronald L. / Brondino, Michael J. 1992. Fact or Fiction: the Effect of the Opening Statement. *Journal of Contemporary Law*, 18. 195-210.
Burke, Kenneth 1984[1954]. *Permanence and Change: An Anatomy of Purpose*. Berkeley: University of California Press.
Burns, Robert 2009. *The Death of the American Trial*. Chicago: The University of Chicago Press.
Cacciaguidi-Fahy, Sophie / Wagner, Anne (eds) 2006. *Legal Language and the Search for Clarity*. Bern: Peter Lang.
Cameron, Deborah 1990. Demythologizing Sociolinguistics: Why Language does not Reflect Society. In Joseph, John E. / Taylor, Talbot J. (eds) *Ideologies of Language*. London: Routledge. 79-93.
Candlin, Christopher 1997. General Editor's Preface. In Gunnarsson, Britt-Louise / Linell, Per / Nordberg, Bengt (eds) *The Construction of Professional Discourse*. London: Longman. ix-xiv.
Candlin, Christopher 2006. Accounting for Interdiscursivity: Challenges to Professional Expertise. In Gotti, Maurizio / Giannoni, Davide S. (eds) New *Trends in Specialized Discourse Analysis*. Bern. Peter Lang. 21-45.
Candlin, Christopher / Bhatia, Vijay K. 1998. *The Project Report on Strategies and Competencies in Legal Communication: A Study to Investigate the Communicative Needs of Legal Professionals*. Hong Kong: The Law Society of Hong Kong.
Candlin, Christopher / Maley, Yon 1997. Intertextuality and Interdiscursivity in the Discourse of Alternative Dispute Resolution. In Gunnarsson, Britt-Louise / Linell, Per / Nordberg, Bengt (eds) *The Construction of Professional Discourse*. London: Longman. 201-222.
Candlin, Christopher / Sarangi, Srikant 2004. Making Inter-relationality Matter in Applied Linguistics. *Journal of Applied Linguistics*, 1/3. 225-229.
Chafe, Wallace 1982. Integration and Involvement in Speaking, Writing, and Oral Literature. In Tannen, Deborah (ed.) *Spoken and Written Language; Exploring Orality and Literacy*. Norwood, NJ: Ablex Publishing Corporation. 35-53.

Charnock, Ross 2006. Clear Ambiguity. In Cacciaguidi-Fahy, Sophie / Wagner, Anne (eds) *Legal Language and the Search for Clarity*. Bern: Peter Lang. 65-103.

Charrow, Robert P. / Charrow, Veda R. 1979. Making Legal Language Understandable: A Psycholinguistic Study of Jury Instructions. *Columbia Law Review*, 79. 1306-1374.

Charrow, Veda R. 1987. Some Guidelines for Clear Legal Writing. *University of Bridgeport Law Review*, 8. 405-08.

Charrow, Veda R. / Crandall, Jo Ann / Charrow, Robert P. 1982. Characteristics and Functions of Legal Language. In Kittredge, Richard / Lehrberger, Johan (eds) *Sublanguage. Studies of Language in Restricted Semantic Domains*. Berlin: Walter de Gruyter. 175-190.

Chatman, Seymour 1969. *Story and Discourse*. Ithaca: Cornell University Press.

Chouliaraki, Lilie / Fairclough, Norman 1999. *Discourse in late modernity*. Edinburgh: Edinburgh University Press.

Clegg, Stewart R. 1989. *Frameworks of Power*. London: Sage.

Clermont, Kevin M. / Eisenberg, Theodore 2002. Litigation Realities. *Cornell Law Review*, 88. 119-154.

Coffin, Caroline / Lillis, Theresa / O'Halloran, Kieran (eds) 2010. *Applied Linguistics Methods: A Reader*. New York: Routledge.

Cohan, Steven / Shires, Linda M. 1988. *Telling Stories: A theoretical Analysis of Narrative Fiction*. London: Routledge.

Coniam, David 2004. Concordancing Oneself: Constructing Individual Textual Profiles. *International Journal of Corpus Linguistics*, 9/2. 271-298.

Conley, John 2000. Epilogue: A Legal and Cultural Commentary on the Psychology of Juror Instructions. *Psychology, Public Policy, and Law*, 6. 822-831.

Conley, John / O'Barr, William 1990. *Rules Versus Relationships: The Ethnography of Legal Discourse*. Chicago: University of Chicago Press.

Conley, John M. / O'Barr, William 1998. *Just words. Law, Language, and Power*. Chicago: University of Chicago Press.

Conley, John / O'Barr, William / Lind, E. Allan 1978. The Power of Language: Presentational Style in the Courtroom. *Duke Law Journal*, 78/6. 1375-1399.

Cornu, Gérard 2005. *Linguistique Juridique*. Paris: Éditions Montchrestien.

Cotterill, Janet 2003. *Language and Power in Court: A Linguistic Analysis of the O.J. Simpson Trial*. Basingstoke: Palgrave.

Crystal, David 1995. *The Cambridge Encyclopedia of the English Language*. Cambridge: Cambridge University Press.

Crystal, David / Davy, Derek 1969. *Investigating English Style*. London: Longman.

Daemmrich, Arthur 1998. The Evidence Does Not Speak for Itself: Expert Witnesses and the Organization of DNA-Typing Companies. Special Issue on Contested Identities: Science, Law and Forensic Practice. *Social Studies of Science*, 28/5-6. 741-772.

Danet, Brenda 1980. Language in the Legal Process. *Law and Society Review*, 14/3. 445-564.

Danet, Brenda 1985. Legal Discourse. In van Dijk, Teun A. (ed.) *Handbook of Discourse Analysis, Vol. 1*. London: Academic Press. 273-291.

Davis, James H., / Bray, Robert M. / Holt, Robert W. 1977. The Empirical Study of Decision Processes in Juries: A critical review. In Tapp, June Louin / Levine, Felice J. (eds) *Law, Justice, and the Individual in Society: Psychological and Legal Issues*. New York: Holt, Rinehart & Winston. 326-361.

Daymon, Christine / Holloway, Immy 2002. *Qualitative Research Methods in Public Relations and Marketing Communications*. London: Routledge.

de Beaugrande, Robert 1997a. The Story of Discourse Analysis. In van Dijk, Teun A. (ed.) *Discourse as Structure and Process*. London: Sage. 35-62.

de Beaugrande, Robert 1997b. *New Foundations for a Science of Text and Discourse*. Norwood: NJ: Ablex.

Del Carmen, Rolando V. 2006. *Criminal Procedure: Law and Practice*. Belmont: Thomson Wadsworth.

den Dikken, Marcel / Tortora, Christina M. (eds) 2005. *The Function of Function Words and Functional Categories*. Philadelphia: John Benjamins.

Denzin, Norman K. [2]1978. *The Research Act: A Theoretical Introduction to Sociological Methods*. New York: McGraw-Hill.

Derrida, Jacques 1972. La Mythologie Blanche. In *Marges de la Philosophie*. Paris: Les Editions de Minuit. 247-324.

Diamond, Shari S. (ed.) 1979. Simulation Research and the Law [Special issue]. *Law and Human Behavior*, 3/1/2.

Diamond, Shari S. 1997. Illuminations and Shadows from Jury Simulations. *Law and Human Behavior*, 21. 561-571.

Dölle, Hans 1949. *Vom Stil der Rechtssprache*. Tübingen: J.C.B. Mohr.

Drew, Paul 1985. Analysing the Use of Language in Courtroom Interaction. In van Dijk, Teun A. (ed.) *Handbook of Discourse Analysis: Vol. 3*. London: Academic Press. 133-47.

Drew, Paul 1992. Contested Evidence in Courtroom Cross-examination: The Case of a Trial for Rape. In Drew, Paul / Heritage, John (eds) *Talk at Work: Interaction in Institutional Settings*. Cambridge: Cambridge University Press. 470-520.

Drew, Paul / Heritage, John (eds) 1992. *Talk at Work: Interaction in Institutional Settings*. Cambridge: Cambridge University Press.

Dumas, Bethany K. 2000. US Pattern Jury Instructions: Problems and Proposals. *Forensic Linguistics*, 7/1. 49-71.

Dunning, Ted 1993. Accurate Methods for the Statistics of Surprise and Coincidence. *Computational Linguistics*, 19/1. 61-74.

Duranti, Alessandro 1986. The Audience as Co-author: An Introduction. *Text*, 6/3. 239-247.

Duranti, Alessandro / Goodwin, Charles (eds) 1992. *Rethinking Context: Language as an Interactive Phenomenon*. Cambridge: Cambridge University Press.

Eades, Diana 1996. Verbatim Courtroom Transcripts and Discourse Analysis. In Kniffka, Hannes (ed.) *Recent Developments in Forensic Linguistics*. Frankfurt: Peter Lang. 241-254.

Edelman, Murray 1972. *The Symbolic Uses of Politics*. Urbana, Ill.: University of Illinois Press.

Ehrlich, Susan 2001. *Representing Rape*. New York: Routledge.

Ellsworth, Phoebe C. / Reifman, Alan 2000. Juror Comprehension and Public Policy: Perceived Problems and Proposed Solutions. *Psychology, Public Policy, and Law*, 6. 788-821.

Elwork, Amiram / Sales, Bruce D. / Alfini, James J. 1977. Juridic Decisions: In Ignorance of the Law or in Light of It? *Law and Human Behavior*, 1. 163-189.

Elwork, Amiram / Sales, Bruce D. / Alfini, James J. 1982. *Making Jury Instructions Understandable*. Charlottesville, Va.: The Michie Co.

Endicott, Timothy 1997. Vagueness and Legal Theory. *Legal Theory*, 3. 37-63.

Endicott, Timothy 2000. *Vagueness in Law*. Oxford: Oxford University Press.

Endicott, Timothy 2001. Law is Necessarily Vague. *Legal Theory*, 7. 377-83.

Erickson, Bonnie / Lind, E. Allan / Johnson, Bruce / O'Barr William 1978. Speech Style and Impression Formation in a Court Setting: The Effects of "Powerful" and "Powerless" Speech. *Journal of Experimental Social Psychology*, 14/3. 266-279.

Faigman, David L. 1999. *Legal Alchemy: The Use and Misuse of Science in the Law*. New York: W. H. Freeman.

Fairclough, Norman 1992a. *Discourse and Social Change*. Cambridge, UK: Polity Press.

Fairclough, Norman 1992b. (ed.) *Critical Language Awareness*. London: Longman.

Fairclough, Norman 1993. Critical Discourse Analysis and the Marketization of Public Discourse: The Universities. *Discourse & Society*, 4/2. 133-168.

Fairclough, Norman 1995a. *Media Discourse*. London: Edward Arnold.

Fairclough, Norman 1995b. *The Discourse Reader*. London: Routledge.

Fairclough, Norman 1995c. *Critical Discourse Analysis: The Critical Study of Language*. London: Longman.

Fairclough, Norman 1996. A Reply to Henry Widdowson's Discourse Analysis: A Critical Review. *Language and Literature*, 5. 1-8.

Fairclough, Norman 2000a. Language and Neo-liberalism. *Discourse & Society*, 11/2. 147-148.

Fairclough, Norman 2000b. *New Labour, New Language?* London: Routledge.

Fairclough, Norman 2001a. Critical Discourse Analysis as a Method in Social Scientific Research. In Wodak, Ruth / Meyer, Michael (eds) *Methods of critical discourse analysis*. London: Sage. 121-138.
Fairclough, Norman [2]2001b. *Language and Power*. Harlow: Longman.
Fairclough, Norman 2003. *Analysing Discourse: Textual Analysis for Social Research*. London: Routledge.
Fairclough, Norman 2008. The Language of Critical Discourse Analysis: Reply to Michael Billig. *Discourse & Society*, 19. 811-19.
Fairclough, Norman / Mauranen, Anna 1997. The Conversationalisation of Political Discourse: A Comparative View. *Belgian Journal of Linguistics*, 11. 89-120.
Fairclough, Norman / Wodak, Ruth 1997. Critical Discourse Analysis. In van Dijk, Teun A. (ed.) *Discourse as Social Interaction*. London: Sage. 258-284.
Fauconnier, Gilles 1997. *Mappings in Thought and Language*. Cambridge: Cambridge University Press.
Feigenson, Neal 2000. *Legal Blame: How Jurors Think and Talk about Accidents*. Washington, DC: American Psychological Association.
Feigenson, Neal 2003. Responsibility and Blame: Psychological and Legal Perspectives, Emotions, Risk Perceptions and Blaming in 9/11 Cases. *Brooklyn Law Review*, 68. 959-998.
Feigenson, Neal / Park, Jaihyun / Slovey, Peter 1997. Effect of Blameworthiness and Outcome Severity on Attributions of Responsibility and Damage Awards in Comparative Negligence Cases. *Law and Human Behavior*, 21. 597-617.
Felman, Shosana 2002. *The Juridical Unconscious: Trials and Traumas in the Twentieth Century*. Cambridge, MA: Harvard University Press.
Festinger, Leon 1964. *Conflict, Decision and Dissonance*. Stanford, CA: Stanford University Press.
Fiske, Susan / Taylor, Shelley E. 2008. *Social Cognition: from Brains to Culture*. New York: McGraw-Hill.
Fjeld, Ruth Vatvedt 2001. Interpretation of Indefinite Adjectives in Legislative Language. In Mayer, Felix (ed.) *Language for Special Purposes: Perspectives for the New Millennium*. Tübingen: Gunter Narr. 643-650.

Fjeld, Ruth Vatvedt 2005. The Lexical Semantics of Vague Adjectives in Normative Texts. In Bhatia, Vijay K. / Engberg, Jan / Gotti, Maurizio / Heller, Dorothee (eds) *Vagueness in Normative Texts*. Bern: Peter Lang. 157-172.

Flesch, Rudolf 1979. *How to Write Plain English: A Book for Lawyers and Consumers*. New York: Harper and Row.

Fletcher, George 2003. Law. In Smith, Barry (ed.) *John Searle*. Cambridge: Cambridge University Press

Flick, Uwe 2002. *An Introduction to Qualitative Research*. 2nd ed. London: Sage.

Foucault, Michel 1980a. *Power/Knowledge: Selected Interviews and Other Writings 1972-1977*. Edited by Colin Gordon. London: Harvester.

Foucault, Michel 1980b. *The History of Sexuality, Vol. 1. An Introduction*. London: Penguin.

Friedman, Lawrence 1973. *A History of American Law*. New York: Simon and Schuster.

Fukurai, Hiroshi 1999. Rethinking the Representative Jury Requirement: Jury Representativeness and Cross-sectional Participation from the Beginning to the End of the Jury Selection Process. *International Journal of Applied and Comparative Criminal Justice*, 23. 55-90.

Fukurai, Hiroshi / Butler, Edgar W. / Krooth, Richard 1993. *Race and the Jury: Racial Disenfranchisement and the Search for Justice*. New York: Plenum Press.

Gaines, Philip 2000. Communicating with Juries: Episodic Representational Structure in Cross-Examination. *Tennessee Law Review*, 67/3. 599-625.

Gaines, Philip 2006. Discourses of the Ideal and the Actual in the Courtroom: The Conflict for Jurors in 'Making Sense' of General Instructions. In Wagner, Anne / Pencak, William (eds) *Images of Law*. Aldershot: Ashgate.

Galdia, Marcus 2009. *Legal Linguistics*. Frankfurt am Main: Peter Lang,

Garner, Bryan A. 2001. *Legal Writing in Plain English*. Chicago: University of Chicago Press.

Garside, Roger 1987. The CLAWS Word-tagging System. In Garside, Roger / Leech, Geoffrey / Sampson, Geoffrey (eds) *The Computational Analysis of English.* London: Longman. 30-41.

Garside, Roger / Leech, Geoffrey / McEnery, Anthony (eds) 1997. *The Computational Analysis of English.* London: Longman.

Garside, Roger / Smith, Nick 1997. A Hybrid Grammatical Tagger: CLAWS4. In Garside, Roger / Leech, Geoffrey / McEnery, Anthony (eds) *Corpus Annotation: Linguistic Information from Computer Text Corpora*. London: Longman. 102-121.

Gee, James Paul 1999. *An Introduction to Discourse Analysis: Theory and Method.* London: Routledge.

Geny, François 1921. *Science et Technique en Droit Privé Positif.* Paris: Société du Recueil Sirey.

Gerbasi, Kathleen / Zuckerman, Miron / Reis, Harry T. 1977. Justice Needs a New Blindfold: A review of Mock Jury Research. *Psychological Bulletin*, 84/2. 323-345.

Gerring, John 2007. *Case Study Research.* Cambridge: Cambridge University Press.

Gibbons, John 1994. *Language and the Law*. Longman: London.

Gibbons, John 2003. *Forensic Linguistics: An Introduction to Language in the Justice System.* Oxford: Blackwell.

Gibbons, John 2006. Language and the Law. In Davies, Alan / Elder, Catherine (eds) *The Handbook of Applied Linguistics*. Malden, MA: Blackwell. 285-303.

Giles, Howard / Coupland, Nikolas 1991. *Language: Contexts and Consequences*. Keynes: Open University Press.

Giles, Howard / Powesland, Peter 1975. A Social Psychological Model of Speech Diversity. In Giles, Howard / Powesland, Peter (eds) *Speech Style and Social Evaluation.* New York: Harcourt Brace.

Glucksberg, Sam 2001. *Understanding Figurative Language: From Metaphors to Idioms*. New York: Oxford University Press.

Goatly, Andrew 1997. *The Language of Metaphor*. London: Routledge.

Goodpaster, Gary 1987. On the Theory of American Adversary Criminal Trial. *Journal of Criminal Law and Criminology*, 78. 118-153.

Goodrich, Peter 1984. Law and Language: An Historical and Critical Introduction. *Journal of Law and Society*, 11/2. 173-206.

Goodrich, Peter 1987. *Legal Discourse: Studies in Linguistics, Rhetoric and Legal Analysis*. London: Macmillan.
Goodwin, Charles 1986. Audience Diversity, Participation and Interpretation. *Text*, 6/3. 283-316.
Goodwin, Jill Tomasson 1994. Trial Advocacy Handbooks: Narratology and Opening Statements. *Mosaic*, 27/4. 215-230.
Gotti, Maurizio [3]2011. *Investigating Specialized Discourse*. Bern: Peter Lang.
Greimas, Algirdas J. 1976. *Sémiotique et Sciences Sociales*. Paris: le Seuil.
Gumperz, John 1982. *Discourse Strategies*. Cambridge: Cambridge University Press.
Gunnarsson, Britt-Louise 1995. Studies of Language for Specific Purposes - A Biased View of a Rich Reality. *International Journal of Applied Linguistics*, 5/1. 111-134.
Gunnarsson, Britt-Louise 1997. Applied Discourse Analysis. In van Dijk, Teun A. (ed.) *Discourse as Social Interaction*. London: Sage. 285-312.
Gunnarsson, Britt-Louise / Linell, Per / Nordberg, Bengt (eds) 1997. *The Construction of Professional Discourse*. London: Longman.
Haack, Susan 2003. Trials & Tribulations: Science in the Courts. *Daedalus*, 132/4. 54-63.
Halliday, Michael A.K. 1978. *Language as Social Semiotic*. London: Edward Arnold.
Halliday, Michael A.K. [2]1994. *An Introduction to Functional Grammar*. London: Edward Arnold.
Halliday, Michael A.K. / Hasan, Ruqaiya 1976. *Cohesion in English*. London: Longman.
Halliday, Michael A.K. / Hasan, Ruqaiya 1989. *Language, Context and Text: a social semiotic perspective*. Oxford: Oxford University Press.
Hannaford-Agor, Paula L. / Waters, Nicole L. 2004. *Examining Voir dire in California*. The National Center for State Courts. Available at: <http://www.ncsconline.org/juries/CAVOIRREP.pdf>. Accessed: January 4, 2010.
Hans, Valerie 2006. *The Jury System*. Burlington, TV: Ashgate.

Hans, Valerie / Hannaford-Agor, Paula L. / Mott, Nicole / Musterman, G. Thomas 2003. The Hung Jury: The American Jury's Insights and Contemporary Understanding. *Criminal Law Bulletin*, 39. 33-50.

Hansen, Lene 2005. *Security as Practice: Discourse Analysis and the Bosnian War*. London: Routledge.

Hardt-Mautner, Gerlinde 1995. *Only Connect: Critical Discourse Analysis and Corpus Linguistics, UCREL Technical Paper 6*. Lancaster: University of Lancaster. Available at: <http://ucrel.lancs.ac.uk/tech_papers.html>. Accessed: January 20, 2009.

Harris, Sandra 1984. Questions as a Mode of Control in Magistrates' Courts. *International Journal of the Sociology of Language*, 49. 5-28.

Harris, Sandra 1988. Court Discourse as Genre. In Fawcett, Robin P. / Young, David J. (eds) *New Developments in Systemic Linguistics, Vol. 2: Theory and Application*. London: Pinter. 94-115.

Harris, Sandra 1989. Defendant Resistance to Power and Control in Court. In Coleman, Hylwel (ed.) *Working with Language: A Multidisciplinary Consideration of Language Use in Work Contexts*. Berlin: de Gruyter. 131-164.

Harris, Sandra 1994. Ideological Exchanges in British Magistrates Courts. In Gibbons, John (ed.) *Language and the Law*. London: Longman. 156-170.

Hastie, Reid 1991. Is Attorney-conducted Voir Dire an Effective Procedure for the Selection of Impartial Juries? *American University Law Review*, 40. 1501-1524.

Hastie, Reid / Penrod, Steven D. / Pennington, Nancy 1983. *Inside the Jury*. Cambridge, Massachusetts: Harvard University Press.

Hathaway, George H. 1983a. An Overview of the Plain English Movement for Lawyers. *Michigan Bar Journal*, 62. 945-949.

Hathaway, George H. 1983b. Plain English in Judicial Opinions. *Michigan Bar Journal*, 62. 976-8.

Hathaway, George H. 1985. The Plain English Movement in Law – Past, Present, and Future. *Michigan Bar Journal*, 64. 1236-1239.

Heffer, Chris 2005. *The Language of Jury Trial: A Corpus-aided Analysis of Legal-Lay Discourse*. Basingstoke: Palgrave Macmillan.

Heffer, Chris 2007. Judgement in Court: Evaluating Participants in Courtroom Discourse. In Kredens, Krzysztof / Gozdz-

Roszkowski, Stanislaw (eds) *Language and the Law: International Outlooks*. Frankfurt am Mein: Peter Lang. 145-179.
Heffer, Chris 2008. The Language and Communication of Jury Instructions. In Gibbons, John / Turell, M. Teresa (eds) *Dimensions of Forensic Linguistics*. Amsterdam / Philadelphia: John Benjamins.
Heritage, John 1984. *Garfinkel and Ethnomethodology*. Cambridge: Polity.
Heuer, Larry / Penrod, Steven D. 1989. Instructing Jurors: A Field Experiment with Written and Preliminary Instructions. *Law and Human Behavior*, 13/4. 409-430.
Hindess, Barry 1982. Power, Interests, and the Outcome of Struggles. *Sociology*, 16/4. 488-511.
Hobbs, Pamela 2003. Is That What We're Here about?: A Lawyer's Use of Impression Management in a Closing Argument at Trial. *Discourse & Society*, 14. 273-290.
Hodger, Robert / Kress, Gunther 1993. *Language as ideology*. London: Routledge.
Hoffman, Morris B. 1997. Peremptory Challenges Should Be Abolished: A Trial Judge's Perspective. *University of Chicago Law Review*, 64. 809-871.
Holdsworth, William S. ^{3}1923. *A History of English Law*. London: Methuen.
Hollien, Harry 2001. *Forensic Voice Identification*. San Diego: Academic Press.
Hunt, Darnell M. 1999. *O. J. Simpson facts and fictions*. Cambridge: Cambridge University Press.
Huntley, Jill E. / Costanzo, Mark 2003. Sexual Harrassment Stories: Testing a Story-Mediated Model of Juror Decision-Making in Civil Litigation. *Law and Human Behavior*, 27. 29-51.
Hymes, Dell 1972. On Communicative Competence. In Pride, John B. / Holmes, Janet (eds) *Sociolinguistics*. Harmondsworth: Penguin. 269-293.
Iedema, Rick / Wodak, Ruth 1999. Introduction: Organizational Discourse and Practices. *Discourse & Society*, 10/1. 5-19.
Isani, Shaeda 2006. Visual Semiotics of Legal Court Dress in England & Wales: a failed vector of professional identity? In Wagner, Anne / Pencak, William (eds) *Images in Law*. London: Cavendish. 51-69.

Jackson, Bernard 1988. *Law, Fact, and Narrative Coherence*. Robey, UK: Deborah Charles.

Jackson, Bernard 1995. *Making Sense in Law: Linguistic, Psychological, and Semiotic Perspectives*. Liverpool: Deborah Charles.

Jacquemet, Marco 1996. *Credibility in Court*. Cambridge: Cambridge University Press.

Jasanoff, Sheila 1990. *The Fifth Branch: Science Advisers as Policymakers*. Cambridge, MA: Harvard University Press.

Jasanoff, Sheila 1995. *Science at the bar*. Cambridge, MA: Harvard University Press.

Jeans, James 1975. *Trial Advocacy*. St. Paul, MN.: West.

Jefferson, Gail 1983. Issues in the Transcription of Naturally-Occurring Talk: Caricature versus Capturing Pronunciational Particulars. *Tilburg Papers in Language and Literature*, 34. 1-12.

Jefferson, Gail 2004. Glossary of Transcript Symbols with an Introduction. In Lerner, Gene H. (ed.) *Conversation Analysis: Studies from the first generation*. Philadelphia: John Benjamins. 13-23.

Johnson-Laird, Philip N. 1983. *Mental Models: Towards a Cognitive Science of Language, Inference, and Consciousness*. Cambridge, MA: Harvard University Press.

Johnstone, Barabara 2008. *Discourse Analysis*. Malden, MA: Blackwell.

Jonakait, Randolph N. 2003. *American Jury System*. New Haven, CT: Yale University Press.

Jones, Carol 1994. *Expert Witnesses*. Oxford / New York: Oxford University Press.

Joos, Martin 1961. *The Five Clocks: A Linguistic Excursion into the Five Styles of English Usage*. New York: Harcourt, Brace and World.

Jorgensen, L. Ronald 2006. *Motion Practice and Persuasion*. Chicago: American Bar Association.

Kagehiro, Dorothy K. / Stanton, W. Clark 1985. Legal vs. Quantified Definitions of Standards of Proof. *Law and Human Behavior*, 9. 159-178.

Kendall, Gavin 2007. What Is Critical Discourse Analysis? Ruth Wodak in Conversation With Gavin Kendall. *Forum: Qualitative Social Research*, 8/2, Art. 29. Available at: <http://www.qualitative-research.net/fqs-texte/2-07/07-2-29-e.htm>. Accessed: June 4, 2009.

Kerr, Norbert. L. / MacCoun, Robert J. / Kramer, Geoffrey P. 1996. Bias in Judgment: Comparing Individuals and Groups. *Psychological Review*, 103/4. 687-719.

King, Nancy Jean 1999. The American Criminal Jury. *Law and Contemporary Problems*, 62. 41-67.

Klonoff, Robert H. / Colby, Paul L. ³2007. *Winning Jury Trials*. Louisville, Colo.: National Institute for Trial Advocacy.

Knight, Alfred H. 1996. *The Life of the Law*. New York: Crown Publishers.

Koch, Chantal Mees / Devine, Dennis J. 1999. Effects of Reasonable Doubt Definition and Inclusion of a Lesser Charge on Jury Verdicts. *Law and Human Behavior*, 23/6. 653-674.

Koller, Veronika / Mautner, Gerlinde 2004. Computer Applications in Critical Discourse Analysis. In Coffin, Caroline / Hewings, Ann / O'Halloran, Kieran (eds) *Applying English Grammar: Functional and Corpus Approaches*. London: Hodder and Stoughton, 216-28.

Koski, Douglas D. / Saks, Micheal J. (ed.) 2003. *The Jury Trial in Criminal Justice*. Durham, NC: Carolina Academic Press.

Kovera, Margaret B. / Dickinson, Jason J. / Cutler, Brian L. 2002. Voir Dire and Jury Selection. In Goldstein, Alan M. (ed.) *Comprehensive Handbook of Psychology: Forensic Psychology, Vol. 11*. New York: John Wiley and Sons. 161-175.

Kramer, Geoffrey P. / Kerr, Norbert L. / Carroll, John S. 1990. Pretrial Publicity, Judicial Remedies, and Jury Bias. *Law and Human Behavior*, 14. 409-438.

Kressel, Neil / Kressel Dorit F. 2002. *Stack and Sway: The New Science of Jury Consulting*. Boulder, CO: Westview press.

Kristeva, Julia 1970. *Le Texte du Roman*. The Hague: Mouton.

Kritzer, Herbert M. 2002. (ed.) *Legal Systems of the World*. Santa Barbara, CA.: ABC–CLIO.

Kuhne, Cecil 2007. *A Litigator's Guide to Expert Witnesses*. Chicago: ABA.

Kurzon, Dennis 1986. *It is Hereby Performed: Explorations in Legal Speech Acts*. Amsterdam/Philadelphia: John Benjamins.

Kurzon, Dennis 1989. Language of the Law and Legal Language. In Laurén, Christer / Nordman, Marianne (eds) *Special Language:*

From Humans Thinking to Thinking Machines. Clevedon: Multilingual Matters. 283-290.
Kurzon, Dennis 1997. Legal Language: Varieties, Genres, Registers. *International Journal of Applied Linguistics*, 7. 119-139.
Labov, William 1966. *The Social Stratification of English in New York City*. Washington D.C.: Center for Applied Linguistics.
Labov, William 1972. *Language in the Inner City*. Philadelphia: University of Pennsylvania Press.
Labov, William 1981. Speech Actions and Reactions in Personal Narrative. In Tannen, Deborah (ed.) *Analyzing Discourse: Text and Talk*. Georgetown University Round Table. Washington, DC: Georgetown University Press. 219-247.
Labov, William / Waletzky, Joshua 1967. Narrative analysis: Oral versions of personal experience. In Helm, June (ed.) *Essays on the Verbal and Visual Arts*. Seattle: University of Washington Press. 12-44.
Lakoff, George / Johnson, Mark 1980. *Metaphors We Live by*. Chicago: University of Chicago Press.
Lakoff, George / Johnson, Mark 1999. *Philosophy in the Flesh: The Embodied Mind and its Challenge to Western Thought*. New York: Basic Books.
Langacker, Ronald W. 1987. *Foundations of Cognitive Grammar. Vol. 1. Theoretical Prerequisites*. Stanford: Stanford University Press.
Lave, Jean / Wenger, Etienne 1991. *Situated Learning: Legitimate Peripheral Participation*. Cambridge: Cambridge University Press.
Lee, David 1992. *Competing Discourse: Perspective and Ideology in Language*. New York: Longman.
Lee, Debra S. / Hall, Charles / Barone, Susan M. [2]2007. *American Legal English*. Ann Arbor, MI: The University of Michigan Press.
Leech, Geoffrey 1997. Introducing Corpus Annotation. In Garside, Roger / Leech, Geoffrey / McEnery, Anthony (eds) *Corpus Annotation: Linguistic Information from Computer Text Corpora*. London: Longman. 1-18.
Lempert, Richard 2001. Citizen Participation in Judicial Decision Making Juries, Lay Judges and Japan. *Saint Louis-Warsaw Transatlantic Law Journal*. 1-14.

Lenoble, Jacques / Ost, François 1980. *Droit, Mythe et Raison. Essai sur la Dérive Mythologique de la Rationalité Juridique*. Bruxelles: Fac. Saint-Louis.

Levi, Judith 1994. *Language and Law: A Bibliographic Guide to Social Science Research in the U.S.A*. Chicago: American Bar Association.

Levi, Judith / Walker, Anne Graffam (eds) 1990. *Language in the Judicial Process*. New York: Plenum.

Lieberman, Joel D. / Arndt, Jamie / Vess, Matthew 2009. Inadmissible Evidence and Pretrial Publicity: The Effects (and Ineffectiveness) of Admonitions to Disregard. In Lieberman, Joel D. / Krauss, Daniel A. (eds) *Jury Psychology: Social Aspects of Trial Processes*. Abingdon: Ashgate.

Lieberman, Joel D. / Krauss, Daniel A. (eds) 2009. *Jury Psychology: Social Aspects of Trial Processes*. Abingdon: Ashgate.

Lieberman, Joel D. / Sales, Bruce D. 1997. What Social Science Teaches us about the Jury Instruction Process. *Psychology, Public Policy, and Law*, 3. 1-56.

Lieberman, Joel D. / Sales, Bruce D. 2000. Jury Instructions: Past, Present, and Future. *Psychology, Public Policy, and Law*, 6/3. 587-590.

Lieberman, Joel D. / Sales, Bruce D. 2006. *Scientific Jury Selection*. Washington: American Psychological Association.

Lind, E. Allen / O'Barr, William M. 1979. The Social Significance of Speech in the Courtroom. In Giles, Howard / St. Clair, Robert (eds) *Language and Social Psychology*. Oxford: Blackwell. 66-87.

Linell, Per / Luckmann, Thomas 1991. Asymmetries in Dialogue: Some Conceptual Preliminaries. In Marková, Ivan / Foppa, Klaus (eds) *Asymmetries in Dialogue*. Hemel Hemstead: Harvester & Wheatsheaf. 1-20.

Lingle, John H. / Ostrom, Thomas M._1981. Principles of Memory and Cognition in Attitude Formation. In Petty, Richard / Ostrom, Thomas / Brock, Timothy (eds) *Cognitive Responses in Persuasion*. Hillsdale, NJ: Erlbaum.

Linz, Daniel / Penrod, Steven 1984. Increasing Attorney Persuasiveness in the Courtroom. *Law & Psychology Review*, 8. 1-47.

Lisnek, Paul M. / Oliver, Eric 2001. *Courtroom Power*. Colorado Springs, CO: Professional Educational Systems.

Little, Laura E. 2001. Negotiating the Tangle of Law and Emotion. *Cornell Law Review*, 86. 974-1002.

Little, Laura E. 2002. Adjudication and Emotion. *Florida Coastal Law Journal*, 3. 205-218.

Locard, Edmond 1920. *L'Enquête Criminelle et les Méthodes Scientifiques*. Paris: Flammarion.

Loftus, Elizabeth 1975. Leading Questions and the Eyewitness Report. *Cognitive Psychology*, 7. 560-72.

Loftus, Elizabeth 1979. *Eyewitness Testimony*. Cambridge, MA: Harvard University Press.

Long, Debra L. / Graessner, Arthur C. 1988. Wit and Humour in Discourse Processing. *Discourse Processes*, 11/1. 35-60.

Lubet, Steven ^{3}2004. *Modern Trial Advocacy: Analysis and Practice*. South Bend, Indiana: National Institute for Trial Advocacy.

Luke, Allan 2002. Beyond Science and Ideology Critique: Development in Critical Discourse Analysis. *Annual Review of Applied Linguistics*, 22. 96-110.

MacIntyre, Alasdair 1981. *After Virtue: A Study in Moral Theory*. Notre Dame, Indiana: Notre Dame University Press.

Maley, Yon 1994. The Language of the Law. In Gibbons, John (ed.) *Language and the Law*. London: Longman. 11-50.

Maley, Yon / Fahey, Rhonda 1991. Presenting the Evidence: Constructions of Reality in Court. *International Journal for the Semiotics of Law*, 4/1, 3-17.

Mandler, Jean Matter 1984. *Stories, Scripts, and Scenes: Aspects of Schema Theory*. Hillsdale, N.J.: Erlbaum.

Marková, Ivan / Foppa, Klaus (eds) 1991. *Asymmetries in Dialogue*. Hemel Hemstead: Harvester Wheatsheaf.

Maroney, Terry A. 2006. Law and Emotion: A Proposed Taxonomy of an Emerging Field. *Law and Human Behavior*, 30. 119-142.

Martineau, Robert 1991. *Drafting Legislation and Rules in Plain English*. St. Paul, Minn.: West Publishing Co.

Matoesian, Gregory 1993. *Reproducing Rape: Domination through Talk in the Courtroom*. Chicago: University of Chicago Press.

Matoesian, Gregory 1997. "I'm Sorry We had to Meet under these Circumstances": Verbal Artistry (and wizardry) in the Kennedy Smith Rape Trial. In Travers, Max / Manzo, John F. (eds). *Law in Action: Ethnomethodological and Conversation Analytic Approaches to Law*. Aldershot: Dartmouth Publishing. 137-82.

Matoesian, Gregory 1999a. The Grammaticalization of Participant Roles in the Constitution of Expert Identity. *Language in Society*, 28/4. 491-521.

Matoesian, Gregory 1999b. "You were Interested in Him as a Person?" Rhythms of Domination in the Kennedy Smith Rape Trial. *Law and Social Inquiry*, 22/1. 55-91.

Matoesian, Gregory 2001. *Law and the Language of Identity: Discourse in the Kennedy Smith Rape Trial*. Oxford: Oxford University Press.

Mattila, Heikki E. S. 2006. *Comparative Legal Linguistics*. Abingdon: Ashgate.

Mauet, Thomas A. 1980. *Fundamentals of Trial Techniques*. Boston: Little Brown.

Mauet, Thomas A. ^{2}2009. *Trials: Strategy, Skills, and the New Powers of Persuasion*. New York: Aspen Publishers.

Mautner, Gerlinde 2008. Analysing Newspapers, Magazines and Other Print Media. In Wodak, Ruth / Krzyzanowski, Michal (eds) *Qualitative Discourse Analysis in the Social Sciences*. Basingstoke: Palgrave-Macmillan. 30-53.

Maynard, Douglas W. 1990. Narratives and Narrative Structure in Plea Bargaining. In Levi, Judith / Walker, Anne Graffam (eds) *Language in the Judicial Process*. New York: Plenum. 65-95.

McEnery, Anthony / Gabrielatos, Costas 2006. English Corpus Linguistics. In Aarts, Bas / McMahon, April (eds) *The Handbook of English Linguistics*. Oxford: Blackwell. 33-71.

McMenamin, Gerald 2002. *Forensic Linguistics: Advances in Forensic Stylistics*. Boca Raton: CRC Press.

Mellinkoff, David 1963. *The Language of the Law*. Boston: Little Brown & Co.

Merry, Sally Engle 1990. *Getting Justice and Getting Even: Legal Consciousness among Working-Class Americans*. Chicago: University of Chicago Press.

Mertz, Elizabeth 1994. Legal Language: Pragmatics, Poetics, and Social Power. *Annual Review of Anthropology*, 23. 435-455.

Meyer, Bernard S. / Rosenberg, Maurice 1971. Questions Juries Ask: Untapped Springs of Insight. *Judicature*, 55. 105-109.

Mogill, Kenneth M. / Nixon, William R. 1986. Practical Primer on Jury Selection. *Michigan Bar Journal*, 65. 52-57.

Morra, Lucia 2010. New Models for Language Understanding and the Cognitive Approach to Legal Metaphors. *International Journal for the Semiotics of Law*, 23/4. 387-405.

Nathan, M. J. / Koedinger, K. R. 2000. An Investigation of Teachers' Beliefs of Students' Algebra Development. *Cognition and Instruction*, 18. 209-237.

Nickerson, Raymond S. 1999. How We Know – and Sometimes Misjudge – What Others Know: Imputing One's own Knowledge to Others. *Psychological Bulletin*, 125. 737-759.

Nieland, Robert G. 1979. *Pattern Jury Instructions: A Critical Look at a Modern Movement to Improve the Jury System*. Chicago: American Judicature Society.

Norman, Donald A. 1983. Some Observations on Mental Models. In Gentner, Dedre / Stevens Albert L. (eds) *Mental models*. Hillsdale, NJ: Lawrence Erlbaum Associates. 7-14.

Norrick, Neal R. 1987. Functions of Repetition in Conversation. *Text*, 7/3. 245-264.

Norton, Michael I. / Sommers, Samuel R. / Brauner, Sara 2007. Bias in Jury Selection: Justifying Prohibited Peremptory Challenges. *Journal of Behavioral Decision Making*, 20. 467-479.

O'Barr, William M. 1981. Language and the Law. In Ferguson, Charles A. / Heath, Shirley Brice (eds) *Language in the USA*. Cambridge: Cambridge University. 386-406.

O'Barr, William M. 1982. *Linguistic Evidence: Language, Power, and Strategy in the Courtroom*. New York: Academic Press.

Ochs, Elinor 1979a. Transcription as Theory. In Ochs, Elinor / Schieffelin, Bambi (eds) *Developmental Pragmatics*. New York: Academic Press. 43-72.

Ochs, Elinor 1979b. Planned and Unplanned Discourse. In Givón, Talmy (ed.) *Discourse and Syntax*. (Syntax and Semantics, Vol. 12). New York: Academic Press. 51-80.

Ochs, Elinor 1997. Narrative. In van Dijk, Teun A. (ed.) *Discourse as Structure and Process*. London: Sage. 185-207.

Olczak, Paul V. / Kaplan, Martin F. / Penrod, Steven 1991. Attorneys' Lay Psychology and its Effectiveness in Selecting Jurors: Three empirical studies. *Journal of Social Behavior and Personality*, 6. 431-452.

Olsson, John 2004. *Forensic Linguistics: An Introduction to Language, Crime and the Law*. London: Continuum.

Ortony, Andrew (ed.) 1979. *Metaphor and Thought*. Cambridge, MA: Cambridge University Press.

Pallotti, Gabriele 2007. Conversation Analysis: Methodology, Machinery and Application to Specific Settings. In Bowles, Hugo / Seedhouse, Paul (eds) *Conversation Analysis and Language for Specific Purposes*. Bern: Peter Lang. 37-67.

Papke, David R. 1991. (ed.) *Narrative and the Legal Discourse: A Reader in Storytelling and the Law*. Liverpool, U.K.: Deborah Charles.

Parker, Ian / Burman, Erica 1993. Against Discursive Imperialism, Empiricism and Constructionism: Thirty-two Problems with Discourse Analysis. In Burman, Erica / Parker, Ian (eds) *Discourse Analytic Research: Repertoires and Readings of Texts in Action*. London: Routledge. 155-172.

Partington, Alan 2003. *The Linguistics of Political Argumentation: The Spin-doctor and the Wolf-pack at the White House*. London: Routledge.

Pascual Olivé, Esther 2002. *Imaginary Trialogues. Conceptual Blending and Fictive Interaction in Criminal Courts*. Utrecht: LOT.

Pennington, Nancy / Hastie, Reid 1986. Evidence Evaluation in Complex Decision Making. *Journal of Personality and Social Psychology*, 51/2. 242-258.

Pennington, Nancy / Hastie, Reid 1991. A Cognitive Theory of Juror Decision Making: the story model. *Cardozo Law Review*, 13/2-3. 519-57.

Pennington, Nancy / Hastie, Reid 1992. Explaining the Evidence: Tests of the Story Model for Juror Decision Making. *Journal of Personality and Social Psychology*, 62/2. 189-206.

Pennycook, Alastair 2001. *Critical Applied Linguistics: A critical introduction*. London, UK: Lawrence Erlbaum Associates.

Perloff, Richard [4]2010. *The Dynamics of Persuasion*. New York: Routledge.

Petty, Richard. E. / Cacioppo, John. T. 1981. *Attitudes and Persuasion: Classic and Contemporary Approaches*. Dubuque, IA: W. C. Brown.

Philips, Susan U. 1987. The Social Organisation of Questions and Answers in Courtroom Discourse. In Kedar, Leah (ed.) *Power through Discourse*. Norwood, NJ: Ablex. 83-112.

Philips, Susan U. 1998. *Ideology in the Language of Judges: How Judges Practice Law, Politics, and Courtroom Control*. Oxford: Oxford University Press.

Pildes, Richard H. 1992. Conceptions of Value in Legal Thought. *Michigan Law Review*, 90. 1520-1559.

Piven, Francis Fox / Cloward, Richard A. 1988. *Why Americans don't Vote*. New York. Pantheon books.

Popper, Karl. R. 1970. Normal Science and its Dangers. In Lakatos, Imre / Musgrave, Alan (eds) *Criticism and the Growth of Knowledge*. Cambridge, UK: Cambridge University Press. 51-8.

Posner, Eric A. 2001. Law and the Emotions. *The Georgetown Law Journal*, 89. 1977-2012.

Pospisil, Leopold 1971. *Anthropology of Law: A Comparative Theory*. New York: Harper & Row.

Pozner, Larry S. / Dodd, Roger J. 1993. *Cross-Examination: Science and Techniques*. Charlottesville, VA: The Michie Company.

Pyszczynski, Thomas / Wrightsman, Lawrence S. 1981. The Effects of Opening Statements on Mock Jurors' Verdicts in a Simulated Criminal Trial. *Journal of applied social psychology*, 11. 301-313.

Pyszczynski, Thomas / Greenberg, Jeff / Mack, Dave / Wrightsman, Lawrence S. 1981. Opening Statements in a Jury Trial: The Effect of Promising More than the Evidence can Show. *Journal of Applied Social Psychology*, 11. 434-444.

Rayson, Paul 2003. *Matrix: A Statistical Method and Software Tool for Linguistic Analysis through Corpus Comparison*. University of Lancaster: Unpublished PhD Thesis.

Rayson, Paul 2008. From Key Words to Key Semantic Domains. *International Journal of Corpus Linguistics*, 13/4. 519-549.

Rayson, Paul 2009. *Wmatrix: a Web-based Corpus Processing Environment*. Computing Department, Lancaster University. Available at: <http://ucrel.lancs.ac.uk/wmatrix/>. Accessed: May 2, 2010.

Rayson, Paul / Archer, Dawn / Piao, Scott / McEnery, Anthony 2004. The UCREL Semantic Analysis System. In *Proceedings of LREC-04 Workshop: Beyond Named Entity Recognition Semantic Labeling for NLP Tasks. Lisbon, Portugal*. 7-12. Available at: <http://www.comp.lancs.ac.uk/~paul/publications/usas_ lrec04ws.pdf>. Accessed: February 2, 2010.

Rayson, Paul / Garside, Roger 2000. Comparing Corpora Using Frequency Profiling. In *Proceedings of the Workshop on Comparing Corpora, 1-8 October 2000, Hong Kong*. 1-6. Available at: <http://www.comp.lancs.ac.uk/~paul/publications/rg_acl2000.pdf>. Accessed: January 3, 2010.

Reddy, Michael J. 1979. The Conduit Metaphor: a Case of Frame Conflict in our Language about Language. In Ortony, Andrew (ed.) *Metaphor and Thought*. Cambridge: Cambridge University Press. 284-324.

Reifman, Alan / Gusick, Spencer M. / Ellsworth, Phoebe 1992. Real Jurors' Understanding of the Law in Real Cases. *Law and Human Behavior*, 16/5. 539-554.

Rembar, Charles 1980. *The Law of the Land*. New York: Simon & Schuster.

Richards, Keith 2006. *Language and professional identity*. Basingstoke: Palgrave.

Rieke, Richard D. / Stutman, Randall K. 1990. *Communication in Legal Advocacy*. Columbia: University of South Carolina Press.

Rimmon-Kenan, Shlomith 1983. *Narrative Fiction: Contemporary Poetics*. London: Routledge.

Ringbom, Håkan 1998. High-Frequency Verbs in the ICLE Corpus. In Renouf, Antoinette (ed.) *Explorations in Corpus Linguistics*. Amsterdam: Rodopi. 191-200.

Römer, Ute / Wulff, Stefanie 2010. Applying Corpus Methods to Written Academic Texts: Explorations of MICUSP. *Journal of Writing Research*, 2/2. 99-127.

Sales, Bruce D. / Elwork, Amiram / Alfini, James J. 1977. Improving Jury Instructions. In Sales, Bruce D. (ed.) *Perspectives in Law*

and Psychology, Vol. 1: The Criminal Justice System. New York: Plenum. 23-90.
Sarat, Austin / Felstiner, William L.F. 1990. Legal Realism in Lawyer-Client Communications. In Levi, Judith / Walker, Anne Graffam (eds) *Language in the Judicial Process*. 133-151.
Šarčević, Susan 2000. *New Approach to Legal Translation*. The Hague: Kluver Law International.
Schane, Sanford 2006. *Language and the Law*. London: Continuum.
Schank, Roger C. 1986. *Explanation Patterns: Understanding Mechanically and Creatively*. Hillsdale, NJ: Erlbaum.
Schank, Roger C. / Abelson, Robert P. 1977. *Scripts, Plans, Goals and Understanding: an Inquiry into Human Knowledge Structures*. Hillsdale, NJ: L. Erlbaum.
Schegloff, Emanuel 1992. In Another Context. In Duranti, Alessandro / Goodwin, Charles (eds) *Rethinking Context: Language as an Interactive Phenomenon*. Cambridge: Cambridge University Press. 191-227.
Schegloff, Emanuel 1997. Whose Text? Whose Context? *Discourse and Society*, 8/2. 165-187.
Schegloff, Emanuel 1998. Reply to Wetherell. *Discourse & Society*, 9/3. 457-60.
Schiffrin, Deborah 1994. *Approaches to discourse*. Oxford: Blackwell.
Schwarzer, William W. 1991. *Reforming Jury Trials. Federal Rules Decisions, vol. 132*. St. Paul: West. 575-96.
Scollon, Ron 1998. *Mediated Discourse as Social Interaction: A study of News Discourse*. London: Longman.
Scollon, Ron 2001a. *Mediated Discourse: The Nexus of Practice*. London: Routledge.
Scollon, Ron 2001b. Action and Text: Towards an Integrated Understanding of the Place of Text in Social (Inter)action, Mediated Discourse Analysis and the Problem of Social Action. In Wodak, Ruth / Meyer, Michael (eds) *Methods of Critical Discourse Analysis*. London: Sage. 139-183.
Severance, Laurence J. / Loftus, Elizabeth F. 1982. Improving the Ability of Jurors to Comprehend and Apply Criminal Jury Instructions. *Law & Society Review*, 17/1. 153-198.

Shapiro, Fred 1993. *Oxford Dictionary of Legal Quotations*. Oxford: Oxford University Press.

Shibles, Warren A. 1971. *Metaphor: An Annotated Bibliography and History*. Whitewater, WI: The Language Press.

Shuy, Roger 1993. *Language Crimes: The Use and Abuse of Language Evidence in the Courtroom*. Oxford: Blackwell.

Shuy, Roger 2007. *Language in the American Courtroom. Language and Linguistics Compass*, 1/1-2. 100-114.

Shuy, Roger / Larkin, Donald K. 1978. Linguistic Considerations in the Simplification/Clarification of Insurance Policy Language. *Discourse Processes*, 1/3. 305-321.

Silverman, David 1993. *Interpreting Qualitative Data: Methods for Analyzing Talk, Text and Interaction*. London: Sage.

Silverstein, Michael 1993. Metapragmatic Discourse and Metapragmatic Function. In Lucy, John A. (ed.) *Reflexive Language, Reported Speech and Metapragmatics*. Cambridge: Cambridge University Press. 33-58.

Simon, Rita James 1969. Judges' Translations of Burdens of Proof into Statements of Probability. *Trial Lawyer's Guide*, 13. 103-114.

Simons, Herbert W. / Berkowitz, Nancy / Moyer, John R. 1970. Similarity, Credibility, and Attitude Change: A Review and a Theory. *Psychological Bulletin*, 73. 1-16.

Sinclair, John 1991. *Corpus, Concordance, Collocation*. Oxford: Oxford University Press.

Sinclair, John 2003. *Reading Concordances*. London: Longman.

Smart, Barry 1983. On Discipline and Social Regulation: a Review of Foucault's Genealogical Analysis. In Garland, David / Young, Peter (eds) *The Power to Punish*. London: Heinemann. 62-83.

Smith, Michael R. 2007. Levels of Metaphor in Persuasive Legal Writing. *Mercer Law Review*, 58. 919-947.

Sommers, Samuel R. / Norton, Michael 2007. Race-Based Judgments, Race-Neutral Justifications: Experimental Examination of Peremptory Use and the Batson Challenge Procedure. *Law and Human Behavior*, 31/3. 261-273.

Sontag, Lorelei 1990. *Deciding Death: A Legal and Empirical Analysis of Penalty Phase Jury Instructions and Capital Decision-making*. Ann Arbor: University Microfilms International.

Sopory, Pradeep / Dillard, James Price 2002. The Persuasive Effects of Metaphor. A Meta-Analysis. *Human Communication Research*, 28/3. 382-419.

Spiecker, Shelley C. / Worthington, Debra L. 2003. The Influence of Opening Statement/Closing Argument Organizational Strategy on Juror Verdict and Damage Awards. *Law and Human Behavior*, 27/4. 437-456.

Steinberg, Edwin R. 1991. *Plain English: Principles and Practice.* Detroit: Wayne State University Press.

Stoffelmayr, Elisabeth / Diamond, Shari Seidman 2000. The Conflict between Precision and Flexibility in Explaining "Beyond a Reasonable Doubt". *Psychology, Public Policy, and Law*, 6/3. 769-787.

Stubbs, Michael 1997. Whorf's Children: Critical Comments on Critical Discourse Analysis. In Wray, Alison / Ryan, Ann (eds) *Evolving Models of Language*. Clevedon: Multilingual Matters. 100-16.

Stubbs, Michael 1996. *Text and Corpus Analysis*. Oxford: Blackwell.

Stubbs, Michael 2001. *Words and Phrases: Corpus Studies of Lexical Semantics*. Oxford: Blackwell.

Stygall, Gail 1994. *Trial Language: Differential Discourse Processing and Discursive Formation.* Amsterdam: John Benjamins.

SunWolf 2007. *Practical Jury Dynamics*. Charlottesville,VA: LexisNexis.

Swales, John M. 1990. *Genre Analysis*. Cambridge: Cambridge University Press.

Swales, John M. 1998. *Other Floors, Other Voices: A Textography of a Small University Building.* Mahwah, NJ: Lawrence Erlbaum.

Swann, Joan 2002. Yes, but is it Gender? In Litosseliti, Lia / Sunderland, Jane (eds) *Gender Identity and Discourse Analysis*. Amsterdam: Benjamins. 43-67.

Tajfel, Henri 1982. *Social Identity and Intergroup Relations*. Cambridge: Cambridge University Press.

Tajfel, Henri / Turner, John C. 1986. The Social Identity Theory of Inter-Group Behavior. In Worchel, Stephen / Austin, L. William (eds) *Psychology of Intergroup Relations*. Chicago: Nelson-Hall.

Tanford, Alexander J. [3]2002. *The Trial Process: Law, Tactics, And Ethics.* Newark, NJ: LexisNexis. Available at: <http://www.law.indiana.

edu/webinit/tanford/reference/04open.pdf>. Accessed: September 4, 2009.

Tannen, Deborah 1982. Oral and Literate Strategies in Spoken and Written Narratives. *Language*, 58/1. 1-21.

Tannen, Deborah 1984. *Conversational Style: Analyzing Talk among Friends*. Norwood, N.J.: Ablex.

Tannen, Deborah 1986. Introducing Constructed Dialogue in Greek and American Conversational and Literary Narratives. In Coulmas, Florian (ed.) *Direct and Indirect Speech*. Berlin: Mouton. 311-322.

Tannen, Deborah 1987a. Repetition in Conversation as Spontaneous Formulaicity. *Text*, 7/3. 215-243.

Tannen, Deborah 1987b. Repetition in Conversation: Toward a Poetics of Talk. *Language*, 63/3. 574-605.

Tannen, Deborah 1987c. Remarks on Discourse and Power. In Kedar, Leah (ed.) *Power through Discourse*. Norwood, NJ: Ablex. 3-10.

Tannen, Deborah ^{2}2007. *Talking voices: Repetition, Dialogue, and Imagery in Conversational Discourse*. New York: Cambridge University Press.

Taylor, Stephanie 2001a. Locating and Conducting Discourse Analytic Research. In Wetherell, Margaret / Taylor, Stephanie / Yates, Simeon J. (eds) *Discourse as Data: A Guide for Analysis*. London: Sage. 5-48.

Taylor, Stephanie 2001b. Evaluating and Applying Discourse Analytic Research. In Wetherell, Margaret / Taylor, Stephanie / Yates, Simeon J. (eds) *Discourse as Data: A Guide for Analysis*. London: Sage. 311-330.

Thakerar, Jitendra / Giles, Howard / Cheshire, Jenny 1982. Psychological and Linguistic Parameters of Speech Accommodation Theory. In Fraser, Colin / Scherer, Klauss eds) *Advances in the Social Psychology of Language*. Cambridge: Cambridge University Press. 205-255.

Thompson, John 1991. Editor's Introduction. In Bourdieu, Pierre. *Language and Symbolic Power*. Cambridge: Polity. 1-31.

Thornburg, Elizabeth G. 1995. Metaphors Matter: How Images of Battle, Sports, and Sex Shape the Adversary System. *Wisconsin Women's Law Journal*, 10. 225-281.

Tiersma, Peter 1993. Reforming the Language of Jury Instructions. *Hofstra Law Review*, 22. 37-78.

Tiersma, Peter 1999a. *Legal Language*. Chicago: The University of Chicago Press.

Tiersma, Peter 1999b. Jury Instructions in the New Millennium, *Court Review*, 36/2. 28-36.

Tiersma, Peter 2001. The Rocky Road to Legal Reform: Improving the Language of Jury Instructions. *Brooklyn Law Review*, 66. 1081-1118.

Tiersma, Peter 2005. *Some Myths about Legal Language*, Loyola-LA Legal Studies Paper No. 2005-26. Available at: <http://ssrn.com/abstract=845928>. Accessed: January 12, 2009.

Tiersma, Peter 2008. The Nature of Legal Language. In Gibbons, John / Turell, M. Teresa (eds) *Dimensions of Forensic Linguistics*. Amsterdam: John Benjamins. 7-25.

Tiersma, Peter 2010. Redrafting California's Jury Instructions. In Coulthard, Malcolm / Johnson, Alison (eds) *The Routledge Handbook of Forensic Linguistics*. London: Routledge. 251-264.

Tiersma, Peter / Curtis, Matthew 2008. Testing the Comprehensibility of Jury Instructions: California's Old and New Instructions on Circumstantial Evidence. *Journal of Court Innovation*, 1. 231-261.

Titscher, Stefan / Meyer, Michael / Wodak, Ruth / Vetter, Eva 2000. *Methods of Text and Discourse Analysis*. London: Sage.

Tomlin, Russell / Forrest, Linda / Pu, Ming Ming / Kim, Myung Hee 1997. Discourse Semantics. In van Dijk, Teun A. (ed.) *Discourse as Structure and Process*. London: Sage. 63-111.

Toolan, Michael J. 1988. *Narrative: A Critical Linguistic Introduction*. London: Routledge.

Trenholm, Sarah 1989. *Persuasion and Social Influence*. Englewood Cliffs, NJ: Prentice-Hall.

Trosborg, Anna 1992. The Performance of Legal Discourse. *Hermes*, 9. 9-19.

Trosborg, Anna 1995. Introduction. Special Issue on 'Laying down the Law – Discourse Analysis of Legal Institutions'. *Journal of Pragmatics*, 23/1. 1-5.

Trosborg, Anna 1997. *Rhetorical Strategies in Legal Language*. Tübingen: Gunter Narr.

Turner, John C. 1982. Towards a Cognitive Redefinition of the Social Group. In Tajfel, Henri (ed.) *Social Identity and Intergroup Relations*. Cambridge: Cambridge University Press.

Ullmann, Stephen 1964. *Language and Style*. Oxford: Blackwell.

van Dijk, Teun A. 1977. *Text and Context. Explorations in the Semantics and Pragmatics of Discourse.* London: Longman.

van Dijk, Teun A. 1993. Principles of Critical Discourse Analysis. *Discourse & Society*, 4/2. 249-283.

van Dijk, Teun A. 1997a. The Study of Discourse. In van Dijk, Teun A. (ed.) *Discourse as Structure and Process.* London: Sage. 1-34.

van Dijk, Teun A. (ed.) 1997b. *Discourse as Structure and Process.* London: Sage.

van Dijk, Teun A. (ed.) 1997c. *Discourse as Social Interaction.* London: Sage.

van Dijk, Teun A. 2001. Multidisciplinary CDA: A Plea for Diversity. In Wodak, Ruth / Meyer, Michael (eds) *Methods of Critical Discourse Analysis*. London: Sage. 95-119.

van Dijk, Teun A. 2006. Discourse, Context and Cognition. *Discourse Studies*, 8/1. Special issue on Discourse, Interaction and Cognition. 159-177.

van Dijk, Teun A. 2007. Comments on Context and Conversation. In Fairclough, Norman / Cortese, Giuseppina / Ardizzone, Patrizia (eds) *Discourse and Contemporary Social Change*. Bern: Peter Lang. 281-316.

van Dijk, Teun A. 2009. *Society and Discourse. How Social Contexts Influence Language and Talk*. Cambridge: Cambridge University Press.

von Mehren, Arthur T. / Murray, Peter L. ^{2}2007. *Law in the United States*. Leiden: Cambridge University Press.

Voss, James F. / van Dyke, Julie A. 2001. Narrative Structure, Information Certainty, Emotional Context, and Gender as Factors in a Pseudo-Jury Decision-Making Task. *Discourse Processes*, 32/2/3. 215-243.

Wagenaar, Willem Albert / van Koppen, Peter J. / Crombag, Hans F. M. 1993. *Anchored Narratives. The Psychology of Criminal Evidence*. New York: Prentice-Hall.

Waldron, Jeremy 1994. Vagueness in Law and Language: Some Philosophical Issues. *California Law Review*, 82. 509-540.

Walker, Anne Graffam 1986. The Verbatim Record: The Myth and the Reality. In Fisher, Sue / Dundas, Alexandra T. (eds) *Discourse and Institutional Authority: Medicine, Education, and Law*. Norwood, NJ: Ablex. 205-222.

Walker, Anne Graffam 1987. Linguistic Manipulation, Power, and the Legal Setting. In Kedar, Leah (ed.) *Power through Discourse*. Norwood, NJ: Ablex Publishing Corporation. 57-80.

Wall, Wilson 2009. *Forensic Science in Court: The Role of the Expert Witness*. Oxford: Wiley.

Walter, Bettyruth 1988. *The Jury Summation As Speech Genre: An Ethnographic Study of What It Means to Those Who Use It*. Amsterdam/Philadelphia: John Benjamins.

Watzlawick, Paul / Beavin, Janet H. / Jackson, Don D. 1967. *Pragmatics of Human Communication*. New York: Norton.

Wells, Gary / Wrightsman, Lawrence / Miene Peter 1985. The Timing of the Defense Opening Statement: Don't Wait until the Evidence is in. *Journal of Applied Social Psychology*, 15. 758-772.

Wenger, Etienne 1998. *Communities of Practice: Learning, Meaning, and Identity*. Cambridge: Cambridge University Press.

Wetherell, Margaret 1998. Positioning and Interpretive Repertoires: Conversation Analysis and Post-Structuralism in Dialogue. *Discourse and Society*, 9/3. 387-412.

Wetherell, Margaret 2001. Themes in Discourse Analysis: The Case of Diana. In Wetherell, Margaret / Taylor, Stephanie / Yates, Simeon (eds) *Discourse Theory and Practice: A Reader*. London: Sage. 14-28.

White, James Boyd 1985. Law as Rhetoric, Rhetoric as Law: The Art of Cultural and Communal Life. *University of Chicago Law Review*, 52/3. 684-702.

Widdowson, Henry 1995. Discourse Analysis: A Critical View. *Language and Literature*, 4/3. 157-172.

Widdowson, Henry 1998. Review Article: The Theory and Practice of Critical Discourse Analysis. *Applied Linguistics*, 19/1. 136-151.

Williams, Christopher 2005. *Tradition and Change in Legal English*. Bern: Peter Lang.

Williams, Glanville [3]1963. *The Proof of Guilt*. London: Stevens.
Williams, Jane M. 2000. Jury Instructions. *Legal Reference Services Quarterly*, 18/1. 123-135.
Williams, Malcolm 2002. Generalization in Interpretive Research. In May, Tim (ed.) *Qualitative Research in Action*. London: Sage. 125-143.
Winter, Steven L. 1989. Transcendental Nonsense, Metaphoric Reasoning, and the Cognitive Stakes for Law. *University of Pennsylvania Law Review*, 137/4. 1105-1237.
Wodak, Ruth 1985. The Interaction between Judge and Defendant. In van Dijk, Teun A. (ed.) *Handbook of Discourse Analysis – Vol. 4: Discourse Analysis in Society*. London: Academic Press. 181-91.
Wodak, Ruth 1996. Critical Linguistics and Critical Discourse Analysis. In Verschueren, Jeff (ed.) *Handbook of Pragmatics*. Amsterdam: Benjamins. 207-210.
Wodak, Ruth 2001a. What CDA is about: A Summary of its History, Important Concepts and its Developments. In Wodak, Ruth / Meyer, Michael (eds) *Methods of Critical Discourse Analysis*. London: Sage. 1-13.
Wodak, Ruth 2001b. The Discourse-Historical Approach. In Wodak, Ruth / Meyer, Michael (eds) *Methods of Critical Discourse Analysis*. London: Sage. 63-94.
Wodak, Ruth / Chilton, Paul Anthony (eds) 2005. *A New Agenda in (Critical) Discourse Analysis*. Amsterdam: John Benjamins.
Wood, Linda A. / Kroger, Rolf O. 2000. *Doing Discourse Analysis: Methods for Studying Action in Talk and Text*. Thousand Oaks, CA: Sage.
Woodbury, Hanni 1984. The strategic Use of Questions in Court. *Semiotica*, 48/3-4. 197-228.
Wydick, Richard C. [5]2005. *Plain English for Lawyers*. Durham, N.C.: Carolina Academic Press.
Yin, Robert K. 2009. *Case Study Research: Design and Methods*. 4th ed. Thousand Oaks, CA: Sage.
Young, Richard M. 1983. Surrogates and Mappings: Two Kinds of Conceptual Models for Interactive Devices. In Gentner, Dedre / Stevens, Albert L. (eds) *Mental Models*. Hillsdale, NJ: Lawrence Erlbaum Associates. 35-52.

Young, William G. 2007. Speech at the Florida Bar's Annual Convention in Orlando June 28, 2007. *The Florida Bar News*, July 15, 2007. Available at: <http://www.floridabar.org/DIVCOM/JN/jnnews01.nsf/8c9f13012b96736985256aa900624829/5d3d1e61610d7e5c852573150051920d!OpenDocument>. Accessed: September 2, 2010.

Zeisel, Hans / Diamond, Shari S. 1978. The Effect of Peremptory Challenges on Jury and Verdict: An experiment in a federal district court. *Stanford Law Review*, 30. 491-531.

Index

Linguistic Insights

Studies in Language and Communication

This series aims to promote specialist language studies in the fields of linguistic theory and applied linguistics, by publishing volumes that focus on specific aspects of language use in one or several languages and provide valuable insights into language and communication research. A cross-disciplinary approach is favoured and most European languages are accepted.

The series includes two types of books:

- **Monographs** – featuring in-depth studies on special aspects of language theory, language analysis or language teaching.
- **Collected papers** – assembling papers from workshops, conferences or symposia.

Each volume of the series is subjected to a double peer-reviewing process.

Vol. 1 Maurizio Gotti & Marina Dossena (eds)
Modality in Specialized Texts. Selected Papers of the 1st CERLIS Conference.
421 pages. 2001. ISBN 3-906767-10-8 · US-ISBN 0-8204-5340-4

Vol. 2 Giuseppina Cortese & Philip Riley (eds)
Domain-specific English. Textual Practices across Communities and Classrooms.
420 pages. 2002. ISBN 3-906768-98-8 · US-ISBN 0-8204-5884-8

Vol. 3 Maurizio Gotti, Dorothee Heller & Marina Dossena (eds)
Conflict and Negotiation in Specialized Texts. Selected Papers of the 2nd CERLIS Conference.
470 pages. 2002. ISBN 3-906769-12-7 · US-ISBN 0-8204-5887-2

Vol. 4 Maurizio Gotti, Marina Dossena, Richard Dury, Roberta Facchinetti & Maria Lima
Variation in Central Modals. A Repertoire of Forms and Types of Usage in Middle English and Early Modern English.
364 pages. 2002. ISBN 3-906769-84-4 · US-ISBN 0-8204-5898-8

Editorial address:

Prof. Maurizio Gotti
Università di Bergamo, Facoltà di Lingue e Letterature Straniere,
Via Salvecchio 19, 24129 Bergamo, Italy
Fax: 0039 035 2052789, E-Mail: m.gotti@unibg.it

Vol. 5 Stefania Nuccorini (ed.)
Phrases and Phraseology. Data and Descriptions.
187 pages. 2002. ISBN 3-906770-08-7 · US-ISBN 0-8204-5933-X

Vol. 6 Vijay Bhatia, Christopher N. Candlin & Maurizio Gotti (eds)
Legal Discourse in Multilingual and Multicultural Contexts.
Arbitration Texts in Europe.
385 pages. 2003. ISBN 3-906770-85-0 · US-ISBN 0-8204-6254-3

Vol. 7 Marina Dossena & Charles Jones (eds)
Insights into Late Modern English. 2nd edition.
378 pages. 2003, 2007.
ISBN 978-3-03911-257-9 · US-ISBN 978-0-8204-8927-8

Vol. 8 Maurizio Gotti
Specialized Discourse. Linguistic Features and Changing Conventions.
351 pages. 2003, 2005.
ISBN 3-03910-606-6 · US-ISBN 0-8204-7000-7

Vol. 9 Alan Partington, John Morley & Louann Haarman (eds)
Corpora and Discourse.
420 pages. 2004. ISBN 3-03910-026-2 · US-ISBN 0-8204-6262-4

Vol. 10 Martina Möllering
The Acquisition of German Modal Particles. A Corpus-Based Approach.
290 pages. 2004. ISBN 3-03910-043-2 · US-ISBN 0-8204-6273-X

Vol. 11 David Hart (ed.)
English Modality in Context. Diachronic Perspectives.
261 pages. 2003. ISBN 3-03910-046-7 · US-ISBN 0-8204-6852-5

Vol. 12 Wendy Swanson
Modes of Co-reference as an Indicator of Genre.
430 pages. 2003. ISBN 3-03910-052-1 · US-ISBN 0-8204-6855-X

Vol. 13 Gina Poncini
Discursive Strategies in Multicultural Business Meetings.
2nd edition. 338 pages. 2004, 2007.
ISBN 978-3-03911-296-8 · US-ISBN 978-0-8204-8937-7

Vol. 14 Christopher N. Candlin & Maurizio Gotti (eds)
Intercultural Aspects of Specialized Communication.
2nd edition. 369 pages. 2004, 2007.
ISBN 978-3-03911-258-6 · US-ISBN 978-0-8204-8926-1

Vol. 15 Gabriella Del Lungo Camiciotti & Elena Tognini Bonelli (eds)
Academic Discourse. New Insights into Evaluation.
234 pages. 2004. ISBN 3-03910-353-9 · US-ISBN 0-8204-7016-3

Vol. 16 Marina Dossena & Roger Lass (eds)
Methods and Data in English Historical Dialectology.
405 pages. 2004. ISBN 3-03910-362-8 · US-ISBN 0-8204-7018-X

Vol. 17 Judy Noguchi
The Science Review Article. An Opportune Genre in
the Construction of Science.
274 pages. 2006. ISBN 3-03910-426-8 · US-ISBN 0-8204-7034-1

Vol. 18 Giuseppina Cortese & Anna Duszak (eds)
Identity, Community, Discourse. English in Intercultural Settings.
495 pages. 2005. ISBN 3-03910-632-5 · US-ISBN 0-8204-7163-1

Vol. 19 Anna Trosborg & Poul Erik Flyvholm Jørgensen (eds)
Business Discourse. Texts and Contexts.
250 pages. 2005. ISBN 3-03910-606-6 · US-ISBN 0-8204-7000-7

Vol. 20 Christopher Williams
Tradition and Change in Legal English. Verbal Constructions in Prescriptive Texts.
2nd revised edition. 216 pages. 2005, 2007. ISBN 978-3-03911-444-3.

Vol. 21 Katarzyna Dziubalska-Kolaczyk & Joanna Przedlacka (eds)
English Pronunciation Models: A Changing Scene.
2nd edition. 476 pages. 2005, 2008. ISBN 978-3-03911-682-9.

Vol. 22 Christián Abello-Contesse, Rubén Chacón-Beltrán, M. Dolores López-Jiménez & M. Mar Torreblanca-López (eds)
Age in L2 Acquisition and Teaching.
214 pages. 2006. ISBN 3-03910-668-6 · US-ISBN 0-8204-7174-7

Vol. 23 Vijay K. Bhatia, Maurizio Gotti, Jan Engberg & Dorothee Heller (eds)
Vagueness in Normative Texts.
474 pages. 2005. ISBN 3-03910-653-8 · US-ISBN 0-8204-7169-0

Vol. 24 Paul Gillaerts & Maurizio Gotti (eds)
Genre Variation in Business Letters. 2nd printing.
407 pages. 2008. ISBN 978-3-03911-681-2.

Vol. 25 Ana María Hornero, María José Luzón & Silvia Murillo (eds)
Corpus Linguistics. Applications for the Study of English.
2nd printing. 526 pages. 2006, 2008. ISBN 978-3-03911-726-0

Vol. 26 J. Lachlan Mackenzie & María de los Ángeles Gómez-González (eds)
Studies in Functional Discourse Grammar.
259 pages. 2005. ISBN 3-03910-696-1 · US-ISBN 0-8204-7558-0

Vol. 27 Debbie G. E. Ho
Classroom Talk. Exploring the Sociocultural Structure of Formal ESL Learning.
2nd edition. 254 pages. 2006, 2007. ISBN 978-3-03911-434-4

Vol. 28 Javier Pérez-Guerra, Dolores González-Álvarez, Jorge L. Bueno-Alonso & Esperanza Rama-Martínez (eds)
'Of Varying Language and Opposing Creed': New Insights into Late Modern English.
455 pages. 2007. ISBN 978-3-03910-788-9

Vol. 29 Francesca Bargiela-Chiappini & Maurizio Gotti (eds)
Asian Business Discourse(s).
350 pages. 2005. ISBN 3-03910-804-2 · US-ISBN 0-8204-7574-2

Vol. 30 Nicholas Brownlees (ed.)
News Discourse in Early Modern Britain. Selected Papers of CHINED 2004.
300 pages. 2006. ISBN 3-03910-805-0 · US-ISBN 0-8204-8025-8

Vol. 31 Roberta Facchinetti & Matti Rissanen (eds)
Corpus-based Studies of Diachronic English.
300 pages. 2006. ISBN 3-03910-851-4 · US-ISBN 0-8204-8040-1

Vol. 32 Marina Dossena & Susan M. Fitzmaurice (eds)
Business and Official Correspondence: Historical Investigations.
209 pages. 2006. ISBN 3-03910-880-8 · US-ISBN 0-8204-8352-4

Vol. 33 Giuliana Garzone & Srikant Sarangi (eds)
Discourse, Ideology and Specialized Communication.
494 pages. 2007. ISBN 978-3-03910-888-6

Vol. 34 Giuliana Garzone & Cornelia Ilie (eds)
The Use of English in Institutional and Business Settings.
An Intercultural Perspective.
372 pages. 2007. ISBN 978-3-03910-889-3

Vol. 35 Vijay K. Bhatia & Maurizio Gotti (eds)
Explorations in Specialized Genres.
316 pages. 2006. ISBN 3-03910-995-2 · US-ISBN 0-8204-8372-9

Vol. 36 Heribert Picht (ed.)
Modern Approaches to Terminological Theories and Applications.
432 pages. 2006. ISBN 3-03911-156-6 · US-ISBN 0-8204-8380-X

Vol. 37 Anne Wagner & Sophie Cacciaguidi-Fahy (eds)
Legal Language and the Search for Clarity / Le langage juridique et la quête de clarté.
Practice and Tools / Pratiques et instruments.
487 pages. 2006. ISBN 3-03911-169-8 · US-ISBN 0-8204-8388-5

Vol. 38 Juan Carlos Palmer-Silveira, Miguel F. Ruiz-Garrido &
Inmaculada Fortanet-Gómez (eds)
Intercultural and International Business Communication:
Theory, Research and Teaching.
2nd edition. 343 pages. 2006, 2008. ISBN 978-3-03911-680-5

Vol. 39 Christiane Dalton-Puffer, Dieter Kastovsky, Nikolaus Ritt &
Herbert Schendl (eds)
Syntax, Style and Grammatical Norms: English from 1500–2000.
250 pages. 2006. ISBN 3-03911-181-7 · US-ISBN 0-8204-8394-X

Vol. 40 Marina Dossena & Irma Taavitsainen (eds)
Diachronic Perspectives on Domain-Specific English.
280 pages. 2006. ISBN 3-03910-176-0 · US-ISBN 0-8204-8391-5

Vol. 41 John Flowerdew & Maurizio Gotti (eds)
Studies in Specialized Discourse.
293 pages. 2006. ISBN 3-03911-178-7

Vol. 42 Ken Hyland & Marina Bondi (eds)
Academic Discourse Across Disciplines.
320 pages. 2006. ISBN 3-03911-183-3 · US-ISBN 0-8204-8396-6

Vol. 43 Paul Gillaerts & Philip Shaw (eds)
The Map and the Landscape: Norms and Practices in Genre.
256 pages. 2006. ISBN 3-03911-182-5 · US-ISBN 0-8204-8395-4

Vol. 44 Maurizio Gotti & Davide Giannoni (eds)
New Trends in Specialized Discourse Analysis.
301 pages. 2006. ISBN 3-03911-184-1 · US-ISBN 0-8204-8381-8

Vol. 45 Maurizio Gotti & Françoise Salager-Meyer (eds)
Advances in Medical Discourse Analysis: Oral and Written Contexts.
492 pages. 2006. ISBN 3-03911-185-X · US-ISBN 0-8204-8382-6

Vol. 46 Maurizio Gotti & Susan Šarcević (eds)
Insights into Specialized Translation.
396 pages. 2006. ISBN 3-03911-186-8 · US-ISBN 0-8204-8383-4

Vol. 47 Khurshid Ahmad & Margaret Rogers (eds)
Evidence-based LSP: Translation, Text and Terminology.
584 pages. 2007. ISBN 978-3-03911-187-9

Vol. 48 Hao Sun & Dániel Z. Kádár (eds)
It's the Dragon's Turn: Chinese Institutional Discourses.
262 pages. 2008. ISBN 978-3-03911-175-6

Vol. 49 Cristina Suárez-Gómez
Relativization in Early English (950-1250): the Position of Relative Clauses.
149 pages. 2006. ISBN 3-03911-203-1 · US-ISBN 0-8204-8904-2

Vol. 50 Maria Vittoria Calvi & Luisa Chierichetti (eds)
Nuevas tendencias en el discurso de especialidad.
319 pages. 2006. ISBN 978-3-03911-261-6

Vol. 51 Mari Carmen Campoy & María José Luzón (eds)
Spoken Corpora in Applied Linguistics.
274 pages. 2008. ISBN 978-3-03911-275-3

Vol. 52 Konrad Ehlich & Dorothee Heller (Hrsg.)
Die Wissenschaft und ihre Sprachen.
323 pages. 2006. ISBN 978-3-03911-272-2

Vol. 53 Jingyu Zhang
The Semantic Salience Hierarchy Model: The L2 Acquisition of Psych Predicates
273 pages. 2007. ISBN 978-3-03911-300-2

Vol. 54 Norman Fairclough, Giuseppina Cortese & Patrizia Ardizzone (eds)
Discourse and Contemporary Social Change.
555 pages. 2007. ISBN 978-3-03911-276-0

Vol. 55 Jan Engberg, Marianne Grove Ditlevsen, Peter Kastberg & Martin Stegu (eds)
New Directions in LSP Teaching.
331 pages. 2007. ISBN 978-3-03911-433-7

Vol. 56 Dorothee Heller & Konrad Ehlich (Hrsg.)
Studien zur Rechtskommunikation.
322 pages. 2007. ISBN 978-3-03911-436-8

Vol. 57 Forthcoming.

Vol. 58 Carmen Frehner
Email – SMS – MMS
294 pages. 2008. ISBN 978-3-03911-451-1

Vol. 59 Isabel Balteiro
The Directionality of Conversion in English: A Dia-Synchronic Study.
276 pages. 2007. ISBN 978-3-03911-241-8

Vol. 60 Maria Milagros Del Saz Rubio
English Discourse Markers of Reformulation.
237 pages. 2007. ISBN 978-3-03911-196-1

Vol. 61 Sally Burgess & Pedro Martín-Martín (eds)
English as an Additional Language in Research Publication and Communication.
259 pages. 2008. ISBN 978-3-03911-462-7

Vol. 62 Sandrine Onillon
Pratiques et représentations de l'écrit.
458 pages. 2008. ISBN 978-3-03911-464-1

Vol. 63 Hugo Bowles & Paul Seedhouse (eds)
Conversation Analysis and Language for Specific Purposes.
2nd edition. 337 pages. 2007, 2009. ISBN 978-3-0343-0045-2

Vol. 64 Vijay K. Bhatia, Christopher N. Candlin & Paola Evangelisti Allori (eds)
Language, Culture and the Law.
The Formulation of Legal Concepts across Systems and Cultures.
342 pages. 2008. ISBN 978-3-03911-470-2

Vol. 65 Jonathan Culpeper & Dániel Z. Kádár (eds)
Historical (Im)politeness.
300 pages. 2010. ISBN 978-3-03911-496-2

Vol. 66 Linda Lombardo (ed.)
Using Corpora to Learn about Language and Discourse.
237 pages. 2009. ISBN 978-3-03911-522-8

Vol. 67 Natsumi Wakamoto
Extroversion/Introversion in Foreign Language Learning.
Interactions with Learner Strategy Use.
159 pages. 2009. ISBN 978-3-03911-596-9

Vol. 68 Eva Alcón-Soler (ed.)
Learning How to Request in an Instructed Language Learning Context.
260 pages. 2008. ISBN 978-3-03911-601-0

Vol. 69 Domenico Pezzini
The Translation of Religious Texts in the Middle Ages.
428 pages. 2008. ISBN 978-3-03911-600-3

Vol. 70 Tomoko Tode
Effects of Frequency in Classroom Second Language Learning.
Quasi-experiment and stimulated-recall analysis.
195 pages. 2008. ISBN 978-3-03911-602-7

Vol. 71 Egor Tsedryk
Fusion symétrique et alternances ditransitives.
211 pages. 2009. ISBN 978-3-03911-609-6

Vol. 72 Cynthia J. Kellett Bidoli & Elana Ochse (eds)
English in International Deaf Communication.
444 pages. 2008. ISBN 978-3-03911-610-2

Vol. 73 Joan C. Beal, Carmela Nocera & Massimo Sturiale (eds)
Perspectives on Prescriptivism.
269 pages. 2008. ISBN 978-3-03911-632-4

Vol. 74 Carol Taylor Torsello, Katherine Ackerley & Erik Castello (eds)
Corpora for University Language Teachers.
308 pages. 2008. ISBN 978-3-03911-639-3

Vol. 75 María Luisa Pérez Cañado (ed.)
English Language Teaching in the European Credit Transfer System:
Facing the Challenge.
251 pages. 2009. ISBN 978-3-03911-654-6

Vol. 76 Marina Dossena & Ingrid Tieken-Boon van Ostade (eds)
Studies in Late Modern English Correspondence. Methodology and Data.
291 pages. 2008. ISBN 978-3-03911-658-4

Vol. 77 Ingrid Tieken-Boon van Ostade & Wim van der Wurff (eds)
Current Issues in Late Modern English.
436 pages. 2009. ISBN 978-3-03911-660-7

Vol. 78 Marta Navarro Coy (ed.)
Practical Approaches to Foreign Language Teaching and Learning.
297 pages. 2009. ISBN 978-3-03911-661-4

Vol. 79 Qing Ma
Second Language Vocabulary Acquisition.
333 pages. 2009. ISBN 978-3-03911-666-9

Vol. 80 Martin Solly, Michelangelo Conoscenti & Sandra Campagna (eds)
Verbal/Visual Narrative Texts in Higher Education.
384 pages. 2008. ISBN 978-3-03911-672-0

Vol. 81 Meiko Matsumoto
From Simple Verbs to Periphrastic Expressions:
The Historical Development of Composite Predicates, Phrasal Verbs,
and Related Constructions in English.
235 pages. 2008. ISBN 978-3-03911-675-1

Vol. 82 Melinda Dooly
Doing Diversity. Teachers' Construction of Their Classroom Reality.
180 pages. 2009. ISBN 978-3-03911-687-4

Vol. 83 Victoria Guillén-Nieto, Carmen Marimón-Llorca & Chelo Vargas-Sierra (eds)
Intercultural Business Communication and
Simulation and Gaming Methodology.
392 pages. 2009. ISBN 978-3-03911-688-1

Vol. 84 Maria Grazia Guido
English as a Lingua Franca in Cross-cultural Immigration Domains.
285 pages. 2008. ISBN 978-3-03911-689-8

Vol. 85 Erik Castello
Text Complexity and Reading Comprehension Tests.
352 pages. 2008. ISBN 978-3-03911-717-8

Vol. 86 Maria-Lluisa Gea-Valor, Isabel García-Izquierdo & Maria-José Esteve (eds)
Linguistic and Translation Studies in Scientific Communication.
317 pages. 2010. ISBN 978-3-0343-0069-8

Vol. 87 Carmen Navarro, Rosa Mª Rodríguez Abella, Francesca Dalle Pezze
& Renzo Miotti (eds)
La comunicación especializada.
355 pages. 2008. ISBN 978-3-03911-733-8

Vol. 88 Kiriko Sato
The Development from Case-Forms to Prepositional Constructions
in Old English Prose.
231 pages. 2009. ISBN 978-3-03911-763-5

Vol. 89 Dorothee Heller (Hrsg.)
Formulierungsmuster in deutscher und italienischer Fachkommunikation. Intra- und interlinguale Perspektiven.
315 pages. 2008. ISBN 978-3-03911-778-9

Vol. 90 Henning Bergenholtz, Sandro Nielsen & Sven Tarp (eds)
Lexicography at a Crossroads. Dictionaries and Encyclopedias Today, Lexicographical Tools Tomorrow.
372 pages. 2009. ISBN 978-3-03911-799-4

Vol. 91 Manouchehr Moshtagh Khorasani
The Development of Controversies: From the Early Modern Period to Online Discussion Forums.
317 pages. 2009. ISBN 978-3-3911-711-6

Vol. 92 María Luisa Carrió-Pastor (ed.)
Content and Language Integrated Learning: Cultural Diversity.
178 pages. 2009. ISBN 978-3-3911-818-2

Vol. 93 Roger Berry
Terminology in English Language Teaching: Nature and Use.
262 pages. 2010. ISBN 978-3-0343-0013-1

Vol. 94 Roberto Cagliero & Jennifer Jenkins (eds)
Discourses, Communities, and Global Englishes
240 pages. 2010. ISBN 978-3-0343-0012-4

Vol. 95 Facchinetti Roberta, Crystal David, Seidlhofer Barbara (eds)
From International to Local English – And Back Again.
268 pages. 2010. ISBN 978-3-0343-0011-7

Vol. 96 Cesare Gagliardi & Alan Maley (eds)
EIL, ELF, Global English: Teaching and Learning Issues
376 pages. 2010. ISBN 978-3-0343-0010-0

Vol. 97 Sylvie Hancil (ed.)
The Role of Prosody in Affective Speech.
403 pages. 2009. ISBN 978-3-03911-696-6

Vol. 98 Marina Dossena & Roger Lass (eds)
Studies in English and European Historical Dialectology.
257 pages. 2009. ISBN 978-3-0343-0024-7

Vol. 99 Christine Béal
Les interactions quotidiennes en français et en anglais. De l'approche comparative à l'analyse des situations interculturelles.
424 pages. 2010. ISBN 978-3-0343-0027-8

Vol. 100 Maurizio Gotti (ed.)
Commonality and Individuality in Academic Discourse.
398 pages. 2009. ISBN 978-3-0343-0023-0

Vol. 101 Javier E. Díaz Vera & Rosario Caballero (eds)
Textual Healing: Studies in Medieval English Medical, Scientific and Technical Texts.
213 pages. 2009. ISBN 978-3-03911-822-9

Vol. 102 Nuria Edo Marzá
The Specialised Lexicographical Approach: A Step further in Dictionary-making.
316 pages. 2009. ISBN 978-3-0343-0043-8

Vol. 103 Carlos Prado-Alonso, Lidia Gómez-García, Iria Pastor-Gómez &
David Tizón-Couto (eds)
New Trends and Methodologies in Applied English Language Research.
Diachronic, Diatopic and Contrastive Studies.
348 pages. 2009. ISBN 978-3-0343-0046-9

Vol. 104 Françoise Salager-Meyer & Beverly A. Lewin
Crossed Words: Criticism in Scholarly Writing?
371 pages. 2011. ISBN 978-3-0343-0049-0.

Vol. 105 Javier Ruano-García
Early Modern Northern English Lexis: A Literary Corpus-Based Study.
611 pages. 2010. ISBN 978-3-0343-0058-2

Vol. 106 Rafael Monroy-Casas
Systems for the Phonetic Transcription of English: Theory and Texts.
280 pages. 2011. ISBN 978-3-0343-0059-9

Vol. 107 Nicola T. Owtram
The Pragmatics of Academic Writing.
A Relevance Approach to the Analysis of Research Article Introductions.
311 pages. 2009. ISBN 978-3-0343-0060-5

Vol. 108 Yolanda Ruiz de Zarobe, Juan Manuel Sierra &
Francisco Gallardo del Puerto (eds)
Content and Foreign Language Integrated Learning.
Contributions to Multilingualism in European Contexts
343 pages. 2011. ISBN 978-3-0343-0074-2

Vol. 109 Ángeles Linde López & Rosalía Crespo Jiménez (eds)
Professional English in the European context: The EHEA challenge.
374 pages. 2010. ISBN 978-3-0343-0088-9

Vol. 110 Rosalía Rodríguez-Vázquez
The Rhythm of Speech, Verse and Vocal Music: A New Theory.
394 pages. 2010. ISBN 978-3-0343-0309-5

Vol. 111 Anastasios Tsangalidis & Roberta Facchinetti (eds)
Studies on English Modality. In Honour of Frank Palmer.
392 pages. 2009. ISBN 978-3-0343-0310-1

Vol. 112 Forthcoming.

Vol. 113 Mihhail Lotman & Maria-Kristiina Lotman (eds)
Frontiers in Comparative Prosody. In memoriam: Mikhail Gasparov.
426 pages. 2011. ISBN 978-3-0343-0373-6

Vol. 114 Merja Kytö, John Scahill & Harumi Tanabe (eds)
Language Change and Variation from Old English to Late Modern English.
A Festschrift for Minoji Akimoto
422 pages. 2010. ISBN 978-3-0343-0372-9

Vol. 115 Giuliana Garzone & Paola Catenaccio (eds)
Identities across Media and Modes: Discursive Perspectives.
379 pages. 2009. ISBN 978-3-0343-0386-6

Vol. 116 Elena Landone
Los marcadores del discurso y cortesía verbal en español.
390 pages. 2010. ISBN 978-3-0343-0413-9

Vol. 117 Maurizio Gotti & Christopher Williams (eds)
Legal Discourse across Languages and Cultures.
339 pages. 2010. ISBN 978-3-0343-0425-2

Vol. 118 David Hirsh
Academic Vocabulary in Context.
217 pages. 2010. ISBN 978-3-0343-0426-9

Vol. 119 Yvonne Dröschel
Lingua Franca English. The Role of Simplification and Transfer.
358 pages. 2011. ISBN 978-3-0343-0432-0

Vol. 120 Tengku Sepora Tengku Mahadi, Helia Vaezian & Mahmoud Akbari
Corpora in Translation. A Practical Guide.
135 pages. 2010. ISBN 978-3-0343-0434-4

Vol. 121 Davide Simone Giannoni & Celina Frade (eds)
Researching Language and the Law. Textual Features and Translation Issues.
278 pages. 2010. ISBN 978-3-0343-0443-6

Vol. 122 Daniel Madrid & Stephen Hughes (eds)
Studies in Bilingual Education.
472 pages. 2011. ISBN 978-3-0343-0474-0

Vol. 123 Vijay K. Bhatia, Christopher N. Candlin & Maurizio Gotti (eds)
The Discourses of Dispute Resolution.
290 pages. 2010. ISBN 978-3-0343-0476-4

Vol. 124 Davide Simone Giannoni
Mapping Academic Values in the Disciplines. A Corpus-Based Approach.
288 pages. 2010. ISBN 978-3-0343-0488-7

Vol. 125 Giuliana Garzone & James Archibald (eds)
Discourse, Identities and Roles in Specialized Communication.
419 pages. 2010. ISBN 978-3-0343-0494-8

Vol. 126 Iria Pastor-Gómez
The Status and Development of N+N Sequences in
Contemporary English Noun Phrases.
216 pages. 2011. ISBN 978-3-0343-0534-1

Vol. 127 Carlos Prado-Alonso
Full-verb Inversion in Written and Spoken English.
261 pages. 2011. ISBN 978-3-0343-0535-8

Vol. 128 Tony Harris & María Moreno Jaén (eds)
Corpus Linguistics in Language Teaching.
214 pages. 2010. ISBN 978-3-0343-0524-2

Vol. 129 Tetsuji Oda & Hiroyuki Eto (eds)
Multiple Perspectives on English Philology and History of Linguistics.
A Festschrift for Shoichi Watanabe on his 80th Birthday.
378 pages. 2010. ISBN 978-3-0343-0480-1

Vol. 130 Luisa Chierichetti & Giovanni Garofalo (eds)
Lengua y Derecho: líneas de investigación interdisciplinaria.
283 pages. 2010. 978-3-0343-0463-4

Vol. 131 Paola Evangelisti Allori & Giuliana Garzone (eds)
Discourse, Identities and Genres in Corporate Communication.
Sponsorship, Advertising and Organizational Communication.
324 pages. 2011. 978-3-0343-0591-4

Vol. 132 Leyre Ruiz de Zarobe & Yolanda Ruiz de Zarobe (eds)
Speech Acts and Politeness across Languages and Cultures.
402 pages. 2012. 978-3-0343-0611-9

Vol. 133 Thomas Christiansen
Cohesion: A Discourse Perspective.
387 pages. 2011. 978-3-0343-0619-5

Vol. 134 Giuliana Garzone & Maurizio Gotti
Discourse, Communication and the Enterprise. Genres and Trends.
451 pages. 2011. ISBN 978-3-0343-0620-1

Vol. 135 Zsuzsa Hoffmann
Ways of the World's Words.
Language Contact in the Age of Globalization.
334 pages 2011. ISBN 978-3-0343-0673-7

Vol. 136 Cecilia Varcasia (ed.)
Becoming Multilingual.
Language Learning and Language Policy between Attitudes and Identities.
213 pages. 2011. ISBN 978-3-0343-0687-5

Vol. 137 Susy Macqueen
The Emergence of Patterns in Second Language Writing.
A Sociocognitive Exploration of Lexical Trails.
325 pages. 2012. ISBN 978-3-0343-1010-9

Vol. 138 Maria Vittoria Calvi & Giovanna Mapelli (eds)
La lengua del turismo. Géneros discursivos y terminología.
365 pages. 2011. ISBN 978-3-0343-1011-6

Vol. 139 Ken Lau
Learning to Become a Professional in a Textually-Mediated World.
A Text-Oriented Study of Placement Practices.
261 pages. 2012. ISBN 978-3-0343-1016-1

Vol. 140 Forthcoming.

Vol. 141 Edith Esch & Martin Solly (eds)
The Sociolinguistics of Language Education in International Contexts.
263 pages. 2012. ISBN 978-3-0343-1009-3

Vol. 142–143 Forthcoming.

Vol. 144 Margrethe Petersen & Jan Engberg (eds)
Current Trends in LSP Research. Aims and Methods.
323 pages. 2011. ISBN 978-3-0343-1054-3

Vol. 145 David Tizón-Couto, Beatriz Tizón-Couto, Iria Pastor-Gómez & Paula Rodríguez-Puente (eds)
New Trends and Methodologies in Applied English Language Research II.
Studies in Language Variation, Meaning and Learning.
283 pages. 2012. ISBN 978-3-0343-1061-1

Vol. 146 Rita Salvi & Hiromasa Tanaka (eds)
Intercultural Interactions in Business and Management.
306 pages. 2011. ISBN 978-3-0343-1039-0

Vol. 147 Francesco Straniero Sergio & Caterina Falbo (eds)
Breaking Ground in Corpus-based Interpreting Studies.
254 pages. 2012. ISBN 978-3-0343-1071-0

Vol. 148 Forthcoming.

Vol. 149 Vijay K. Bhatia & Paola Evangelisti Allori (eds)
Discourse and Identity in the Professions. Legal, Corporate and Institutional Citizenship.
352 pages. 2011. ISBN 978-3-0343-1079-6

Vol. 150 Maurizio Gotti (ed.)
Academic Identity Traits. A Corpus-Based Investigation.
363 pages. 2012. ISBN 978-3-0343-1141-0

Vol. 151 Priscilla Heynderickx, Sylvain Dieltjens, Geert Jacobs, Paul Gillaerts & Elizabeth de Groot (eds)
The Language Factor in International Business.
New Perspectives on Research, Teaching and Practice.
320 pages. 2012. ISBN 978-3-0343-1090-1

Vol. 152 Paul Gillaerts, Elizabeth de Groot, Sylvain Dieltjens, Priscilla Heynderickx & Geert Jacobs (eds)
Researching Discourse in Business Genres. Cases and Corpora.
215 pages. 2012. ISBN 978-3-0343-1092-5

Vol. 153 Yongyan Zheng
Dynamic Vocabulary Development in a Foreign Language.
262 pages. 2012. ISBN 978-3-0343-1106-9

Vol. 154 Forthcoming.

Vol. 155 David Hirsh (ed.)
Current Perspectives in Second Language Vocabulary Research.
180 pages. 2012. ISBN 978-3-0343-1108-3

Vol. 156–157 Forthcoming.

Vol. 158 Bárbara Eizaga Rebollar (ed.)
Studies in Linguistics and Cognition.
301 pages. 2012. ISBN 978-3-0343-1138-0

Vol. 159 Giuliana Garzone, Paola Catenaccio, Chiara Degano (eds)
Genre Change in the Contemporary World. Short-term Diachronic Perspectives.
329 pages. 2012. ISBN 978-3-0343-1214-1

Vol. 160 Carol Berkenkotter, Vijay K. Bhatia & Maurizio Gotti (eds)
Insights into Academic Genres.
468 pages. 2012. ISBN 978-3-0343-1211-0

Vol. 161 Forthcoming.

Vol. 162 Patrizia Anesa
Jury Trials and the Popularization of Legal Language. A Discourse Analytical Approach.
247 pages. 2012. ISBN 978-3-0343-1231-8

www.ingramcontent.com/pod-product-compliance
Ingram Content Group UK Ltd.
Pitfield, Milton Keynes, MK11 3LW, UK
UKHW021851100926
8556IPUK00020B/1175

9 783034 312318